MULTICULTURAL EDUCATION SERIES

James A. Banks, Series Editor

City Schools and the American Dream: Reclaiming the Promise of Public Education
PEDRO A. NOGUERA

Thriving in the Multicultural Classroom: Principles and Practices for Effective Teaching
MARY DILG

Educating Teachers for Diversity: Seeing with a Cultural Eye
JACQUELINE JORDAN IRVINE

Teaching Democracy: Unity and Diversity in Public Life
WALTER C. PARKER

The Making—and Remaking—of a Multiculturalist
CARLOS E. CORTÉS

Transforming the Multicultural Education of Teachers: Theory, Research, and Practice
MICHAEL VAVRUS

Learning to Teach for Social Justice
LINDA DARLING-HAMMOND, JENNIFER FRENCH, AND SILVIA PALOMA GARCIA-LOPEZ, EDITORS

Culture, Difference, and Power
CHRISTINE E. SLEETER

Learning and Not Learning English: Latino Students in American Schools
GUADALUPE VALDÉS

Culturally Responsive Teaching: Theory, Research, and Practice
GENEVA GAY

The Children Are Watching: How the Media Teach About Diversity
CARLOS E. CORTÉS

Race and Culture in the Classroom: Teaching and Learning Through Multicultural Education
MARY DILG

The Light in Their Eyes: Creating Multicultural Learning Communities
SONIA NIETO

Reducing Prejudice and Stereotyping in Schools
WALTER STEPHAN

We Can't Teach What We Don't Know: White Teachers, Multiracial Schools
GARY R. HOWARD

Educating Citizens in a Multicultural Society
JAMES A. BANKS

City Schools and the American Dream

RECLAIMING THE PROMISE OF PUBLIC EDUCATION

PEDRO A. NOGUERA

Teachers College, Columbia University
New York and London

Published by Teachers College Press, 1234 Amsterdam Avenue,
New York, NY 10027

Library of Congress Cataloging-in-Publication Data

Noguera, Pedro A.
City schools and the American dream : reclaiming the promise of public education / Pedro A. Noguera
p. cm—(Multicultural education series)
Includes bibliographical references and index
ISBN 0-8077-4382-8—ISBN 0-8077-4381-X (pbk.)
1. Urban schools—United States. 2. Educational equalization—United States. 3. School improvement programs—United States. I. Title. II. Multicultural education series (New York, N.Y.)
LC5131 .N64 2003
371/.009173/2—dc21
[B] 2003053342

ISBN 0-8077-4381-X (paper)
ISBN 0-8077-4382-8 (cloth)

Printed on acid-free paper
Manufactured in the United States of America

14 13 12 11 10 9 8 7 6

Contents

Series Foreword

The nation's deepening ethnic texture, interracial tension and conflict, and increasing percentage of students who speak a first language other than English make multicultural education imperative in the 21st century. The U.S. Census Bureau (2000) estimated that people of color made up 28% of the nation's population in 2000, and predicted that they would make up 38% in 2025, and 47% in 2050.

American classrooms are experiencing the largest influx of immigrant students since the beginning of the 20th century. About a million immigrants are making the United States their home each year (Martin & Midgley, 1999). More than seven and one-half million legal immigrants settled in the United States between 1991 and 1998, most of whom came from nations in Latin America and Asia (Riche, 2000). A large but undetermined number of undocumented immigrants also enter the United States each year. The influence of an increasingly ethnically diverse population on the nation's schools, colleges, and universities is and will continue to be enormous.

Forty percent of the students enrolled in the nation's schools in 2001 were students of color. This percentage is increasing each year, primarily because of the growth in the percentage of Latino students (Martinez & Curry, 1999). In some of the nation's largest cities and metropolitan areas, such as Chicago, Los Angeles, Washington, D.C., New York, Seattle, and San Francisco, half or more of the public school students are students of color. During the 1998–1999 school year, students of color made up 63.1% of the student population in the public schools of California, the nation's largest state (California State Department of Education, 2000).

Language and religious diversity is also increasing among the nation's student population. Sixteen percent of school-age youth lived in homes in which English was not the first language in 1990 (U.S. Census Bureau, 2000). Harvard professor Diana L. Eck (2001) calls the United States the "most religiously diverse nation on earth" (p. 4). Most teachers now in the classroom and in teacher education programs are likely to have students from diverse ethnic, racial, language, and religious groups in their classrooms during their careers. This is true for both inner-city and suburban teachers.

An important goal of multicultural education is to improve race relations and to help all students acquire the knowledge, attitudes, and skills needed to participate in cross-cultural interactions and in personal, social, and civic action that will help make our nation more democratic and just. Multicultural education is consequently as important for middle-class White suburban students as it is for students of color who live in the inner city. Multicultural education fosters the public good and the overarching goals of the commonwealth.

The major purpose of the *Multicultural Education Series* is to provide preservice educators, practicing educators, graduate students, scholars, and policy makers with an interrelated and comprehensive set of books that summarizes and analyzes important research, theory, and practice related to the education of ethnic, racial, cultural, and language groups in the United States and the education of mainstream students about diversity. The books in the *Series* provide research, theoretical, and practical knowledge about the behaviors and learning characteristics of students of color, language minority students, and low-income students. They also provide knowledge about ways to improve academic achievement and race relations in educational settings.

The definition of multicultural education in the *Handbook of Research on Multicultural Education* (Banks & Banks, 2001) is used in the *Series*: "Multicultural education is a field of study designed to increase educational equity for all students that incorporates, for this purpose, content, concepts, principles, theories, and paradigms from history, the social and behavioral sciences, and particularly from ethnic studies and women's studies" (p. xii). In the *Series*, as in the *Handbook*, multicultural education is considered a "metadiscipline."

The dimensions of multicultural education, developed by Banks (2001) and described in the *Handbook of Research on Multicultural Education*, provide the conceptual framework for the development of the books in the *Series*. They are: *content integration*, *the knowledge construction process*, *prejudice reduction*, *an equity pedagogy*, and *an empowering school culture and social structure*. To implement multicultural education effectively, teachers and administrators must attend to each of the five dimensions of multicultural education. They should use content from diverse groups when teaching concepts and skills; help students to understand how knowledge in the various disciplines is constructed; help students to develop positive intergroup attitudes and behaviors; and modify their teaching strategies so that students from different racial, cultural, language, and social-class groups will experience equal educational opportunities. The total environment and culture of the school must also be transformed so that students from diverse groups will experience equal status in the culture and life of the school.

Although the five dimensions of multicultural education are highly interrelated, each requires deliberate attention and focus. Each book in the series focuses on one or more of the dimensions, although each book deals with all of them to some extent because of the highly interrelated characteristics of the dimensions.

Urban schools that serve mostly low-income, ethnic minority, and language minority students have many critics and few defenders in these times of shrinking budgets, high stakes testing, and accountability. Most critics of urban schools do not reveal the significance of these schools to the children and communities they serve and consequently undermine efforts to transform and reimagine them. In this readable, informative, and engaging book, Pedro Noguera not only describes why urban schools are the last hope for most of the low-income and language minority students who attend them, he explains why urban schools need "critical support," "pragmatic optimism," and imagination to be transformed. Noguera set forth thoughtful and workable strategies that can be used to improve and restructure schools in the nation's inner cities.

Noguera draws upon his rich experiences as a junior high school teacher, a school board member, a researcher, and a college professor to construct a complex image of urban schools and to describe the myriad factors that must be considered to successfully reform them. His incisive sociological analysis compels him to conclude that because schools are deeply embedded within the social context and political economy of society, urban schools cannot be reformed until serious efforts are made to solve the social and economic problems in inner-city communities, such as unemployment, housing, and health care. Noguera reminds us that "extreme disparities in wealth" are the major reason that so many urban schools fail. His astute observations are especially timely today, when politicians frequently blame schools for their shortcomings and raise the bar for achievement and accountability, without providing them with the capital and human resources they need to improve. The high-stakes state testing as well as the No Child Left Behind Act have been implemented without adequate funding and resources (Amrein & Berliner, 2002) and without an understanding or appreciation of the complex issues that Noguera makes explicit in this book. Noguera believes that high-stakes tests, as they are being conceptualized and implemented in most states, are "fundamentally flawed and morally irresponsible."

Noguera's background as a sociologist leads him to conclude that schools are limited by their social and political contexts. However, his experiences as a teacher, parent, and school board member are the source of his strong belief that schools can transform the lives of students and promote equality and social justice. This hopeful and inspiring book restores our faith in the nation's urban schools and in the ability of schools to create possibilities for students who have been written off and are victims of "benign neglect." It also reminds us that urban schools are desperately needed by the students and communities they serve, and consequently are essential for the realization of the American dream of social justice and equality for all.

I can think of no other time within the last three decades when the message of this incisive and compassionate book was more needed. I hope Noguera's message will be heard by the wide audience this book deserves, and that readers will respond by taking actions that will create caring schools in the nation's cities that will transform lives and promote equality, freedom, and democracy.

James A. Banks
Series Editor

REFERENCES

Amrein, A. L., & Berliner, D. C. (2002). High-stakes testing, uncertainty, and student learning. *Education Policy Analysis Archives, 10*(8). Retrieved February 14, 2003, from http://eppa.asu.edu/eppa/v10n18/

Banks, J. A. (2001). Multicultural education: Historical development, dimensions, and practice. In J. A. Banks & C. A. M. Banks (Eds.), *Handbook of research on multicultural education* (pp. 3–24). San Francisco: Jossey-Bass.

Banks, J. A., & Banks, C. A. M. (Eds.). (2001). *Handbook of research on multicultural education.* San Francisco: Jossey-Bass.

California State Department of Education. (2000). On-line: http://data1.cde.ca.gov/dataquest

Eck, D. L. (2001). *A new religious America: How a "Christian country" has become the world's most religiously diverse nation.* New York: HarperSanFrancisco.

Martin, P., & Midgley, E. (1999). Immigration to the United States. *Population Bulletin, 54*(2), pp. 1–44. Washington, DC: Population Reference Bureau.

Martinez, G. M., & Curry, A. E. (1999, September). *Current population reports: School enrollment—Social and economic characteristics of students* (update). Washington, DC: U.S. Census Bureau.

Riche, M. F. (2000). America's diversity and growth: Signposts for the 21st century. *Population Bulletin, 55*(2), pp. 1–43. Washington, DC: Population Reference Bureau.

U.S. Census Bureau. (2000). *Statistical abstract of the United States* (120th edition). Washington, DC: U.S. Government Printing Office.

Preface

I spend a great deal of time in schools. Most often, the schools I visit and work with are city schools, the kind of schools that are better known for their failures than their successes. Most of these are schools that serve poor children from poor neighborhoods: kids whose lives are so difficult and complicated that, for some, just getting to school each day represents a major feat and accomplishment.

I also spend a great deal of time working with policy makers on the issues confronting urban schools. More often than not, I am struck by how little they understand about the lives of the children served by failing schools and the complicated nature of the problems they seek to address. Typically, my conversations with them about solutions to the problems facing urban schools become reduced to a search for blame. Should we blame the lazy, unmotivated kids, or the irresponsible and neglectful parents? What about the ineffective and burned-out teachers, or the mindless bureaucrats and unreliable administrators who run the school districts? Of course, the policy makers are least likely to blame themselves. Pointing fingers and assigning blame are typically easier than accepting responsibility.

Somehow the politicians manage to see themselves as being above and beyond the fray. Often when they speak of failing schools and urban poverty it is as if they were speaking about issues in a foreign land, not jurisdictions that they bear indirect responsibility for. From micro-managing school board members, to media-crazed mayors, congresspeople, and governors, I have found that consistently those who know the least about education end up having the most say about what should be done.

Typically, when politicians offer solutions to the problems confronting failing inner-city schools, they fixate on a policy gimmick or a cure-all—more testing, charter schools, choice, vouchers—as if there were a silver bullet or special formula that quickly and easily could solve the problems and fix the schools. The inevitable failure of these gimmicks and the wasted resources applied in their pursuit add to the frustration and cynicism of the public. Unfulfilled promises and the long record of failure in the most troubled schools fuel the perception that the task of improving public education is simply too big, too complex, and too intractable for the

United States, the most powerful, wealthiest, and most technologically advanced nation in the world.

Occasionally, I am asked by a journalist, a parent, or even a policy maker about what should be done to improve failing urban schools. I often start out by quoting the opening line of a song by hip-hop singer Lauryn Hill in which she calls on her listeners to see that "it should be so simple but you'd rather make it hard." Of course, Hill is referring to relationships and not public education, but I think the same point applies. It should be simple to educate all children, even those who are poor and reside in the inner city. Simple, because from the time a child is born, he or she begins to learn. Learning to communicate, to reason, and to assimilate information is as natural a part of human development as learning to crawl or walk. To keep children from learning, one literally would have to lock them in a closet and deny them any stimulation and human contact.

The question is, why is it that many students don't learn very much or very well in many of our urban schools? What is there about the schools we have created, and invested billions of dollars in, that has led some students to reject school entirely and turned so many of them off to learning? Why are so many urban schools utterly inept at carrying out this basic task, a task nearly as old as human civilization itself?

I have written this book to attempt to provide answers to these questions, and to restore a sense of hope for the possibility that urban schools can be significantly improved. I fundamentally believe that educating all children, even those who are poor and non-White, is an achievable goal, *if* we truly value all children. Of course, that is the real question: Does American society truly value all of its children? Do we care enough to do what it takes to ensure that all children receive a quality education? Do we genuinely believe that education should serve as the "great equalizer" of opportunity, as the early architects of public education envisioned, that it should serve as a beacon of hope and a source of mobility for the poor and the powerless?

Achieving these goals is the great promise of American education. It is a promise that led this country to be the first among Western nations to develop a system of public education. And it is a promise that is integral to the American dream. Universal access to public education is what makes the Declaration of Independence's call for "life, liberty, and the pursuit of happiness" seem even remotely believable.

We now have an administration that has pledged to fulfill this promise by boldly calling on the nation to "leave no child behind." This is powerful rhetoric, and even those who question the commitment behind it find it difficult to question the sentiment and noble ambition that it conjures. Whether we believe in the veracity of the pledge or not, the fact is that the

President of the United States has raised the expectations of the entire nation by setting a goal that has been held out as a utopian ideal, but has never before been achieved.

If we believe that it is possible, or at least desirable, to try to fulfill the promise of American education, then the critical question confronting the nation is: What will it take to truly leave no child behind? Throughout this book, I make the case that answering this question will require us to recognize that educational problems in poor inner-city neighborhoods cannot be addressed without also responding to the social and economic conditions in the communities where schools are located. It is unfair and unrealistic to expect schools to raise test scores and focus narrowly on the task of educating children when a broad array of unmet nonacademic needs (e.g., food, housing, and health care) invariably affect their ability to learn. Put more simply, we cannot address educational issues in a social vacuum, and we cannot treat all schools or children the same when we know that life is much harder for some children than for others.

Throughout this book I show how external conditions affect the ability of schools to serve the needs of children, and I attempt to show what it would take to respond adequately to these needs. To make these points as clear and concrete as possible, I draw heavily on my years of experience working in schools as a researcher, teacher, policy maker, and activist in the San Francisco Bay Area. Although the region may not be typical of other areas in the United States, the problems plaguing its schools are. Each chapter is developed around one or more of the large external challenges confronting urban schools. I attempt to show how schools are affected by these external challenges and make suggestions for how they might respond.

In Chapter 1 I begin by laying out my approach to understanding the issues facing urban schools, an approach I characterize as pragmatic optimism. This approach is rooted in an analysis of the ways in which the social context affects children's lives and the character of schools. I also situate these issues within a framework that Brazilian educator Paulo Freire has termed "limit situations." Freire's framework calls for a careful assessment of the conditions that constrain the lives and potential of the poor and oppressed, and it implores those who would take on these challenges to devise creative and imaginative ways to respond to and subvert those conditions. Most important, it is a perspective based on the idea that the poor must play the leading role in finding solutions to the sources of their oppression and to the conditions that limit and restrict human potential.

In Chapter 2 I use the high-wealth (San Francisco and Berkeley) and high-poverty (Oakland and Richmond) cities of the Bay Area to show how social boundaries relating to race and class shape the character of schools and neighborhoods. Demographic change in the composition of urban school districts is intimately connected to the problems and issues they face and to the ways in which policy makers respond. In this chapter I show how terms such as "urban" and "community" are increasingly less related to geography and spatial proximity and more tied to identity and perceptions of interests.

The complex relationship between race and educational performance is tackled in Chapter 3 in an attempt to shed light on the factors influencing the persistence of disparities in student achievement. I wade through the arguments and rationalizations that are made most frequently by scholars and educators in relation to why minority children tend to achieve at lower rates than White students. I take on these arguments because belief in them contributes to the idea that children, families, and some amorphous notion of "culture" are the causes of the so-called achievement gap, and leads to the perception that there is nothing that schools can do to close the gap. Also, given that urban schools in the United States disproportionately serve students of color, the need to address issues directly related to race is especially important.

I follow this discussion with an examination of how racial inequality is reproduced in schools, through a case study analysis of Berkeley High School in Chapter 4. Drawing on 4 years of research at the school, I show how patterns of privilege and failure are maintained and describe some of the measures that have been taken to reverse these long-standing trends. In so doing, I scrutinize the way in which race has been used to frame educational challenges facing minority students and suggest different ways of formulating the problems and solutions. I also show how research can be used as an instrument of reform and how collaborations can be built between university-based and school-based practitioners.

The ways in which poverty and racial segregation have limited possibilities for democratic governance and the ability of poor people to hold their schools accountable in Oakland is the subject of Chapter 5. I take up a point frequently expressed by conservative advocates of privatization but generally ignored by liberals: Schools that serve a "captured consumer market" have little incentive to improve or to serve their constituents well. I show how poverty makes it possible for elected officials and district administrators to ignore the needs of the children and families they serve. I also describe ways in which schools can be improved from the outside-in through the development of social capital and civic capacity in low-income communities.

Chapter 6 is focused on the ways in which student perceptions and experiences with violence shape their attitudes toward it, and how these in turn influence safety within schools. I present research and describe my experience working with Lowell Middle School in west Oakland to demonstrate the importance of understanding what students think and feel about these issues. Through a study carried out at the site, I show how an understanding of student attitudes toward violence can be used to devise strategies to promote safety. I also critique the ways in which policy makers and educators have responded to fears about school violence, and show how ineffective these approaches have been in producing genuine safety in schools.

In the final chapter, I return to Paulo Friere's notion of limit situations to show how some of the most difficult problems facing urban schools can be approached. The failures of educational policy and policies related to urban poverty are documented and analyzed. As an alternative to these failed approaches, I use individual and community cases to illustrate how thoughtful and significant responses can be devised to respond to difficult problems, and I use these to suggest that there is still a reasonable basis for hope that change can be made.

Throughout this book I use the names of real schools and real people. This is not typical for books of this kind. In most cases, authors who write about schools change the names of people and places so that they can protect those they have worked with. I use the names of individuals only if the reference is positive; however, with respect to the schools I name, the commentaries about them are mixed. To be helpful to the schools I've worked with and to my readers, I feel that a strong degree of honesty and transparency is essential. Using pseudonyms for people and schools would make this work safer and potentially less controversial, but also would make it easier for me to be less forthright and honest.

ACKNOWLEDGMENTS

In keeping with my interest in openness, I also must thank all of the individuals who have assisted me in different aspects of the work that led to this book. First, I want to thank Ronnie Stevenson and George Perry, two individuals who convinced me that working in urban schools with kids who had been written off as unteachable, was worthwhile and important. I also want to thank Timiza Wagner, whose patience and tireless commitment to her students served as a source of inspiration to me in my work. Rosalyn Upshaw, Joe Coats, and Betty Maze helped me to understand the challenges confronting schools and children and West Oakland, and helped me to make sense of the issues I encountered. Ronald Glass, Jean Yonemura Wing, Anne Okahara, Susan Groves, Julia González Luna, Dick LeBlanc, Rick Ayers, Tamara Friedman, Emma Fuentes, Jabari Mahiri, Anthony Rojo, Dana Moran, Flora Russ, Miriam Stahl, LaShawn Routé-Chatmaon, James

Williams, Antwi Akom, Elena Silva, Beth Rubin, Kysa Nygreen, Anne Gregory, Robin Ortiz-Young, Isabel Parra, Cheryl Roberts, Juana Villegas, Julina Bastidas-Bonilla, Regina Segura, Pamela Doolan, Betty Spillman, Vajra Watson, Dave Stevens, Marie Roberts, Lance McCready, Amy Crawford, Pharmicia Mosely, Annie Johnston, Rory Bled, Amy Hansen, Alicia Rodriguez, Miriam Topel, Louis Thomas, Colette Cann, Ted Shultz, Hodari Davis, Doris-Wallace Tanner, Terry Doran, Joey Christiano, Jamie McMaryion, Barbara Mellion, Anthony Santangelo, Nancy Spaeth, Siobhan Acosta, Eleanor Mayer, Leticia Brown, Kysa Nygreen, Patricia Sanchez, Soo Ah Kwan, Maika Watanabe, Andrea Dyrness, Daniel Liou, and Irma Parker were all partners who worked with me at various times over the course of 4 years to try to make Berkeley High School a fairer and more equitable place. I also want to thank Shauna Cagan, Karen Wisniewski, and Kristen Prentice for their assistance in editing and preparing this book for publication.

Of course, a project like this could not have been completed without considerable support and forbearance from my family. I want to thank my four children: Joaquin, Amaya, Antonio, and Naima, each of whom is mentioned in the book because their experiences in school provided me with yet another window through which to understand what was happening in urban schools. Too often they were deprived of my time and attention because my energies were focused on the needs of other children. Last but not least, I want to thank my wife Patricia, who for 21 years has been my toughest critic, my conscience, and my most important source of moral support.

In big and small ways, all of these individuals helped to make this book and the work that went into it possible, and I thank them all for the support, encouragement, and feedback they have provided along the way.

City Schools and the American Dream

RECLAIMING THE PROMISE OF PUBLIC EDUCATION

CHAPTER 1

Finding Hope Among the Hopeless

It was an overcast, Thursday afternoon. The fog was rolling in across the Bay and the temperature was dropping. It was the kind of day that is more typical of summer than fall in the Bay Area.

It was late in the day and I was feeling particularly uninspired about my job. When I first started working as the Executive Assistant to Mayor Loni Hancock, I thought I had the best job in the city. I was at the center of power in local government, and I thought I was in a position to make things happen. From the very first day the job had been demanding, but in a good way. Every day I was presented with new challenges and new issues to work on. At first I thought that I was in a position to have an impact on issues I cared about—homelessness, drug abuse, and the plight of the city's youth. About 3 months into the job, my optimism had given way to the grim reality that change comes slowly in municipal government.

I soon realized that the Mayor's office was not a place where sweeping reforms would be launched and fundamental changes would be initiated. Even more depressing for me was the realization that rather than power, what I had was responsibility. I was responsible for figuring out what the city should do about the homeless who were camping out in the park behind City Hall. I was responsible for explaining to frightened residents why the police couldn't stop the drug dealers who were terrorizing their neighborhood. I was responsible for meeting with protesters who wanted to make Peoples Park into a national shrine, and old ladies who wanted their neighbors to trim their trees so that their view of the Bay would not be obstructed.

I was growing tired of Berkeley politics, and for the first time in my life I felt discouraged, despondent, and downright depressed about my work. Perhaps I had been too naive. Why should I have thought that crime and poverty could be solved by one city, even as they plagued communities throughout the United States?

The year was 1988 and crack cocaine and the violence that accompanied it were devastating the Black community in Berkeley. As the Mayor's representative, I was frequently the person who had to respond to community complaints about drive-by shootings and crack houses that operated like open markets. I quickly learned that city government lacked the resources to solve any of the major problems facing residents. As the person most likely to hear the pain and anguish of the community and to be blamed for the city's failures, I had grown extremely frustrated after just 2 years on the job.

Feeling beleaguered and burdened by the responsibilities of the job, I was miraculously drawn back into education by the principal of a local high school who came to my office that foggy afternoon accompanied by one of his students. My friend George Perry recently had been assigned to serve as principal of the local continuation school, East Campus (a school for students who had been removed from the traditional high school due to poor behavior and/or grades). It turned out that he had been assigned to his new job as punishment for the trouble he had caused in the district. However, instead of scaring him into retirement as the higher-ups had hoped, the assignment renewed George's sense of purpose about his work in education.

He came to see me because I once had served as the student body president at UC Berkeley, and he wanted me to convince his student, John Peters, to run for student body president of his school. As George sang the praises of his student leader, I took a good look at John and immediately surmised that he was probably a street-level drug dealer. With gold teeth in his mouth, a thick gold chain around his neck, and a beeper at his waist, John fit a profile I had come to know well. I looked at John and then back at George, and my look revealed my confusion about what he had in mind. But instead of voicing my doubts, I listened as George told me why he wanted John to run for student body president and I listened closely as John told me about himself. Within minutes I understood what George was thinking. John was intelligent, articulate, and extremely charismatic. George knew that if he could co-opt John by convincing him to play a positive role at his school, he might be able to find a way to get other students to begin to take their education more seriously. John was a natural leader and George understood that he needed John on his side. He needed John to be a force for good at the school.

East Campus once had served as an alternative school for kids who did not fit in at the large, impersonal environment at Berkeley High School. Over time, it had become a dumping ground for troubled kids like John. Tucked away at the margins of the school district, East Campus was a school in name only. The first time I visited the school there were more kids in the parking lot blasting their car radios and smoking pot, than there were in the classrooms. In a city that took great pride in its commitment to racial integration, the school was over 90% Black. Hardly any students attended class, and those that did seemed to be there in body only.

Despite the sorrowful state of the school, I was so taken by John and by what my friend George Perry was trying to accomplish, that I immediately was convinced that working at the school was where I should be, given my desire to make a difference. I saw the potential to transform this small forgotten school into a place that could become a genuine alternative for kids who were being killed and imprisoned each day because of the drug trade on the streets. Shortly after my visit, I left my job with the Mayor to join George as a teacher at East Campus.

CONFRONTING THE "CRISIS" IN URBAN PUBLIC SCHOOLS

I begin this book with this story about my entry into the field of education because it is reflective of how I have come to understand the promise and the potential of urban public schools in the United States. Like East Campus, many other urban schools have been written off as failures. Failure is the word used most frequently to describe urban public schools in the United States, because the lists of problems confronting these institutions is so long and daunting. Low test scores, low grades, high drop-out rates, poor attendance, and generally unmotivated students usually top the lists of failings. Burned-out and ineffective teachers, who care more about protecting their jobs than helping students, typically follow complaints about students. Those more intimately familiar with conditions in urban districts point to dilapidated and unsafe buildings, administrations hopelessly mired in politicized and inefficient bureaucracies, and an endless series of reforms that never seem to lead to genuine improvement (F. Hess, 1999).

If these characterizations were limited to a handful of urban schools or districts, the "problem" might not seem so daunting, but this is not the case. Urban school failure is pervasive. It is endemic in the nation's largest cities—New York, Chicago, Los Angeles, and Philadelphia, and not uncommon in small towns such as East St. Louis, Poughkeepsie, Camden, and Compton. In fact, wherever poor people are concentrated and employment is scarce, public schools are almost always very bad. In many parts of the country, the problems present within urban schools are perceived as so numerous and intractable that the term "crisis" frequently is applied to describe the situation; and this is how it is described by those who haven't given up hope completely.

Yet, although the problems and issues confronting urban public schools in the United States are profound and deeply discouraging, characterizing their plight as either one of crisis or utter hopelessness is inaccurate. Nor do such grim portrayals serve as a genuine diagnosis of the problems or shed light on what should be done to address them. Such descriptions do, however, play an important role in influencing popular conceptions of urban schools, and ultimately they influence how policy makers approach the task of "fixing" the schools.

Were the situation in urban schools truly a "crisis," one might expect to see urgent responses from leaders at the local, state, and federal levels. After all, the education and welfare of millions of children are at stake, and if a crisis were genuinely perceived, would not drastic measures be taken to alleviate the suffering, not unlike the actions taken following an earthquake or a hurricane? However, even during a period in which educational issues are receiving more media coverage and more attention from policy makers than ever before,[1] there is a stunning lack of urgency associated with official responses to the issues confronting urban public schools.

Moreover, in everyday parlance, the term *crisis* typically is thought of as a temporary condition, a temporary although serious deviation from the status quo. Injured individuals and beleaguered communities affected by a storm or fire generally are not thought of as being in a permanent state of crisis. Even if the problems have devastating long-term consequences, over time the condition ceases to be described as a crisis. Eventually, there is a recovery and a return to a state of normalcy. Crises that persist or become more severe, like illnesses that take a turn for the worse and are deemed incurable, generally are characterized as chronic and debilitating conditions, unfortunate but permanent states for which solutions may never be found.

Similarly, while the term *crisis* may not appropriately characterize the situation in urban schools, those who describe them as doomed and hopelessly unfixable are also off the mark. There is no question that the problems of urban schools are entrenched and intractable. However, compelling evidence suggests that despite their failings and weaknesses, urban public schools are in fact indispensable to those they serve. Without any viable alternative available, urban public schools cannot be written off as rotten structures in need of demolition.

THE INDISPENSABLE INSTITUTION

Despite the severity of the conditions present in many urban schools, and despite the intractability of the problems they face, these deeply flawed institutions continue to serve millions of children throughout the United States. In fact, the largest school districts in the nation are classified as "urban" and they serve nearly one-third of school-aged children (Council of Great City Schools, 2001). In a profound demonstration of faith, millions of parents voluntarily take their children each day to the very schools that have been described as "desperate hell holes" (McGroarty, 1996). Certainly, many do so with reluctance and considerable consternation. In many cases, parents enroll their children only because they lack options or access to schools they regard as better or safer. However, many others do so willingly, hoping against the odds that for their child, or at the particular school their child attends, something good will happen, and a better future through education will be possible.[2] At a minimum, they may enroll their sons and daughters because they know that even at a failing public school their children will have access to a warm meal and adult supervision while they are there.

I was reminded of the difficult choices facing poor parents during conversations with Salvadoran refugees in a run-down neighborhood of inner-city Los Angeles. I was meeting with a group of parents at the Central American Refugee Center shortly after the Rodney King uprising of 1991. We met in an area of downtown LA called Pico Union, one of the most densely populated neighborhoods in the United States and home to thousands of undocumented war refugees from Central America. Although it did not receive much media attention, it had been one of the epicenters of violence and looting during the riot. The parents I met with described the riot as the product of rising frustrations, and while others debated whether the outburst should be called a riot or a rebellion, these refugees of brutal civil wars termed it "*un explosion social*" (a social explosion).

As they described the perils they faced raising children in this crime-ridden, drug-infested neighborhood, they made me aware of how important the public schools were to them. They did not complain about the overcrowded classrooms, the absence of certified teachers, or the dismal state of the facilities. Instead, they spoke with genuine appreciation about how happy they were to have a safe place to send their children. The fact that their children were fed, and in at least one school provided health care, added to their sense of gratitude. "*Somos probes, sin poder o derechos. Por los menos nuestro hijos teinen una educacion. Si, hay problemas en las escuelas, pero tenemos esperanza que el futuro de los hijos va estar mejor.*" (We are poor, without power or rights. At least our children have an education. Yes, there are problems in the schools, but we have hope that the future for our children will be better.)

In economically depressed inner-city communities like Pico Union, public schools play a vital role in supporting low-income families. Even when other neighborhood services, including banks, retail stores, libraries, and other public services, do not exist, are shut down, or are abandoned, public schools remain (Noguera, 1995a). They are neighborhood constants, not because they succeed in carrying out their mission or because they satisfy the needs of those they serve, but because they have a relatively stable source of funding ensured by the legal mandate to educate children.

Urban public schools frequently serve as important social welfare institutions.[3] With meager resources, they attempt to address at least some of the nutritional and health needs of poor children. They do so because those charged with educating poor children generally recognize that it is impossible to serve their academic needs without simultaneously addressing their basic need for health and safety. For many poor children, schools provide a source of stability that often is lacking in other parts of their lives, and while many urban public schools are plagued by the threat of violence and intimidation, most are far safer than the communities in which they are located (Casella, 2001). The bottom line is that even when there is little evidence of educational efficacy, urban public schools still provide services that are desperately needed by poor families, and federal and state policies offer few alternatives.

In the absence of genuine alternatives, even failing public schools retain a dependent although disgruntled constituency base because they are typically the only social institution that provides a consistent source of stability and support to impoverished families. For this reason, those who castigate and disparage urban public schools without offering viable solutions for improving or replacing them jeopardize the interests of those who depend on them. Politicians who often lead the chorus of criticisms have largely failed to devise policies to address the deplorable conditions present in many inner-city schools and communities. Even in the few cases where drastic measures, such as state takeovers of troubled districts (most often, urban school systems), have been taken, the results achieved generally have failed to live up to the expectations or promises. Most of the popular educational reforms enacted by states and the federal government (e.g., standards and accountability through high-stakes testing, charter schools, phonics-based reading programs, etc.) fail to address the severe social and economic conditions in urban areas that invariably affect the quality and character of public schools.

The central argument of this book is that until there is a genuine commitment to address the social context of schooling—to confront the "urban" condition—it will be impossible to bring about significant and sustainable improvements in urban public schools. The complex and seemingly intractable array of social and economic problems in urban areas must be addressed and school-based policies that respond to these problems must be devised; otherwise, pervasive school failure in cities across the United States will continue to be the norm.

Public schools are the only institutions in this country charged with providing for the educational needs of poor children. Given the role they play, it would be a mistake to allow them to deteriorate further or to become unsalvageable. Undeniably, they often carry out their mission poorly, without adequately serving the educational needs of the children under their charge. However, public schools in the United States are the only social institutions that cannot by law turn a child away regardless of race, religion, immigration status, or any other trait or designation (Kirp, 1982). Access to public education in the United States is complete, universal, and compulsory (Tyack, 1980), and, as such, it is also the only public service that functions as a form of social entitlement: a "positive right"[4] and social good provided to citizens and noncitizens alike (Carnoy & Levin, 1985). For all of these reasons, public education, even in the poorest sections of the inner city, constitutes a vital public resource. Rather than being regarded as hopelessly unfixable, urban public schools, particularly those that serve poor children, must be seen for what they are: the last and most enduring remnant of the social safety net for poor children in the United States.

Seen in this light, the problems confronting urban public school must be approached from a different perspective. Instead of castigating and decrying their failures, and inadvertently joining the chorus clamoring for their total demolition, those who recognize the value and the importance of the services schools provide must instead adopt a position of critical support. In the same way that it would be unwise for criticisms of overcrowded buses or trains to prompt calls to abandon mass transportation, those who deplore conditions in urban public schools must recognize that, despite their weaknesses, urban public schools are desperately needed by those they serve. Just as complaints about long lines and poor service should not be used to justify the elimination of public hospitals and clinics that provide health services to the poor and elderly, the failures of urban public schools should not be used as a rationale for their elimination. At least until a genuine, superior alternative for all children is available, public education, with all its faults and weaknesses, remains "the one best system," or at least the only system we have (Tyack, 1980).

However, critical support should not be confused with unquestioning loyalty to public education. Parents, especially those whose children are forced to attend the worst schools, generally have very little loyalty to the "system," and for good reason. The parents I spoke with in Pico Union appreciated the support their children received from struggling schools in their neighborhood, but in all likelihood would jump at the opportunity to enroll their children in better schools if it were possible. Few parents are willing to sacrifice the needs of their children because they wish to show support for the democratic principles underlying the existence of public schools. Given the opportunity, most parents actively seek schools they think have the greatest potential to meet the needs of their children. Whether this occurs in a public, private, or charter school is generally less relevant than whether the school is accessible, affordable, safe, and educationally viable. Defenders of public education who refuse to recognize this reality of parenting undoubtedly will feel betrayed when those who were once their most reliable consumers, namely, poor parents, abandon public schools when provided with options they perceive as superior.

Critical supporters of public education must recognize that it is the rights of children and their families to a good education, and not a failed system, that must be supported. Critical supporters must not be afraid to honestly identify and call attention to the failures of the system, whether these are related to unresponsive leadership or the poor quality of teaching. Critical supporters must demonstrate active support for change and improvement, and, given the sorrowful plight of many schools, they must be open to considering a variety of strategies for innovation. This should not be interpreted as a naive willingness to embrace every new fad in educational reform that comes along. Rather, critical supporters should recognize that all reforms should be evaluated and assessed by the academic and social outcomes obtained by children. With calls for privatization gaining support and momentum, the only way to save public education is to radically alter it. Ensuring that the needs of students and their parents are treated as the highest priority, may be the most radical reform of all.

PRAGMATIC OPTIMISM AS A GUIDE

This book was written to show how urban schools are affected by the social environment in which they are located and to put forward a set of strategies to transform, improve, and fundamentally restructure them. The ideas presented are the product of years of research, teaching, and service in urban schools throughout the United States. These years of experience have provided me with a strong sense of the grim reality present in many urban public schools, and also insights into what I believe it will take to make change possible. I characterize my perspective on the issues and problems confronting urban public schools as one of critical support and pragmatic optimism.

My pragmatism comes from personal and direct experience grappling with the problems facing urban public schools; and so does my optimism. As a middle and high school teacher in Providence, Rhode Island, and in

Oakland and Berkeley, California, I have seen firsthand how hard it can be to work within schools and districts where the academic failure of large numbers of students has been the norm for a very long time. In such places, patterns of failure for certain kinds of students are so commonplace and so deeply entrenched that failure tends to be accepted as inevitable and unavoidable. Through research carried out at numerous urban schools, I have seen how easy it is for teachers and administrators to rationalize and therefore accept failure. Given the abundance of unmotivated and underprepared students, dysfunctional and distressed families, unresponsive and incompetent administrators and teachers, and, most of all, misguided and foolhardy politicians, there is no shortage of compelling excuses for persistent failure. Yet, ultimately even this litany of charges just provides the person espousing them with a justification for the inability to make a difference with the children he or she serves. The tendency for some educators to cast blame elsewhere, while accepting responsibility for very little, provides me with a strong sense of pragmatism as I consider what it will take to bring about change.

Additionally, having served as an elected Director and President of the School Board in Berkeley, California, I also realize how difficult it is to reverse negative trends and change things for the better. Serving from 1990 to 1994, a period during which many schools faced severe financial hardships, I realized that my job was to manage what I came to regard as a miserable status quo. My responsibility as a board member required me to eliminate vital programs in order to balance the district budget. I was forced to take the heat for strained relations with our labor unions because we were unable to satisfy their legitimate demands for higher wages. Worst of all, I was forced to vote to expel some of our neediest students, setting them loose on the streets without adequate provision for their education or welfare, because they engaged in violent or dangerous behavior.

If I had not become a pragmatist from such experiences, I undoubtedly would have abandoned my interest in working for the betterment of urban public schools long ago. Pragmatism makes it possible for one to act even in difficult circumstances when one must accept and recognize the limitations of what may be possible. Pragmatism also makes it possible to avoid demonizing beleaguered administrators, angry parents, and frustrated teachers, because it allows one to understand the legitimate source of their resentment, even if it does not provide a way to adequately respond to it.

However, my pragmatism has not given way to cynicism or disillusionment. I remain profoundly aware of the unique potential inherent in education; it alone has the ability to transform and improve the lives of even the neediest and most downtrodden individuals. At the most basic level, I know that all children, regardless of their race or class background, can learn and grow in positive and productive ways when provided the opportunity, and that even in the poorest communities it is possible to create schools that serve children well. I know these things not because of blind faith but largely from direct experience. I have taught in schools that were dumping grounds for "at-risk" adolescents, and I have worked with students who had been written off as incorrigible and unteachable. I have seen these same students learn, grow confident in their abilities, and aspire to achieve goals that previously seemed impossible.

GAINING A PERSPECTIVE ON SUCCESS AND FAILURE

My faith in the possibility that education can serve as a vehicle of individual transformation, and even social change, is rooted in an understanding that human beings have the ability to rise above even the most difficult obstacles, to become more than just victims of circumstance. I have seen education open doors for those who lacked opportunity, and open the minds of those who could not imagine alternative ways of being and living. Like Brazilian educator Paulo Freire (1970), I have seen education enable students to "perceive critically the way they exist in the world; to see the world not as a static reality, but as a reality in process, in transformation" (p. 71).

My optimism is rooted in my faith in people. It is a faith affirmed by teachers like Timiza Wagner, who, unlike me, spent nearly 20 years teaching at East Campus, tirelessly working to instill a sense of hope among young people who had been written off as hopeless by the schools that served them. It is a faith that is renewed by finding schools like Henshaw Middle School in Modesto, California, where most of the children are recent immigrants, speak Spanish as their first language, and have parents who work at the dirty jobs that most Americans refuse to take. Yet, this is a school whose students consistently achieve at high levels (Carnegie Foundation, 1994/1995), and a school where parents are respected as genuine partners despite all the things they do not have. I have worked with other schools that provide an oasis of hope to children who live in neighborhoods and housing projects that seem unfit for human habitation, whose lives are so difficult and arduous that coming to know them well can be a painful experience. I also have had the privilege of working with schools that gradually have been transformed from dumping grounds for bad kids and poor teachers, into model schools that provide students with genuine alternatives from the uncaring, impersonal environments present in many urban public schools. Finally, I have observed teachers who consistently create educational magic in their classrooms, who incite and motivate their students to want to learn, who set high standards for themselves and their students and make it clear that not learning simply is not an option.

Experiences such as these enabled me to overcome the pessimism I felt while working in the Mayor's office: a pessimism that so often overwhelms those who work in urban schools in the United States. As a university professor, of course, I have the luxury to visit both good and bad schools, but unlike those I observe and work with, I get to leave the despair and return to the comfort of the university. I work with and speak to thousands of teachers, students, and parents, and I hear them express their frustrations about politicians who either do not understand or do not care about the conditions in inner-city schools. I also serve on national committees that are charged with studying the problems confronting urban education, and occasionally I am asked to testify before policy makers about what should be done. I use these opportunities to voice the concerns of those who are never heard because their plight and suffering simply are not seen as important.

Yet despite my extensive involvement, I still get to leave the schools whenever I want. I get to return to my office at the university where I can escape the daily grind and the mind-numbing routine of so many schools. I can escape the loud hallways and the tedious faculty meetings that drive even idealistic and committed teachers to cynicism or out of teaching altogether. I get to see the big picture, to keep one foot in and one foot out of urban public schools, and I am allowed time to reflect on what I have seen. I have time to review the data I have collected, to reflect on the stories I have heard, and the opportunity to write and speak about my experiences at some distance from the places where the drama of school plays itself out. I am mindful of the many privileges I enjoy in relation to this work, and I feel compelled to use my position to speak on behalf of those who do not possess similar opportunities and advantages. I do not take this responsibility lightly. My experience leaves me compelled to be accountable for my words and deeds.

When I compare my situation with the reality of most teachers, counselors, and administrators who work within urban public schools, or with the lives of the children who attend them, I am forced to reflect on my own life and the privileges I enjoy. As a former student in New York City's public schools, I am keenly aware that things could have turned out differently for me. Most of my closest friends did not go to college, much less an Ivy League university. The fortunate found dead-end jobs that provide them and their families with a degree of stability. The less fortunate are either dead or wasting away their lives in prison. The long list of those who met such a fate suggests their demise was more than the result of poor choices made or a lack of self-discipline.

My personal fortune does not lead me to the conclusion that if I, a working-class kid from Brooklyn, can find success through education, then so can anyone else who makes the effort. Unlike individuals such as John McWhorter (2000) and Shelby Steele (1990), who use their personal success as a basis for castigating others, especially Black people, for laziness and anti-intellectualism,[5] my experience has taught me that there is more to achieving academic and personal success than effort alone. Children don't get to choose their parents, the neighborhood they'll grow up in, the school they'll attend, or the teachers to whom they'll be assigned. While growing up, I knew many kids who tried hard to do well in school, whose parents supported them and who valued education as strongly as did mine. Yet, most of them were not as fortunate. Due largely to circumstances beyond their control, their dreams and those of their parents were never realized, not because of a lack of effort, but because of a lack of luck and opportunity.

As the second of six children from working-class Caribbean immigrant parents, neither of whom graduated from high school or attended college, I benefited from having learned at an early age to understand the importance of education. Even though neither of my parents had the time or knowledge to navigate the school system, they still managed to convey the importance of academic success to their children, and succeeded in sending all six to some of the most highly regarded universities in the nation. We didn't attend elite private or suburban schools. There was no money for private tutors, computers, or expensive vacations. Yet, education worked for us, even though, for the most part, we succeeded in spite of the system, not because of it. As new immigrants, my parents rejected the idea that the skin color and culture made us racially inferior. We were taught that character and hard work mattered more than race, and that none of the White children we went to school with were inherently superior. Ours is an old success story, one of immigrants who are able to reap the rewards of American opportunity through hard work and determination. Yet, such stories do not negate the fact that, without a Herculean effort, the vast majority of those who are born poor, stay poor.

Now, as the parent of four children, all of whom have attended urban public schools, I continue to enjoy a position of privilege. Unlike me, my children have access to the resources available to most middle-class families—summer enrichment programs, music lessons, and foreign travel. They attend public schools but we have the know-how to make the system work for them and the resources to make up for what they do not receive in school. I know how to advocate for my children and I know how to help them navigate schools that consistently fail large numbers of students. My education grants me class privileges, and generally I am treated with courtesy and respect when I visit my children's schools. Unlike many other parents, I am treated like a valued customer: a client who has the ability and wherewithal to exit the system if I feel unsatisfied with the quality of service.

My experience as a parent and student in urban public schools has taught me that while effort is a key ingredient for individual success, for those who are born poor it is not a guarantee. My understanding of the broad patterns of failure and success in American society leads me to conclude that under the present conditions, academic failure for large numbers of poor and working-class children is inevitable. Although we may be in a "new economy" in which many jobs require advanced skills and education (Murnane & Levy, 1996), there is still a need for people who are willing to accept low-status, low-wage work. As long as some schools (suburban and private) are able to generate a sufficient number of academically qualified students for high-skill, high-wage labor, or as long as such labor can be imported, the failure of low-performing schools does not pose a problem for the economy.

Politically, the quality of schools corresponds closely to the strength of electoral constituencies. This is a point that will be developed further in Chapter 2, where I examine the effects of poverty and racial segregation on local control over schools. Since the end of World War II, political power has shifted in most states from the cities to the suburbs (Clark, 1985; Gratz & Mintz, 1998). Moreover, in high-poverty urban areas, voter participation tends to be low, and ties to political parties are often weak (Schorr, 1997). Cities increasingly lack the political clout needed to obtain much-needed resources from state government. In some cases, cities still serve as important centers of economic and cultural activity. But even when they retain a degree of viability, they are more likely to employ those who reside elsewhere than those who live within city limits.[6]

Throughout the United States, failing schools are treated as local matters, and responsibility for improving them is delegated to those who reside in the communities they serve. This continues to be the case whether or not communities can generate the resources to address the needs of poor students. From afar, state governments have established academic standards and systems for holding schools accountable (Blasi, 2001; Elmore, 1996), even though it is widely recognized that there are many schools where basic "opportunity to learn standards" have not been met (Oakes, 2002). Of course, state governments do find ways to commit resources to an ever-expanding penal system that stands ready to absorb those who have encountered failure elsewhere.

The consistency of patterns of success and failure, both academic and ultimately economic, and the predictability of these patterns—their correlation with the racial and socioeconomic backgrounds of children—explain why the problems of America's urban public schools are written off as inevitable. Although academic failure in urban schools may be lamented by politicians and deplored by the media, and although those seen as responsible may be viciously castigated, such posturing should not be confused with a serious response to the problem. Ultimately, the lack of a concerted and sustained effort to respond to failing urban public schools can be explained only by understanding that America simply does not care that large numbers of children from inner-city schools and neighborhoods are not properly educated.

This is not a conspiracy theory. For me, it is simply a starting point for my pragmatism. The plight of inner-city schools and many rural schools that serve poor children throughout the United States is not a secret or unknown fact. It is widely recognized that many urban public schools are places that should be avoided because they are dangerous, chaotic, and potentially damaging to those who go there. Yet, it also is understood that certain children—the poorest and neediest—will end up there. For this reason, the possibility that low-performing schools will be forced to close and that other schools will be required to educate their students, as called for in a new policy from the Bush administration, seems implausible. Just as it was true during the bitter and bloody conflicts over busing, it continues to be true today: There aren't many schools in affluent areas that want to serve poor children, especially those who are not White. For this reason it is highly unlikely that the new policy—various forms of school choice or even vouchers—will provide the least powerful children access to schools that are as good as those that serve affluent children.[7]

Urban schools and the children who attend them languish under third world-like conditions, even as President George W. Bush boldly promises to "leave no child behind." Millions of dollars from private and public sources are spent in the name of reform and restructuring, and an entire industry of education experts has been created to go about the work of improving America's schools, but the situation in inner-city schools remains largely unchanged.

In my travels across the United States, I frequently encounter a small number of effective schools that cater to poor children. However, I realize that their scarcity is not an accident.[8] In the San Francisco Bay Area, elementary schools such as Washington in Richmond, Emerson in Berkeley, and Hawthorn in San Francisco serve as living proof that it is possible to create schools that serve poor children well. Their existence, like the 4,000 high-performing, high-poverty schools throughout the nation identified by the

Education Trust, reminds us that the problem is not the children but the schools they attend (Education Trust, 2002). Still, knowing that such schools exist forces me to ask why we continue to allow them to be exceptions amid a sea of miserable inadequacy.

The extreme disparities in wealth that pervade U.S. society are largely responsible for the plight of young people and the state of education in urban areas. However, the dearth of good schools is also the inevitable by-product of a system that is almost completely unaccountable to those it serves. Public education is one of few enterprises where the quality of service provided has no bearing whatsoever on the ability of the system to function. Even when there is little evidence that schools are able to fulfill their basic mission—educating children—the system continues to chug along and all employees get paid (some quite well). This is why I believe that the high-stakes exams that have been adopted in states such as Massachusetts and California are fundamentally flawed and morally irresponsible. The exams are used to hold students accountable for their achievement even though the authorities who have imposed the exams know that they cannot guarantee the quality of the education students receive.

As long as we are able to convince ourselves that simply providing access to education is equivalent to providing equal opportunity, we will continue to treat failing schools as a nonissue. We also will continue to delude ourselves with the notion that the United States is a democracy based on genuine meritocratic principles: a society where social mobility is determined by individual talent and effort. We hold on to this fantasy even as a quarter of the nation's children are denied adequate educational opportunity.

Ultimately, this denial relegates the problems and issues confronting urban public schools to the margins of public life in American society. The media frequently carries stories about deplorable conditions in urban public schools, but typically it does so as if they occurred far away in some third world nation. Occasionally, the media will report on the triumphant stories of poor children like Cedric Jennings, the lead character in *A Hope in the Unseen* (Suskind, 1999). Cedric manages to overcome tremendous obstacles while going to school in southeast DC, and he manages to succeed against great odds. Yet, even in telling his story, the idea that individual effort rather than structural change is the solution is reinforced. As a society we are generally far more comfortable extolling the virtues of individual responsibility and merit, even as the structural nature of the problems affecting poor kids and schools in poor neighborhoods go unexplored and unaddressed in policy.

The fact that the United States tolerates the failure of so many of its urban schools suggests that there is either a pervasive belief that poor children are not entitled to anything better, or an active conspiracy to ensure that the majority of children who are born poor, stay poor. Whether we accept either of these explanations is ultimately less important than what critical supporters actually do to ensure that present and future generations of children are provided with the opportunity to attend better schools.

LIMITS AND POSSIBILITIES OF CHANGING URBAN PUBLIC SCHOOLS

One of the goals of this book is to put forward a framework that can be used to guide the improvement of urban public schools, one that takes the social context—or what I have termed the urban condition—into account. Drawing on my research and teaching experience, and from a perspective based on pragmatic optimism, my starting point for such a framework is to recognize the limits and possibilities of what can be changed in the current circumstances.

My own thinking about limits and possibilities is influenced by the work of Brazilian educator Paulo Freire (1972). Freire uses the concept of a "limit situation" in theorizing about his work in adult literacy. For Freire, illiteracy is much more than a failure to master the mechanics of reading and writing. It is rather a symptom of a larger condition of oppression and powerlessness and therefore cannot be fixed through traditional approaches to adult education. Instead, through dialogue and communication based on mutual respect and reciprocity, Freire calls upon educators to teach students to "read the world." This entails helping students to acquire an understanding of the forces that maintain imbalances in wealth and power so that the students can see their "situation as an historical reality susceptible to transformation" (p. 73). It also involves a move away from fatalistic perspectives that lead individuals to accept and adapt to oppressive circumstances, and calls for the adoption of a critical stance toward relations of power.

Freire recognized that a critical perspective (he uses the term *critical consciousness*) is not enough to transform social conditions, so he calls on teachers to treat conditions of oppression as "limit situations": problems that require critical reflection, engagement, and praxis. By this he meant that in any historical period, the possibilities for change must constantly be assessed and reflected upon so that strategies for countering these conditions can be devised. Freire conceived of human liberation and social justice as states of being that people must aspire to and devise courses of action to realize. By viewing the constraints on their freedom and dignity as limited situations, Freire believed the oppressed would be less inclined to see their situation as having been ordained by God. He hoped that such a shift in perspective would open the possibility that the oppressed would consider ways to act on these constraints and gradually expand possibilities for a greater degree of freedom. Freire (1970) writes:

> As they separate themselves from the world and locate the seat of their decisions in themselves and in their relations in the world and with others, men overcome the situations which limit them: the "limit situations." Once perceived as fetters, as obstacles to their liberation, these situations stand out in relief from the background, revealing their true nature as concrete historical dimensions of a given reality. . . . As critical perception is embodied in action, a climate of hope and confidence develops which leads men to attempt to overcome the limit situations. (p. 89)

If we apply Freire's approach to understanding the limit situations that confront urban schools, there is a greater likelihood that we can devise creative approaches that make it possible to move beyond the dismal status quo. In the case of urban public schools, the constraints that stand in the way of change are both internal and external to school systems. Externally, the constraints are related primarily to the effects of poverty and social isolation on families in economically depressed inner-city neighborhoods. External conditions related to poverty invariably affect schools and have an impact on teaching and learning (Anyon, 1996; Maeroff, 1988; Schorr, 1997). Many inner-city communities have been in a constant state of economic depression for a very long time, and in many areas even the prosperity of the 1990s failed to significantly lower unemployment or bring about significant improvements in the quality of life (Phillips, 2002). The absence of well-paying jobs and a vibrant retail sector has converted many of these communities into what some economists refer to as "no zones"—no banks, no stores, no pharmacies, no community services. In the absence of a functioning formal economy, many residents generate income through the informal economy where many of the transactions and economic activities are illegal (e.g., drug trafficking, prostitution, gambling, "off-the-books" labor). Consistently, research has shown that when poverty is concentrated and poor people are socially isolated, the health and welfare of children and families suffer (Greenberg & Schneider, 1994; Massey & Denton, 1993; Wilson, 1987).

The role that local and state politicians play vis-à-vis urban schools and communities is another important external factor that influences the operation of schools. In many cities, the public school system is the leading employer, and the jobs available within the school system often offer higher pay than similar jobs in the private sector. The officials who manage schools are often quite powerful. The contracts that officials grant for construction, food services, and maintenance constitute a significant source of revenue for external suppliers. When those responsible for schools treat the economic activities of the school system as a cash cow and source of patronage, educational issues often become a low priority. In such cases, it is not uncommon for resources that should be directed to support schools, to be redirected into questionable activities. Political corruption, instability in leadership, institutional indifference, and administrative interference and/or ineptness can all have a profound effect on the ability of schools to function (Anyon, 1996; Henig et al., 1999). Finally, when battles for political control of schools take on greater importance than fulfilling their educational mission, key players and constituencies can become too distracted to focus on the critical educational work that needs to be done.

A broad array of demographic and socioeconomic factors, including the arrival of new immigrants (Suarez-Orozco & Suarez-Orozco, 2001) and neighborhood instability, also exert powerful influences over schools and the children who attend them. For example, as middle-class families have moved out of rust-belt cities like Buffalo, Detroit, Cleveland, and Hartford since the 1960s, the quality of schools has declined precipitously. Schools decline partially because there is less money available as the tax base is eroded, but also because when household income goes down and the percentage of low-income, single-parent families goes up, the challenges facing schools increase significantly. Likewise, other trends, such as housing affordability and stability, the accessibility of health care, and the impact of welfare reform, profoundly affect schools and the quality of children's lives.

These external constraints cannot be ignored or treated as factors that are beyond the reach of schools and therefore impossible to address. The tendency to ignore the environmental context is commonplace, even though a vast body of research has shown that external factors such as poverty play highly significant roles in influencing the quality of schooling provided to children (Anyon, 1996; Coleman et al., 1966; Jencks, 1972; Noguera, 1995c). Despite widespread recognition of the dire social problems confronting urban public schools, it is rare for politicians to devise policies that take social context into account. Instead, there are numerous examples of policies that treat schools uniformly and subject both rich and poor to the same laws and regulations.

Internal constraints also limit and hinder the possibilities for schools to improve. High turnover among superintendents, principals, and teachers adds to the sense of instability present in some schools and results in inexperienced professionals being assigned the most difficult and complex educational jobs (Darling-Hammond, 1997). Even when turnover is not as great a problem, urban districts often have large numbers of teachers who are demoralized and/or burned-out as a result of poor working conditions and low salaries. The morale of school personnel and the culture and organizational climate within schools and administrative offices have a tremendous bearing on the capacity of schools to change and improve. Genuine reform and improvement are impossible to achieve in schools where disorder and chaos are prevalent (Payne, 1984, 2001).

Similarly, inadequate facilities, which in many urban areas may include broken windows, poor heating and ventilation, and a wide array of cosmetic and structural deficiencies, as well as a shortage of instructional materials such as computers and textbooks, also constitute important internal constraints on schools. Finally, the common tendency to pursue costly reforms without a commitment to evaluate the effectiveness of new measures adds to the sense of demoralization experienced by school personnel and contributes to a profound cynicism among them about the possibility of reform itself. Commenting on the tendency of policy makers to issue new recommendations for reform without evaluating or learning from past failures, Sarason (1971) writes:

> When you read the myriad of recommendations these commission reports contain, it becomes clear that they are not informed by any conception of a system. This is a charitable assessment. It deserves emphasis that none of these reports confronts the question of why these recommendations for changing this or that part of the system have been ineffective. More upsetting is the question of why so many people think the situation has not remained the same but deteriorated. Why, in the quiet of night, do so many people think that the situation is hopeless? (p. 15)

Many of the conditions described above are not unique to urban schools, but are present to varying degrees within schools throughout the United States (Cuban & Tyack, 1995; Wagner, 1994). However, they are more likely to be present and to be particularly severe in urban public schools that are located in economically depressed neighborhoods.

Yet, despite the real obstacles created by internal and external constraints, there are realistic possibilities for improvement and reform. The most compelling evidence that such openings exist in spite of these constraints is the existence of what are now recognized widely as "effective schools" that serve poor children and operate in low-income urban areas. Isolated and few in number though they may be, a significant number of schools that serve poor children manage to demonstrate that it is possible for students to achieve at high levels. Research on such schools has shown that they succeed both because they find ways to develop the internal capacity of schools to support good teaching and learning, and because they face the external constraints head-on (Haycock, 2002). They do this by explicitly devising strategies that enable them to cope with, and in some cases overcome, the obstacles present within the external environment. Such schools find ways to provide coats to children in the winter and additional food to children who don't eat regularly at home. By finding ways to mitigate the impact of external constraints, such schools provide a reasonable basis for pragmatic optimism.

Furthermore, possibilities for change and improvement are enhanced when capable and committed educators are organized to serve the needs of children. Programs such as the Omega Boys Club in San Francisco, Young Black Scholars in Los Angeles, and the Paul Robeson Institute in New York have been highly effective in furthering academic achievement of poor minority students.[9] Of course, the success of such programs is contingent on the availability of competent and committed personnel, a fact that often makes replication difficult. However, this fact should not negate the possibility that similar programs can be adopted to help schools to improve. Rather, it should underscore the importance of the most critical ingredient of school success—the availability of highly skilled and dedicated professionals without whom success simply is not possible. Furthermore, the success of certain interventions, as well as even the temporary success of certain schools, serves as proof that the possibility for transforming urban public schools is real.

Finally, and most important, the possibility for better education exists because children are fundamentally educable and capable of learning at high levels. This fact must be articulated repeatedly because in too many cases it is not the premise on which reforms are based. When the adults who serve children do not believe their students are capable of learning and achieving at high levels, they are less likely to provide students with an education that challenges them to fully realize their intellectual potential. Invariably, adults who question the ability of students to learn set lower standards and hold lower expectations (Ladson-Billings, 1994). Most disturbing of all is the fact that such educators provide an education to their students that they would regard as unacceptable for their own children.

Working with an awareness of the limits and possibilities for school improvement, we are compelled to revisit the issue of commitment, effort, and will. While such subjective characteristics may not suffice as explanations for student achievement, they are indispensable features of any school change process. Put most simply, schools improve when people work harder and smarter (Elmore, 1996). When they invest greater time and energy into improving their practice and coordinating the services they provide to children and their families in a more coherent manner, increased achievement is more likely. This is not to suggest that hard work alone is all that is needed to improve urban schools. However, even if all of the key ingredients are in place and optimal conditions have been created to support teaching and learning, success will still require hard work.

The work required to improve schools that serve poor children entails much more than a mechanistic adherence to a set of prescribed reforms or the adoption of a new curriculum. One consistent feature of schools that succeed at educating poor children is that they are guided by a coherent mission: one that is embraced enthusiastically by teachers, students, and parents (Edmonds, 1979; Meier, 1995; Sizemore, 1988). Such schools almost always are led by dedicated and exemplary principals who motivate and inspire their staff while simultaneously generating a sense of accountability to those they serve. Successful schools, especially those that succeed over a long period of time, often have an intangible quality about them that produces high morale, and an *esprit de corps* that compels those who teach or learn there to approach their work with a sense of purpose and commitment.

I was reminded of this characteristic of effective schools when I went to see an old friend from college. I sought out my college roommate, Amateka Morgan, after nearly 20 years without contact, hoping that he might have some wisdom to share with my 17-year-old son Joaquin, who was about to enroll in college in New York City. We found Amateka working in a private Islamic primary school in the Williamsburgh section of Brooklyn. Two weeks before school was to begin, he was hard at work waxing floors, painting walls, and moving furniture. He explained that he recently had resigned from Girls and Boys High School (a large comprehensive public school in Brooklyn) where he had been employed for over 10 years as a science teacher and track coach. He told us that although he enjoyed working at the school, he had grown tired of hearing people say that if he could save one or two children, he would have accomplished something. Smiling broadly, he informed us, "At this school, we know we can save all of our children. The only thing limiting us is the size of the building. Even though we don't have facilities like the public schools we can do a better job because we love the children, and it shows in what they can do" (personal communication, September 2, 2000).

Without the kinds of qualities demonstrated by my old friend—commitment, enthusiasm, compassion, solidarity, and love—it is doubtful that public schools can be reformed. Individuals possessing such qualities also need support derived from structural changes aimed at easing the effects of poverty. However, without such individuals change may not be possible at all. The nature of work in urban schools is simply too difficult, the working conditions too harsh, and the external obstacles too numerous. Without the extra boost provided by an emotional or philosophical motivation for doing the work, success cannot be achieved. Unfortunately, such traits cannot be invoked by policy makers, or mandated by superintendents or school boards;

if they are not rooted within an individual's value system, often they cannot be cultivated. In some cases, individuals can be inspired to manifest these qualities, but they cannot be coerced to do so. Hence, to a large degree, the possibility for transforming urban public schools is contingent on our ability to find ways either to attract highly motivated and competent professionals to work in them, or to inspire and support those who are already there. Assessing the situation in urban schools with a healthy dose of pragmatism forces us to recognize that neither task is easy.

IMPROVING THE QUALITY OF PUBLIC EDUCATION IN THE SAN FRANCISCO BAY AREA

For nearly 20 years I taught and conducted research in several schools in the San Francisco Bay Area. These experiences provide the empirical basis for my analysis of the limits and possibilities of improving urban schools. Widely regarded as one of the most prosperous regions in the United States due to its proximity to Silicon Valley, the national center of the "new economy," the Bay Area would seem to have every ingredient needed to make the probability for success in public education high. Yet, like urban schools throughout the rest of the nation, public schools in the Bay Area exhibit most of the familiar signs of failure and distress, despite their location in this affluent region.

In the forthcoming chapters I will explain why public education in the Bay Area has largely failed to live up to its promise and potential. Through a series of case studies, I will show how several schools have been affected by and have attempted to respond to the challenges of the urban environment. I will do this by drawing attention to both the reasons for failure and the factors that have enabled some schools to produce a degree of success.

It is my hope that this book will not only inform readers about the peculiarities of this region, but also provide insights that can help us to understand what it will take to reverse trends in urban education generally. It is my hope that by grounding this analysis in the experience of real schools and communities, I will make a credible and realistic case for radically improving urban public schools. Drawing on my position of critical support and pragmatic optimism, I will describe how schools can respond to the forces of social inequality and fulfill the promise of American education. That promise is rooted in Horace Mann's belief that schools should function as the great "equalizer" of opportunity: an arena where inherited privileges do not determine one's opportunities (Tyack, 1980). Improving the state of America's urban schools necessarily will be a central element of any effort to realize that promise.

CHAPTER 2

The Social Context and Its Impact on Inner-City Schooling

RETHINKING THE "URBAN"

Increasingly, the term *urban* is less likely to be employed as a geographic concept used to define and describe physical locations than as a social or cultural construct used to describe certain people and places. Although demographers and planners may regard any neighborhood or residence within a standard metropolitan area as urban, in common parlance the term has attained specific socioeconomic and racial connotations. When media reports describe a neighborhood or group of residents as "urban," we can almost always be sure that those being described are relatively poor and, in many cases, non-White. Such references are made even more explicit when terms like *inner-city* are used instead of urban, or when they are replaced by more blatantly pejorative words such as *ghetto, slum, barrio,* or *hood*. However, with the change of language that came about with the attempt to use more sensitive words to refer to marginalized groups, *urban* is generally the more acceptable adjective used in reference to certain people who reside within certain neighborhoods in cities.

Changes in nomenclature reflect more than just ideological and political trends. The association between the term *urban* and people and places that are poor and non-White is tied to the demographic and economic transformations that occurred in cities throughout the United States during the past 50 years (Clark, 1998; Wilson, 1978, 1987). With the exception of a small number of "global cities," since the end of World War II cities across the United States have declined in importance as economic, political, and commercial centers. For many northeastern and midwestern cities, the decline began as early as the late nineteenth century as the textile, furniture, and garment industries moved south or out of the United States entirely in search of cheaper labor (Friedland, 1983). In the 1950s, federal policies hastened the decline of cities as new highways were constructed, making it easier for the middle class to move out of cities to obtain a piece of the American dream: a single-family home located in the suburbs. With the advent of shopping malls and Levittown-style tract housing, suburban living became possible even for the working class (Gans, 1967). In the 1970s, continued de-industrialization and the globalization of the economy further eroded the economic base of many cities, particularly those that were dependent on a single industry such as steel production or auto manufacturing (Castells, 1998).

Court-ordered busing and the desegregation of housing and public education in the 1960s also played a role in the transformation of cities (See Table 2.1). With jobs and housing moving to the suburbs and African Americans—and later other minorities—moving to cities in greater numbers, many cities experienced a "darkening" and precipitous "White flight." Declining White enrollment in schools and the gradual process of ethnic succession in neighborhoods dramatically changed the racial and socioeconomic character of cities. In several cities, "dark ghettos" (Wade, 1995) replaced White working-class neighborhoods, and more often than not the transition was neither smooth nor peaceful. Several cities—for example, Boston, Philadelphia, and Chicago—experienced protracted conflicts, some of which became violent, as a result of White resistance to school and neighborhood desegregation. Even in places such as the Bay Area where there was less open resistance to dismantling of racial segregation, genuine integration in the make-up of schools or neighborhoods was the exception and not the norm in most communities.

Despite the resistance, White backlash largely failed to deter the racial transformation of cities. In several of the largest cities, separate and distinct White neighborhoods—some poor, some affluent—still remain, but the majority population became non-White.[1] Eventually, changes in the

Table 2.1. White Flight—Percent Population White over Three Decades

	1960s		1970s		1980s	
	Percent White	Percent Change*	Percent White	Percent Change	Percent White	Percent Change
Berkeley	73.8	-14.6	68.5	-7.7	66.0	-3.8
Oakland	73.6	-16.2	59.2	-24.3	38.2	-55.0
Richmond	78.0	-9.9	51.6	-51.2	39.7	-30.0
San Francisco	81.6	-9.7	71.7	-13.8	58.2	-23.2

* Percent change based on 1950s data. *Source:* U.S. Census Bureau.

racial composition of cities made it possible for Black and in some cases Latino mayors to be elected in major cities such as Los Angeles, Denver, Chicago, and Washington, DC, during the 1970s and 1980s. Changes in the leadership of municipal governments in turn brought about changes in the make-up of the civil service and the administration of public schools (Bush, 1984; Pinkney, 1984).[2] By the 1980s, the transformation was nearly complete: Cities throughout the United States no longer wielded the power they once held within the American economy and politics, and increasingly they were disproportionately comprised of residents who were poor and non-White.

THE SAN FRANCISCO BAY AREA: CONTRASTING CONDITIONS IN HIGH-WEALTH AND HIGH-POVERTY CITIES

I want to examine four cities in the San Francisco Bay Area—San Francisco, Oakland, Berkeley, and Richmond—in order to illustrate the challenges and dilemmas confronting urban public schools. These are also cities where I have done most of my research and teaching over the past 20 years. Although each city and region has its own particular history and unique cast of historical characters, many of the changes that have occurred in the Bay Area have occurred in cities throughout the United States. Hence, the region serves as an appropriate and useful locale from which to analyze and discuss trends in cities and schools that have transpired elsewhere.

In the Bay Area, two distinct national trends among cities are also evident: the emergence of high-wealth and high-poverty cities. Oakland and Richmond, two mid-sized, formerly industrial cities, vividly illustrate the problems and challenges confronting high-poverty cities. Following the end of World War II, both cities experienced substantial job loss when Kaiser Aluminum moved or reduced its shipping- and defense-related operations from the area. Economic changes also contributed to major demographic changes as White middle- and working-class residents moved away from Richmond and Oakland in the 1960s and 1970s (Moore, 2000).

With a declining tax base, the downtown commercial districts of both Oakland and Richmond experienced gradual deterioration. Once vibrant retail, financial, and cultural centers, these areas declined dramatically and became like ghost towns, particularly after 6 p.m. By the 1980s, vacant shops and boarded up office buildings filled the historic downtown areas, eventually outnumbering viable enterprises. It was during this period of economic decline that Black leadership emerged to assume control of city government, including the police and fire departments, and the administration of public schools. The election of former judge Lionel Wilson in Oakland and George Livingston in Richmond broke the color barriers in politics and elevated the hopes and expectations of low-income, minority communities. Their ascension was heralded as a sign that better days were coming.

Unfortunately for the new leadership, changes in administrative leadership occurred during a period of fiscal austerity. Instead of delivering new programs and economic development initiatives, the new leadership met the high expectations of the electorate with lamentations about budget shortfalls and diminished public resources. As the number of impoverished residents increased in the 1980s, the situation worsened considerably. In the local media, both cities became known as havens for drug trafficking, drive-by shootings, and homelessness, and the plight of their public schools soon came to epitomize the widespread sense of despair. With the dreams of progress unfulfilled, faith in politics as the solution to local problems gradually dissipated.

The 1990s briefly brought signs of economic revival to Oakland and Richmond as the growth generated by the "new economy," especially in the high tech and biotech sectors, finally stimulated growth in other sectors. However, in comparison to their richer counterparts, the two cities continue to lag far behind. With the recession of 2000 still inflicting damage, it is now clear that those who hoped improved economic conditions in the two cities would lead to tangible benefits for low-income city residents, will have to wait a while longer. It seems more likely that in certain desirable neighborhoods a different scenario will play itself out and poor people gradually will be displaced by more affluent residents.

Whereas poverty rates increased in Oakland and Richmond in the 1970s and 1980s, San Francisco and Berkeley experienced a steady decline in the number of low-income households during the same period. Significantly, the decline in poverty largely was not due to government interventions such as the development of affordable housing or the enactment of rent control, although these policies were pursued and implemented in both cities (Nathan & Scott, 1978). Instead, San Francisco and Berkeley experienced a steady decline in the number of low-income residents as a result of rising property values and a dramatic slowdown in construction of low-income housing. Increasingly, poor and working-class people, especially African Americans, found it difficult to find affordable housing in the two cities and were forced to move to working-class neighborhoods in the suburbs. Both cities also have experienced aggressive and steady gentrification as neighborhoods, such as the Western Addition in San Francisco and the Oceanview neighborhood in West Berkeley, saw the gradual departure of poor, elderly, and minority residents and their replacement by White, middle-class professionals.

Interestingly, although San Francisco and Berkeley did not experience the White flight that occurred in Oakland and Richmond, Blacks, and to a lesser extent Asians and Latinos, did rise to positions of leadership in both cities (See Table 2.2). Warren Widener became the first Black mayor of Berkeley in the 1970s, while Willie Brown, former Speaker of the California Assembly, was elected Mayor of San Francisco in the 1990s. Like Oakland and Richmond, minorities experienced significant employment gains in the public sector, including the public schools, over the past 30 years. The superintendency in San Francisco was a bastion of patronage for Italian American politicians until the first minority superintendent, Ray Cortinez, was appointed in the 1980s. Following Cortinez, a succession of minorities—a Puerto Rican man (Waldemar Rojas) and two Black women (Linda Davis and Arlene Ackerman)—have held the post. Berkeley appointed its first Black superintendent, Laval Wilson, in the 1970s, and in the 1980s, Blacks rose to positions of leadership throughout the city, including city manager and chief of the police and fire departments.

Although the contrast between the high-wealth and high-poverty cities of the Bay Area is striking, with respect to the demographic make-up of their schools the four cities share a great deal. In all four cities, the majority of children enrolled in the public schools are poor and minority. Of the four, Berkeley remains relatively integrated, with White enrollment in most schools hovering at 35–40%. However, in a city that is nearly 70% White, and where an estimated 25% of all school-aged children are enrolled in private schools, racial imbalance is still quite evident.[3]

Table 2.2. White Flight—Changes in White Enrollment over Four Decades

	1960s	**1970s**		**1980s**		**1990s**	
	Percent White	Percent White	Percent Change	Percent White	Percent Change	Percent White	Percent Change
Berkeley	**46.2**	45.8	<-1.0	39.6	-15.7	**33.6**	-17.9
Oakland	**30.9**	13.5	-128.0	9.1	-48.4	**6.1**	-49.2
Richmond	**66.9**	47.6	-41.0	33.5	-42.1	**20.0**	-67.5
San Francisco	**41.2**	20.5	-100.1	14.8	-38.5	**12.5**	-18.4

Source: School district website or archives.

In San Francisco the imbalance in the racial and socioeconomic composition of the public schools as compared with the city is even more dramatic. From 1975 to 2003, fewer than 10% of all students enrolled in the district have been White, compared with a White population in the city that is over 60%. White enrollment in San Francisco public schools is particularly noteworthy when one considers that as recently as 1968 it was as high as 40%. Much of the change in the San Francisco student population can be explained by the dramatic increase in Asian enrollment brought about by a steady influx of Asian immigrants during this 20-year period (Clark, 1998). However, the steady exodus of White working-class families, triggered at least in part by the advent of court-ordered desegregation and school busing, was equally important in prompting White flight from the public schools (Kirp, 1982). Like Berkeley, San Francisco still has a large White population (49.7%); however, much of this population is affluent and relatively few White households have school-aged children (U.S. Census Bureau, 2000).

In Oakland and Richmond, White flight from the schools mirrored White flight from the cities and neighborhoods (Moore, 2000). In both cities, an increase in the number of African American residents corresponded closely to a steady decline in the number of White residents. This pattern is captured most vividly through a perusal of high school yearbooks at Castlemont High School in East Oakland and Kennedy High School in Central Richmond. Both schools were predominantly White throughout the 1960s, and Kennedy High School was widely regarded as one of the best high schools in the Bay Area. However, as one turns the pages of yearbooks from the late 1960s, it becomes evident that as the number of Black faces increases, the number of White faces decreases. In the case of Castlemont, the White faces in the senior class are nearly all gone by the early 1970s, while at Kennedy the disappearance of White students was not complete until the end of the 1970s.

In the following pages, I will examine how changes in the composition of these cities and their schools influenced the character and quality of public education. The point of such an exercise is to illustrate the complex relationship between economic and demographic change in the social context and the challenges confronting urban public schools. Such an analysis will be used to establish a framework for understanding the limits and possibilities of schooling in urban areas today (See Tables 2.3 and 2.4). It is important to note the significant differences in the racial compositions of the four cities (over half of the population in both Richmond and Oakland are Black and Hispanic) and also the contrast in the percentage of households with school-aged children.

Table 2.3. Economic Profile of Four Cities—Housing, Education, Employment, and Poverty Rates

	Berkeley	Oakland	Richmond	San Francisco
Housing Tenure (%)				
Owner-occupied housing units	42.7	41.4	53.3	35.0
Renter-occupied housing units	57.3	58.6	46.7	65.0
Educational Attainment				
< 9th grade	3.4	13.3	11.2	10.5
9th–12th grade, no diploma	4.4	12.8	13.5	8.3
High school graduate and equivalent	8.6	17.7	21.8	13.9
Bachelor's degree	29.9	18.0	14.1	28.6
Graduate/professional degree	34.3	12.9	8.3	16.4
Grandparents as Caregivers	30.2	34.6	35.4	27.6
Employment Status				
% unemployed in labor force	3.6	5.1	4.8	3.0
% not in labor force	34.2	38.4	38.1	33.7
% employed in labor force	62.1	56.5	57.0	63.3
Poverty Rates				
% families living below poverty level	8.3	16.2	13.4	7.8
% families with children under 18	24.8	47.0	39.4	24.5
% families with female-headed household	19.4	29.5	24.8	16.6
% families with female-headed household with children under 18	60.8	80.5	69.0	58.4
Home Value (Homeowners Only)				
% whose homes valued over $200,000	85.6	55.6	35.1	83.8

Source: U.S. Census Bureau, 2000.

Table 2.4. Four Bay Area Cities by Race, and Percentage of Households with School-Aged Children

	Berkeley	Oakland	Richmond	San Francisco
White	59.2	31.3	31.4	49.7
Black	13.6	35.7	36.1	7.8
American Indian	0.5	0.7	0.6	0.4
Asian	16.4	15.2	12.3	30.8
Hispanic	9.7	21.9	26.5	14.1
Household with child	19.8	33.5	4.0	19.4

Source: U.S. Census Bureau, 2000.

RACE VERSUS SPACE: FRAGMENTATION AND SOCIAL BOUNDARIES IN THE POSTMODERN CITY

Characterizing the differences among the Bay Area's four major cities on the basis of their wealth and racial composition, fails to accurately capture the complexity that is manifest at the neighborhood level. While there are a greater number of affluent households in San Francisco and Berkeley, and a greater number of impoverished households in Oakland and Richmond, all four cities contain affluent and impoverished enclaves. In fact, the differences in wealth and quality of life among neighborhoods is so pronounced and striking that, with respect to the socioeconomic character of an individual neighborhood, there are relatively few differences among the four cities.

For example, although the homes in the Point Richmond neighborhood are somewhat more affordable, the quality of life there is more like that of San Francisco's affluent Marina District than that of the Iron Triangle neighborhood located less than 2 miles away in central Richmond. With Point Richmond's waterfront homes abutting the San Francisco Bay, one does not feel even remotely connected to the city of Richmond where crime, poverty, and toxic emergencies are frequent and widespread. Similarly, neighborhoods in the Oakland and Berkeley hills, with their stunning views of the San Francisco Bay and proximity to the wooded open spaces in Tilden Regional Park, have more in common with each other than they do with the low-income neighborhoods located in the flatlands of both cities.

As real estate agents put it, "location is everything," but in the Bay Area, as is true in many cities throughout the United States, the cultural and economic boundaries separating neighborhoods are as important as those created by space and distance. Even in high-wealth cities like San Francisco and Berkeley, where rising property values, gentrification, and a return of middle-class Whites have transformed the economic and social character of the landscape, pockets of poverty remain. Disparities in wealth and living conditions actually have widened in these cities despite their booming economies and dramatic revitalization.[4] In Berkeley and San Francisco, the beleaguered communities where poor people are concentrated—the Tenderloin, Hunters Point, and the Mission District in San Francisco, and the flatland neighborhoods of south and west Berkeley—are cut off and isolated, economically and socially, from the prosperity that is prevalent elsewhere. Like their counterparts in Oakland and Richmond, such neighborhoods have a disproportionate number of liquor stores but no grocery stores; pawn shops and check cashing outlets are plentiful, but not banks or pharmacies. Furthermore, poor people residing in such neighborhoods are confronted with the realistic prospect that they eventually will be driven out of these cities entirely, as market forces make even what once were seen as undesirable areas, attractive to developers and Yuppie pioneers.

Several neighborhoods in the Bay Area vividly illustrate how race and class differences between neighborhoods serve as boundaries that effectively eliminate a sense of shared identity based on geography and spatial proximity. For example, although Montclair is located less than 3 miles from the Fruitvale area, in social, cultural, and psychological terms, these areas in Oakland might as well be hundreds of miles apart. Montclair is an affluent neighborhood located in the foothills of Oakland. It is a multiracial area comprising largely affluent families who reside in expensive homes. With its beautiful trees and stunning vistas of the San Francisco Bay, Montclair feels much more suburban than urban. In fact, with its sidewalk cafes, fashionable boutiques, and own neighborhood newspaper, Montclair feels much more like neighboring Piedmont (an affluent city located next to Oakland) than like part of Oakland.

In contrast, the Fruitvale area is a lower-class neighborhood located in the flatlands of central east Oakland and comprises predominantly Latinos, Blacks, and recent Asian immigrants. Although it takes only a few minutes to drive from Montclair to Fruitvale, once there, one literally feels as though one has entered another world. With its street vendors and bargain retailers hawking their wares in a variety of languages (none of them English), Fruitvale bears little similarity to its affluent neighbor. Its streets are congested with cars, trucks, and buses, and the mix of factories, warehouses, single-family homes, and apartments gives it all of the features commonly associated with immigrant enclaves in urban America today (Portes, Haller, & Guarnizo, 2002). The Fruitvale area is not even one of

Oakland's most distressed neighborhoods (Office of Economic Development, 2000). Unlike parts of east and most of west Oakland, it has a thriving low-end commercial district, and housing prices have been steadily rising for the past 10 years. Although they are located near each other and within the same city, it is clear that these two neighborhoods have little in common.

Interestingly, although schools in the Montclair and Fruitvale neighborhoods are part of the Oakland Unified School District, there are significant differences with respect to academic performance indicators and other characteristics. For example, Montera Middle School, which is located in Montclair, received a statewide academic performance index (API) ranking of 8, and an API ranking of 9 when compared with schools with similar characteristics (10 is the highest possible rank).[5] In contrast, Calvin Simmons Middle School, located in the Fruitvale area, received a ranking of 1 on both sets of indicators. Table 2.5 shows how the two schools compare with respect to a variety of indicators.

Two schools in the same district; two neighborhoods located in the same city. Yet, despite their association with common jurisdictional and municipal structures, there are dramatic differences in the educational opportunities available to students and in the quality of education provided. How do we explain such significant variation among schools and neighborhoods located in the same city? Unless one subscribes to con-

Table 2.5. Comparison Between Montera and Calvin Simmons Middle Schools

	Montera	Calvin Simmons
Racial Make-up (%)		
Black	41.0	24.0
Native American	2.0	0.0
Asian/Filipino	18.0	17.0
Latino	8.0	55.0
White	30.0	3.0
API rank *	9.0	1.0
Parent education **	3.77	2.22
% free lunch	17.0	52.0
% credentialed teachers	74.0	51.0

* Academic performance index, similar schools.
** 1 represents high school graduate, 5 represents college graduate.
Source: Ed Data, 2002.

spiracy theories and believes that there is a deliberate effort to shortchange poor communities, the only plausible answer must be that public institutions, in this case schools, reflect and respond to the characteristics—cultural, demographic, and socioeconomic—of the constituencies they serve. To a large degree, differences in quality can be explained by sheer political clout, or by what social scientists refer to as social capital (Putnam, 1995; Saegert, Thompson, & Warren, 2001; Sampson, 1998). Constituencies that have the ability to effectively apply pressure on the public institutions that serve them often receive better service. This is more than just a matter of the squeaky wheel getting the grease. Poor parents may protest and organize in an effort to demand better services from schools and other public agencies, as they have on numerous occasions in Fruitvale and other parts of Oakland (Noguera, 2001b). However, those who manage public institutions often respond differently to different constituencies.

Differences in the way public agencies respond to the needs of their constituents became apparent to me when I served as Assistant to the Mayor of Berkeley from 1986 to 1988. During those 2 years one of my responsibilities was to find ways to respond to the crime and violence that dramatically increased with the proliferation of drug trafficking in south and west Berkeley neighborhoods during this period. After just a few weeks on the job, I learned that the police and other city departments responded differently to requests for service emanating from different neighborhoods. Consistently, the neighborhoods experiencing the most serious crime had the longest wait when urgent calls were made for police service, while residents in more affluent neighborhoods generally received prompt attention, even for relatively minor incidents. The difference in police response became even more apparent when I realized that the police department knew the precise location of what were referred to as drug "hot spots." These high-crime areas, in which drive-by shootings frequently occurred, were policed by a strategy that I came to regard as a form of containment. Although they regularly arrested street-level dealers and responded vigorously to violent incidents, they did relatively little to root out drug dealing altogether, so long as it was contained to certain neighborhoods.

In more affluent areas, the police department took aggressive action to prevent crimes by responding with speed and a great show of force to reports of prowlers or suspicious activity. But differences in response based on the needs of neighborhoods were not limited to the police department. For example, I was called on to help mediate a conflict among neighbors in the Berkeley hills who were involved in a heated dispute over whether a homeowner should be required to trim a tree if it blocked the view of his or her neighbor. The thorny dispute (no pun intended) pitted the right to see the sunset unfettered by branches against the right to allow the trees in one's yard to grow naturally. As the Mayor's representative, I was expected to spend as much time as it took to help these neighbors find a resolution to this conflict. With easy access to members of the City Council and lawyers ready to file suit at a word's notice, these residents had no doubt that they would get the service from city government to which they felt entitled.

In contrast, when confronted by angry residents from south and west Berkeley about the inadequacy of police protection, the most common refrain from the police was that concerns about the civil liberties of suspected drug dealers prevented them from doing more to address the crime problem. In meetings with neighbors who were afraid to leave their homes because drug dealers controlled the streets, I often heard police say they were doing all they could given the resources available and the constraints placed on them by the courts. However, I knew from my own experience and observations that drug dealers, loiterers, or even panhandlers who strayed into wealthier neighborhoods could not expect a similar level of sensitivity to their civil liberties when police officers were called.

Scholars such as Coleman (1988) and Wacquant (1998) have argued that social capital plays a tremendous role in determining how communities are served by schools and other public institutions. A number of scholars also have used the concept of social capital to analyze and measure the tangible benefits that an individual or group may obtain from participation within social networks (Saegert, Thompson, & Warren, 2001). Bonds of reciprocity derived from participation in social networks and political influence generated by money and organization can produce better service from public institutions (Sampson, 1998; Woolcock, 1998). Coleman has argued that the quality of service provided in schools is directly related to the degree to which there are shared values and expectations between school personnel and the parents that they serve. The greater the degree of social closure, the more likely it is that service providers will feel obligated and able to provide high-quality service (Coleman, 1988).

The closure described by Coleman is generally a scarce commodity in inner-city schools and communities. More often than not, relations between parents and school personnel are weak, if not strained or even hostile (Noguera, 2001a). Wacquant (1998) has argued that poor inner-city neighborhoods often are served by public institutions that generate negative rather than positive social capital. Although the services they provide are essential, public agencies in the inner city, such as schools, hospitals, and police departments, often exhibit indifference and even hostility toward those they serve. Wacquant argues that public institutions actually contribute to the deterioration of the quality of life in inner-city neighborhoods when they treat residents with contempt and disdain. They can even undermine the efficacy of community efforts to improve conditions, through poor or inefficient service. Compared with middle-class residents who typically are able to exert control over the institutions that serve them, poor residents of inner-city neighborhoods are more likely to feel estranged and underserved by neighborhood-based public institutions. For that reason, they may perceive public institutions as the source of problems rather than as a valued community asset.

Working for several years in a variety of capacities, I saw firsthand how schools in the Bay Area failed to enhance the social capital of the communities they served. Often, the actors involved—school board members, administrators, and teachers—were completely unaware of their attitudes and behavior. For example, at one school I worked with in Oakland, the school receptionist, the first person to greet visitors and parents, had a sign on her desk that read, "This ain't Burger King. We do it my way here!" Although I am certain that she saw her sign as a joke, to a parent visiting the school for the first time such a greeting might be somewhat off-putting. In a similar vein, following a workshop on how to increase parental involvement at schools in Richmond, a principal seated at my table announced jokingly that she didn't want parents at her school to get more involved because they were "nothing but low lifes and crack heads." At yet another meeting that I held with a group of teachers in Berkeley to discuss negotiations over the union contract, I was told that teachers were concerned about the flight of White middle-class children from the district. One veteran teacher asserted that "the cream is leaving our schools, and we are being left with the dregs and the crack babies. If we don't do something soon to keep the kids from the hills from leaving, we will soon be just like Oakland" (Noguera, 1995c).

Such statements of contempt typically were matched by deep distrust and antagonism on the part of minority parents toward the schools that served them in all four cities. At a conference for parents in San Francisco, a group of Vietnamese parents told school officials that the schools were teaching their children to be disrespectful toward them. They complained that the longer their children attended the public schools, the more embarrassed the children became about the old ways and customs of their families. The parents also explained that as their children became more estranged from them, the children were more likely to join gangs and to get into trouble. Speaking with the assistance of a translator, one mother implored district officials to "teach our children to respect us so that we can help them" (May 15, 1998).

Similar concerns about the lack of respect displayed toward parents by school personnel were expressed in other schools throughout the Bay Area. At a tense community forum in Richmond held to discuss the causes of interracial violence in the schools, the only moment of intergroup solidarity occurred in response to a statement by a Latino parent. To rousing applause from the diverse group of parents who were assembled, the mother of four asserted that "our children don't learn to respect each other because they see that even their parents are not respected by the schools" (October 7, 1999).

Even within the same district and city, differences in social capital among residents can be extreme. For example, while I served on the school board, parents from the Berkeley hills convinced the board to rebuild Cragmont Elementary School, even though the site had been declared a risk by the Office of the State Architect due to its proximity to an earthquake fault line. They did this by implying that they would campaign against a pending school bond measure and threatening to withdraw their children from the district if the school was not rebuilt. In contrast, parents in west Berkeley struggled to secure funding for their new school because the plan they supported called for comprehensive family services to be located at the school. The new proposal exceeded the original budget allocation for the school by $1 million. To their credit, the parents succeeded in raising the funds with the support of well-connected and savvy fund raisers, but support from the district was minimal.

Differences in the way school districts respond to the concerns of parents cannot be explained merely by race or class bias on the part of school board members or district officials. In the case of construction funds for the two schools in Berkeley, both groups of petitioning parents were well organized, and both were multiracial in their make-up. I attribute the difference in the response of the board to differences in social capital. While affluent parents from the hills can use the threat of departure from the district as leverage, parents in west Berkeley have no equivalent weapon at their disposal. Both groups engaged in protest and presented demands to the school district, but only the more affluent constituency had the wherewithal to get the board to do what it wanted.[6] Individual and collective power, which is one of the by-products of social capital, has a profound influence on the ways that schools and other social institutions respond to the needs of their constituents in the Bay Area and elsewhere.

INEQUITY AS A CAUSE OF TENSION AMONG NEIGHBORS

In many communities, race and class differences serve as boundaries that undermine the sense of community one might expect would be generated by spatial proximity. In the absence of bonds of solidarity that could be created through reliance on shared services, social institutions, and civic organizations, the significance associated with differences in status often is increased. Even when they reside within the same neighborhood, individuals and families from diverse cultural and socioeconomic backgrounds often lack a basis for developing networks and connections that might enable them to transcend their differences in pursuit of common interests. In such neighborhoods, tensions can develop among residents when conflicting interests become politicized and when residents compete openly over resources or the direction of a neighborhood.

In the San Francisco Bay Area, this trend is most evident within neighborhoods such as West Berkeley, West Oakland, and the Mission District and Western Addition in San Francisco. Because of their attractive locations, each of these low-income communities experienced rapid gentrification during the 1980s. Since the 1990s, it is no longer uncommon to find poor and affluent residents living side-by-side in these communities. Yet, while they may share sidewalks, parks, and public libraries, low-income residents typically have little in common with the more affluent newcomers, and from a sociological standpoint, they might as well live in different worlds. Lacking the bonds that might be created through participation in civic associations, churches, or public institutions such as schools, these neighborhoods often experience considerable tension and conflict due to competition over various quality of life issues. In such communities, shared space fails to foster a sense of solidarity due to the perception that differences related to race and class are insurmountable.

I experienced these tensions firsthand while working as Assistant to the Mayor. During those 2 years, south and west Berkeley were in the midst of substantial demographic change, as affluent White professionals began purchasing homes in neighborhoods that historically had comprised working-class African American and Latino families. As mentioned previously, these neighborhoods also were besieged by a dramatic increase in crime and violence due to fierce competition among crack dealers over control of the drug market. One of my jobs was to meet with neighborhood groups to discuss crime prevention strategies and ways of making the police department more responsive to community needs. On several occasions, community meetings deteriorated into intense conflicts between new and old residents regarding how the police and city government should respond to the crime problem.[7]

In one case, a group of new, White middle-class residents began circulating a petition for the city to shut down a neighborhood park because drugs were being sold and several violent incidents had occurred there. This action incensed older, predominantly African American residents who deeply resented the idea that Greg Brown Park, which had been named after a young man who had been killed while serving in the U.S. military during the Vietnam War, would be closed to appease the newcomers. In contrast, the older residents saw the park as a vital neighborhood asset, and they called for greater police presence and supervised recreational activities for young people living in the area.

As the conversation became more heated and polarized, one of the new White residents charged that the elderly woman chairing the neighborhood watch meeting had a grandson who was selling drugs in the park. Rather than striking back, the previously combative woman lowered her head and admitted, "Yes, he's selling drugs and I don't know what to do about it" (November 16, 1986). To the White residents, her admission served as proof that their neighbors could not be trusted because of their complicity with criminal activity. However, for the mostly elderly Black members, the confession of their neighbor was evidence of the problem's complexity. In my private conversations with these older residents, they acknowledged that the roots of the drug problem were economic—unemployed young people and poor families had grown dependent on the income they gained from drug sales. Even though they felt the brunt of the violence inflicted by the drug traffickers, they were deeply conflicted about how to respond. Unlike their White neighbors who felt comfortable simply demanding that the police lock up the drug dealers, they believed that more was needed to address the economic and social dimensions of the problem. As one of the people responsible for mediating this dispute, I found it nearly impossible to arrive at a compromise that would satisfy both constituencies, because of the different ways in which each constituency defined its needs and interests.

Such cleavage among residents within neighborhoods and cities is reflective of patterns present in many urban areas throughout the United States. In many cases public schools, which once provided a basis for neighborhood solidarity, no longer serve this purpose because new residents either have no children (see Table 2.4) or send their children to private schools. Jane Jacobs (1961), one of the best-known writers on urban planning and design, has argued for years that diversity in terms of class, race, and usage, is important to the health, safety, and well-being of urban neighborhoods. But increasingly, urban areas are fragmented along these very dimensions, and urban public schools have become places that disproportionately serve the children of the poor and powerless: people who lack access to better educational options (Anyon, 1996; Kozol, 1991).

In cities such as Berkeley and San Francisco, where the overwhelming majority of residents are middle or upper-middle class, the public schools overwhelmingly comprise low-income African American, Latino, and Asian children (see Table 2.4). Even when a degree of integration in terms of race and class does exist, as in the case of most Berkeley public schools, there are significant differences in academic outcomes and perceptions of service among the constituencies that are served. As I will describe in Chapter 4, finding ways to respond to the different needs of poor and affluent children in Berkeley schools has been as difficult as finding ways to respond to the conflicting needs of residents in south and west Berkeley.

Immigration is another factor changing the composition of schools and communities in the Bay Area (Clark, 1998). With new residents arriving from Latin America and Asia especially, and other parts of the world as well, new conflicts and tensions have emerged (Suarez-Orozco & Suarez-Orozco, 2001). Low-income immigrants typically have settled in neighborhoods that previously were populated by African Americans. With their arrival, new tensions created by competition over housing, jobs, and public services, add yet another source of friction to the social fabric. In several Bay Area high schools, these tensions have resulted in violent confrontations among students, some of which have become quite large and dangerous (Noguera & Bliss, 2001). In contrast to the situation of middle-class newcomers in gentrified neighborhoods, schools have served as the meeting place for new immigrants and older residents in other parts of the region. However, more often than not, schools have been unprepared to respond to the needs of the new arrivals or to the conflicts that have accompanied their increased presence.

Due to the fragmentation that characterizes many Bay Area neighborhoods, mobilizing community support for public education often becomes a difficult and challenging task. With middle-class constituents largely absent from the school system, the ability of community residents to hold schools accountable is substantially weakened (Nocera, 1991). Affluent cities like San Francisco and Berkeley are still able to approve bond measures and supplemental taxes to support public schools because of the liberal sentiments of the community. However, additional funding has not led to community buy-in and support for public education. Moreover, with neighbors divided by race and class differences, and with public schools catering almost exclusively to the neediest segment of the population, it is not surprising that schools in affluent communities taken on characteristics more typically associated with inner-city schools despite their location.

Hence, the condition of urban public schools in the Bay Area, and in cities throughout the United States, is related less to the socioeconomic character of where the schools are located, than it is to the socioeconomic and cultural characteristics of the children that are served. Increasingly, the student population of schools in urban areas is poorer and more likely to be non-White than the overall population of the city in which the schools are located. With the exception of magnet and some charter schools, urban schools generally serve an impoverished population, and more often than not, who is served has direct bearing on the quality of education that is provided.

THE URBAN SCHOOL AS A SOURCE OF SOCIAL SUPPORT

Although I could cite numerous examples of schools in the Bay Area that undermine the social capital of those they serve, I would be remiss if I did not also mention the growing number of schools that are actively working to develop supportive relationships with parents in impoverished communities. Following a growing national trend (Comer, 1980; Dryfoos, 2001), several schools in the Bay Area now have health clinics located on the site that provide a range of services (such as first aid, dental care, pregnancy counseling, and immunizations) to students and their families. During the 1990s, a number of schools applied for and received Healthy Start grants that allowed them to develop plans for after-school tutorial programs and other youth services.[8] At Lowell Middle School in west Oakland, the staff decided to use a school improvement grant to provide three meals a day to students because they realized that for many students school meals were their only consistent source of nutrition. The same school also provided children in need with coats in the winter and new shoes at the beginning of the school year.[9]

Several of the teachers I have worked with at Bay Area schools consistently extend themselves above and beyond their role as teachers to provide assistance to kids and families in need. Flora Russ, a teacher at Berkeley High School and coordinator of the Computer Academy, is legendary among students for her willingness to help kids find jobs, get into college, or get out of jail. Jeffery Duncan, an English teacher and girls basketball coach at Oakland High School, provided year-round tutoring to all his players. He also worked long hours to make sure that each of his players received a scholarship for college after graduation. Finally, Joan Cone, an English teacher at El Cerrito High School, led the effort to end tracking in the English department and to open up access to advanced placement courses. Her efforts and those of her colleagues made it possible for numerous minority students to win scholarships and gain admission to prestigious colleges.

These are just a few examples of teachers and administrators who actively seek to help students and their families in tangible and important ways. I mention them because even though their presence may not offset the effects of institutional indifference, they play important roles in providing personal support for many kids. For the students who have been fortunate enough to be served by these kinds of teachers, their presence literally has meant the difference between success or failure, school or jail, life or death. Moreover, the actions of these individuals, like those of the schools that have sought to provide essential services and closer ties to the families they serve, show us what it might take for schools to become genuine assets to distressed and disadvantaged communities. There is no question that such schools and teachers are desperately needed. The sad thing is that they are in short supply.

What sets teachers and schools like those I've just described apart from so many others is their willingness to broaden and redefine the traditional mission of schools. Given the hardships present in so many inner-city communities, and given the difficult circumstances that so many young people in these areas are forced to endure, such redefinition is essential. If urban schools are to become a source of support and stability to young people and their families in economically depressed urban areas,[10] they must find ways to address the academic and nonacademic needs of children that affect their welfare and ability to learn.

Of course, it is not fair or reasonable to expect that underresourced schools and overburdened teachers can do this on their own. Addressing the academic needs of poor children is more than most inner-city schools can handle as it is. To provide the extra services that disadvantaged children require, schools will need to form partnerships with local governments, churches, and neighborhood-based service agencies. A small number of such school-based partnerships already exist, such as the handful of schools supported by the Children's Aid Society in New York (Dryfoos, 2001). Beyond these small but valiant efforts, state and federal policies, backed by the requisite funding, are needed to ensure that all schools in impoverished areas have the ability to meet the needs of the distressed communities they serve.

In the following chapters, I will describe some of the ways schools in the Bay Area have grappled with the constraints, both internal and external, that limit their ability to effectively serve students. For the most part, these will not be success stories. The point of such an exploration is to uncover lessons about what it takes to create urban schools that are successful in serving the needs of children, so that we might gain some insight regarding how to approach the difficult task of improving urban public schools throughout the United States. I recognize at the outset that even these lessons may be insufficient as a guide for how to proceed with the work of school reform and improvement, but at a minimum they may serve as a source of renewed hope in the possibility that change can be brought about.

CHAPTER 3

The Role of Schools in Reducing Racial Inequality: Closing the Achievement Gap

UNDERSTANDING THE LINK BETWEEN RACE AND ACADEMIC ACHIEVEMENT

The relationship between race, class, and school performance has been one of the most consistent features of education in the United States (Fass, 1989; Tyack, 1980). The educational outcomes of racial minorities and poor children typically have reflected broader patterns of inequality: Minority and disadvantaged children tend to do less well in school than affluent White students (Jencks & Phillips, 1998; Miller, 1995). Rather than serving as the "great equalizer" as envisioned by Horace Mann, one of the early architects of American public education (Katznelson & Weir, 1985), schools in the United States more often have been sites where patterns of privilege and inequality are maintained and reproduced. Even in places such as Berkeley where children of different backgrounds attend the same schools, it is common for White children to outperform non-Whites, and for the children of the poor to do less well than their more affluent counterparts.

The consistency and predictability of these patterns contribute to the commonsense notion that differences in academic performance among children are "normal" and can be explained by "essential" (such as biological, cultural, or familial) differences that exist within the U.S. population. Historically, differences in achievement and academic performance have been attributed to innate differences in intelligence and genetic endowments (Hernstein & Murray, 1994; Jensen, 1969). Although such explanations presently are regarded as politically objectionable, the fact that they are reintroduced into the public discourse periodically by scholars and journalists (although generally not geneticists)[1] suggests that they have an enduring appeal. It also should be remembered that the presumption that non-Whites generally—and Blacks, Native Americans, Hawaiians,

Mexicans, and Puerto Ricans specifically—were inferior peoples, served as the primary means through which slavery, colonization, and more contemporary forms of subordination and exploitation have been justified (Fredrickson, 1981; Horseman, 1981). While the influence of the ideology of White supremacy may seem less relevant today in post-civil rights America, there is considerable evidence that its legacy and concomitant presumption of non-White inferiority are still very much a part of the present.

An analysis of schools in the East Bay (Richmond, Berkeley, and Oakland) reveals in a stark and graphic manner the ways in which the academic outcomes of children are linked to the racial and class characteristics of a neighborhood. It turns out that the higher the elevation of the school, the higher its aggregate test score. Conversely, the closer the school is to sea level, the lower the test scores of its students. Such a pattern is perplexing unless one knows about the characteristics of neighborhoods in the East Bay. Generally, poor and working-class people of color live in flatland neighborhoods, while more affluent White people live in the hills. Given these demographic patterns with respect to the composition of neighborhoods and schools, the relationship between school location and the test scores of children hardly seems surprising or unusual; the scores follow a pattern that Americans historically have come to expect as "normal."

RELATIONSHIP BETWEEN CULTURE AND ACADEMIC ACHIEVEMENT

Since the 1960s, explanations of school performance that have the greatest popularity tend to emphasize the importance of cultural differences. For example, it is widely believed that Asian American students tend do well academically because their culture emphasizes the importance of hard work and the pursuit of academic excellence (Lee, 1996; Sue & Okazaki, 1990; Takaki, 1989). Over the past 25 years, the number of Asian American students entering the most elite universities in the United States has increased substantially (Takagi, 1992). In many parts of the United States, the fact that students from the broad assortment of groups labeled as "Asian" outperform Whites and other groups on a number of academic indicators has reinforced their status as a "model minority."

In contrast, African American, Native American, and Latino students are perceived as being held back by their culture. Oppositional attitudes, a poor work ethic, and, in some instances, a culture of poverty frequently are identified as causes of lower academic achievement for students from these groups (Ogbu, 1987b). Repeating the arguments of Shelby Steele

(1990), Berkeley linguist John McWhorter (2000) argues that African Americans suffer from a culture of "victimology." He contends that "victimology stems from a lethal combination of this inherited inferiority complex with the privilege of dressing down the former oppressor," and he adds that it "condones weakness and failure" (p. 28).

Books like those of Steele and McWhorter generally sell quite well. There seems to be an insatiable appetite for work by Black scholars that blames Black people for the problems they experience. Books like theirs sell well even though cultural explanations of academic performance fail to account for those who deviate from established patterns, including individuals like Steele, McWhorter, and me. More significantly, such theories occupy a dominant position among researchers and practitioners. Even though cultural arguments cannot explain, for example, the large number of Asian students at Galileo High School in San Francisco or Richmond High School who drop out of school, the idea that Asian students constitute a model minority persists. There is no evidence that these students do less well in school because they have an insufficient amount of Asian culture. However, their difficulties are dismissed as some sort of odd exception, while stereotypes about the cultural origins of Asian student success remain firmly intact (Lee, 1996). Broad generalizations about culture are so widely embraced and so deeply embedded in popular thinking about race and school performance that they manage to survive even when there is empirical evidence that appears to undermine their validity.

One of my former students at the University of California, Berkeley, Julian Ledesma (1995), tested the strength of the Asian model minority stereotype in a paper that he wrote for one of my courses. He surveyed students and teachers at Fremont High School in Oakland about which ethnic group they believed was most academically talented. The vast majority of those he surveyed identified Asian students as the highest performers. This was true even for the Asian students he interviewed who were not doing well in school. Given that Asian students were overrepresented in honors and advanced placement courses at the school, and given that several of the school's valedictorians had been Asian, their responses were hardly surprising. However, in his analysis of student performance data, Julian showed that the academic stars at the school who happened to be Asian were not representative of Asian students as a whole. In fact, the grade point average for Asian students at the school was 1.9. He pointed out that because Asian students were perceived as academically successful, little effort had been expended to provide them with the kind of academic support or special services that had been made available to other students.

In addition to reinforcing inaccurate stereotypes, cultural explanations of academic ability also fail to account for the high degree of diversity within racial groups. Differences related to class and income, the educational background of parents, the quality of school students attend, or the kind of neighborhood students live in significantly affect student achievement (Miller, 1995). Such factors influence the academic performance of all students, but because of the tendency to generalize about the performance of racial groups, they often are ignored. Consequently, although there are a considerable number of White students who do poorly in school, substantially less attention is paid to this problem than to the issues facing minority students. Academic failure among White students, like the existence of poverty among White people in the United States, is a phenomenon that is rendered invisible by the overemphasis on race in American social policy. Because racial disparities in measurements of intelligence and academic performance have been used to rationalize racial inequality and discrimination in the United States (Hernstein & Murray, 1994; Lehman, 1999), deviations from established patterns often have been overlooked. It is even more troubling that because culture is treated as an overriding explanation of academic ability, we often have ignored other factors that influence school performance and that we actually might be able to do something about.

During the late 1980s, I was one of several researchers working with the Task Force on Black Student Eligibility that was established by the University of California to study the factors influencing the enrollment of Black students in the University system. The Task Force had been created because the number of Black students who were eligible for admission to the University had been declining steadily for several years (Making the Future Different, 1990). For one of my assignments, I was asked to identify urban public high schools across the state that consistently produced a significant number of high-achieving Black students. My search identified three high schools that for 3 or more years had produced seven or more Black students eligible for the University of California. As I learned more about these schools, I discovered that high academic standards and high-quality academic programs were common to all three. It also turned out that the three schools were led by strong African American principals who devised and implemented academic enrichment programs to support student achievement.

Explanations of academic performance that emphasize the importance of culture generally ignore the fact that what we think of as culture—customs, beliefs, and practices associated with particular groups—is constantly subject to change. Particularly in a country like the United States where the steady influx of immigrants and the popular culture produced by the mass media exert profound influence over values and norms, the idea that culture could be treated as a static independent variable is very misleading and results in misconceptions. Yet, this is precisely what a number of scholars who study the relationship between race and education have done. Even though several of the better-known scholars are regarded as experts in the study of culture (e.g., Anderson, 1988; Fordham, 1996; McWhorter, 2000; Ogbu, 1987b), they continue to propagate the idea that culture determines academic performance. With knowledgeable scholars uncritically embracing broad generalizations about the relationship between culture and academic achievement, it is not surprising that we also find widespread acceptance of this perspective among educational practitioners and the general public.

Undoubtedly, one reason for the popularity of cultural explanations of academic performance is that they are less overtly racist; placing the blame on culture is less controversial than locating the problem in the genetic make-up of a racial group. Unlike genes, culture is not immutable. Through education, social mobility, and assimilation, one can be freed from a "deprived" or even "pathological" culture and become part of mainstream America.[2] This is undoubtedly why African American scholars such as John McWhorter and Shelby Steele go to great lengths to describe their personal backgrounds. By describing their own accomplishments at length (McWhorter in particular does this in the most self-serving way), they can distinguish themselves as high achievers relative to other African Americans. In so doing, they set themselves up as model individuals and living proof that it is possible to escape the harmful effects of African American culture.

The fact that scholars like Steele and McWhorter blame Black students and Black people generally for academic failure, has made them extremely popular with conservatives. Cultural explanations are attractive because by placing the cause of disparities in achievement within the attitudes and behaviors of students and their families, they absolve schools and U.S. society generally from any responsibility for reversing academic trends. After all, there is little that schools or for that matter any other social institution can do to change a person's culture. If those who fail or underperform are from groups that are "culturally disadvantaged" and do not value education, is it fair to hold schools responsible? Of course, this logic shares a disturbing consistency with a broad array of deeply embedded racially biased beliefs that historically have permeated American society—beliefs that have rationalized the differential treatment accorded to Black people and other racial minorities on the basis of their presumed inferiority. Yet, when they are used to explain the relationship between race and academic achievement and framed in terms of culture, such arguments are more palatable because they are perceived as less racist (especially because often they are made by minority scholars) or pernicious.

MOVING FROM CULTURAL EXPLANATIONS TO DECISIVE ACTION

Genetic and cultural explanations of differences in achievement continue to circulate widely throughout U. S. society. In my work with schools, such explanations come up frequently whenever disparities in student achievement are discussed. Too often I have found that such explanations are used to rationalize why schools are unable to help students achieve at higher levels.

For example, I was invited to speak at a high school located in an affluent community in Marin County, California, one of the wealthiest counties in the United States. The school had spent the previous 3 years engaged in various reform projects—restructuring class schedules, adopting an integrated curriculum, and creating two new career academies. As the school was approaching the end of its reform process, I was invited to speak to the faculty on the topic of diversity. Their interest in the topic stemmed from the fact that over the course of 10 years, the school had gone from serving a predominantly White and affluent student population to one in which 90% of the students were poor Mexican immigrants. During that period several major problems had developed at the school, including a rising drop-out rate, lower SAT scores and college attendance, and gang-related conflicts among students.

Before addressing the topic of diversity, I asked the teachers whether they believed that the changes they had adopted at the school would lead to an improvement in academic outcomes for their students. After a good deal of discussion on this question, a consensus emerged among the faculty. Several teachers stated that little change in academic performance would occur because the families of their students simply did not value education. As one veteran teacher put it, "These people are just barely getting by. They're working two and three jobs for very little money. How can we expect them to support their kids' education?" Others were less sympathetic but echoed this teacher's sentiment that the students came from a culture that did not value education. They believed that their students simply were conforming to the low expectations they had learned at home.

I then probed to learn more about their knowledge of their students' culture and to find out what they actually knew about the families of the students they served. In particular, I wanted to know whether they had spoken to any parents while they were carrying out the reforms, or if they could tell me anything about their students' families and the neighborhoods where they lived. As it turned out, most of the teachers knew very little about the lives of their students outside of school, and no one present could even say where most of the students lived. Where poor people could live in this affluent community is not readily apparent because the average home in the area was valued at over $700,000 in 2000. Several of the teachers said that they had heard their students talk about a "zone" located near a canal, and they believed that was where most of the students lived. However, not one of the teachers present had ever visited the area. Growing defensive because of my questions, the teachers explained that they had not spoken to any parents because their planning meetings occurred during the school day while parents were working.

As I started my workshop focused on "diversity," I pointed out that without a partnership with parents and others who knew and understood the social reality of the students, finding a way to reach them in school and improve their academic performance would be extremely difficult. This assertion generated no opposition since the teachers had already acknowledged that their attempts at working with students without the support of parents had been futile. I also pointed out that since many of the students were old enough to drop out of school if they wanted to, there was a strong possibility that many of them and their families believed that education was important.

Interestingly, these two revelations seemed to have a dramatic effect on the tenor of our conversation. At the teachers' insistence, the remainder of our workshop focused on a discussion of how the school might go about engaging parents in a constructive dialogue over how to support the education of their children. We also spent time identifying agencies and churches that provide services to the Mexican immigrant community. We discussed how these organizations could be enlisted to support the efforts of the school.

My experience at this high school illustrates how easy it is for stereotypes and assumptions about the values and culture of students and their families to influence the way schools respond to their needs. A great deal of research on teaching has shown that educators often equate differences (such as in culture, language, or race) with intellectual deficiencies, and that such beliefs often have a profound influence on the expectations that are held toward students (Banks, 1981; Davidman & Davidman, 1994; Nieto, 1992). In the case of this school, race, class, and linguistic barriers limited the ability of the faculty to conceive of educational programs and interventions that they believed would elevate the academic performance of their students. These barriers also had the effect of negating the possibility that parents would be engaged as partners in the process of delivering high-quality education to their children. In my experience working with schools, I often have found that even when educators assert that they want to get parents involved in the education of their children, parents are more likely to be excluded and treated with disregard if they are poor, uneducated, and non-White.

This example also sheds light on why many schools fail in their efforts to raise the academic performance of low-income minority students, and why it is that high levels of academic failure among such students often are treated as inevitable and impossible to alter. In schools where low student achievement has been present for a long time, it is not uncommon for educators to develop a variety of ways to rationalize their students' failure. Blaming uncaring parents, lazy students, or a society that does not provide adequately for the needs of poor children serves as an effective means to avoid taking responsibility for one's role as an educator. Once failure is normalized and the causes of failure are attributed to some set of factors beyond one's control, reversing patterns of achievement can be nearly impossible.

Yet, this case also reveals a kernel of possibility. When given the chance, the faculty at this school was very much interested in learning more about the needs of the students and their families. As they learned more, they were willing to consider how they might make modifications in their work to improve the quality of teaching and learning. Moreover, when prompted to examine the assumptions they had made about the culture of their students, many readily conceded that they had formed judgments that were not based on accurate information. Finally and most important, the vast majority of these teachers genuinely wanted to see the academic outcomes of their students improve, and although they had little faith that the changes they had made would bring this about, I have no doubt that their desire for greater academic success was real. From my own experience, I have learned that when the hopes of teachers are encouraged and transformed into concrete actions for improving the quality of teaching, the possibility of bringing about substantial change in schools can be realized.

EXCEPTIONS TO RACIAL PATTERNS: IMMIGRANT AND MIDDLE-CLASS BLACK STUDENTS

The issues surrounding the relationship between race and achievement seem to be particularly complex when we consider what appears to be a paradox in the performance of two broad categories of students: recent immigrants and middle-class Black students. Several studies reveal that immigrant students of color, many of whom are from low-income families, often are academically successful (Kao & Tienda, 1995; Ogbu, 1987b; Suarez-Orozco & Suarez-Orozco, 2001).[3] This finding shows up not just for Asian immigrants but for immigrants from a variety of other nations and regions as well. As a result of their academic success in high school, a disproportionate number of immigrant students, especially from certain Asian countries (e.g., Taiwan, South Korea, China, and Vietnam), presently are overrepresented at several leading universities in the United States (Takaki, 1989).

Of course, the relative success of immigrant students should not be overstated. Many immigrant students are not doing well at school. Latino immigrants in particular, such as the students at the high school previously mentioned in Marin, are at greater risk of dropping out of school (Garcia, 2001; Valencia, 1991), less likely to attend college, and more likely to join gangs (Vigil, 2002) than students in the general population. Additionally, school and community conditions in the areas where immigrants settle and the amount of education they received prior to arriving in the United States significantly influences academic performance (Suarez-Orozco & Suarez-Orozco, 2001). Even with these important qualifiers, the significant number of low-income immigrant children who excel in school is an undeniable phenomenon, and one that requires an explanation given the rampant failure and mediocre performance of so many domestic minority and nonminority students in the United States.

In contrast to the disproportionate success of many immigrant students, many middle-class Black students tend to underperform academically even though they come from relatively privileged families (Ferguson, 2000; Jencks & Phillips, 1998). On most standardized tests, including the SAT, middle-class Black students tend to perform less well than even low-income White and Asian students (Ferguson, 2000). This is one of the reasons why the new percentage-based admissions policies that have been adopted in California, Florida, and Texas as a replacement for affirmative action have failed to significantly increase Black and Latino enrollment at state-run public universities (Frost, 2003). Even in racially segregated high schools, the highest-achieving students, who are most likely to benefit from these new policies, are more likely to be immigrants than U. S.-born Blacks or Latinos (Frost, 2003).[4]

While several factors directly and indirectly influence the relative success of immigrants and the underachievement of middle-class Blacks and Latinos, I believe that these patterns are related largely to the ways in which racial and gender identities are constructed in school settings. Several studies have shown that students are influenced by the perceptions and expectations of the adults who teach them (Brookover & Erickson, 1969; Weinstein, Madison, & Kuklinski, 1995). We know relatively less about how student perceptions of their racial identities affect their outlook and performance in school. Patterns of achievement suggest that race, class, and gender are related to academic performance. Certain categories of students, namely, African American and Latino males, are consistently overrepresented at the lower rungs of the achievement ladder (Jencks & Phillips, 1998; Miller, 1995). However, we know relatively little about the subjective dimension of this phenomenon or how awareness of these patterns might affect how students see themselves.

We do know that race is more than just a social identity (Omi & Winant, 1986). Race is also an ideological construct, one that is loaded with meanings and beliefs about superiority and inferiority (Miles, 1989). When one identifies as a member of a racial group in the United States, one necessarily takes on the history, stigma, and stereotypes associated with that group. For subordinate groups in particular, membership within racial categories carries with it certain political commitments. These commitments often generate a sense of solidarity among members that can create a shared outlook and perspective on social and political issues. For some young people, the commitments associated with racial membership can lead them to shut off possibilities of participating in activities and courses that are perceived as being outside the invisible but real racial boundaries. When this occurs, individual options can be severely limited.

Schools are rarely neutral on matters related to race. In many U.S. schools, a firm and clear racial hierarchy is in place, one in which Blacks and Latinos are overrepresented in categories related to negative behavior, and Whites are overrepresented in positive categories. Race shows up as a salient feature in friendships and peer groups (Peshkin, 2000), course enrollment patterns (Oakes, 1985), club membership (Steinberg, 1996), and matters related to punishment and discipline (Meier, Stewart, & England, 1989). For this reason, understanding the process through which young people come to see themselves as belonging to particular racial categories is important because it can have profound implications for the norms and behaviors they embrace in connection with their social and academic performance.

For many years, a number of researchers have recognized the significance of the link between the process of identity development (unrelated to race) as it occurs among adolescents, and academic performance. The subjective positioning of students has been found to have bearing on motivation and persistence (Newman, 1992), on relationships with peer groups and teachers (Phelan, Davidson, & Yu, 1998; Stienberg, 1996), on conformity and deviance (Gottfredson, 2001), and on overall self-esteem (Obiakor,

1992). Yet, despite the substantial body of research in this area, there is far less agreement among scholars about how the development of racial identities among adolescents influences the stance and orientation they adopt in relation to school.

There is a large body of research on racial identity development (Cross, Parnham, & Helms, 1991; Phinney, 1990; Tatum, 1997), but most of these studies have not considered the process through which racial identities evolve and shape academic performance. Despite overwhelming evidence of a strong correlation between race and academic performance, there is considerable confusion about how and why American minority students come to perceive a linkage between their racial identities and their academic ability, and how these in turn shape their aspirations and behaviors toward education and school.

The scholars whose work has had the greatest influence on these issues are Ogbu (1987a, 1987b, 1990) and Fordham (1996), both of whom argue that Black students from all socioeconomic backgrounds develop "oppositional identities" that lead them to view schooling as a form of forced assimilation. Having positioned themselves as marginal outsiders, Ogbu and Fordham argue that Black students and other "non-voluntary minorities" (e.g., Chicanos, Puerto Ricans, and Native Americans) come to equate academic success with "acting White" (Fordham & Ogbu, 1986). For these researchers, such perceptions lead to the devaluation of academic pursuits and the adoption of self-defeating behaviors that inhibit possibilities for academic success. The few who aspire to achieve academically (kids like Cedric Jennings, mentioned in Chapter 1) must pay a heavy price for success. According to these researchers, Black students who perform at high levels often are ostracized by their peers as traitors and "sell outs," and are compelled to adopt a "raceless" persona to avoid the stigma associated with membership in their racial groups (Fordham & Ogbu, 1986).

In contrast, others (Gibson, 1988; Matut-Biachi, 1986; Suarez-Orozco & Suarez-Orozco, 2001) have argued that immigrant students of color are largely immune to the insidious association between race and achievement that traps students from domestic minority backgrounds. So-called "voluntary minorities," whether Mexican, Asian, African, or West Indian, are more likely to perceive schooling as a pathway to social mobility, and for this reason they are also more likely to adopt behaviors that increase the likelihood of academic success. Having been raised in societies where people of their race or ethnic group are in the majority, they typically have not been subjected to socialization processes that lead them to see themselves as members of subordinate or inferior groups. Less influenced or cognizant of the history of racial oppression in the United States, these students are more likely to accommodate the dominant culture and conform to the prescriptions that are regarded as essential for achieving success in school (Spring, 1994; Waters, 1990). Even if they avoid complete assimilation, they are more likely to conform to the expectations of their teachers and adopt behaviors that contribute to school success (Gibson, 1988; Ogbu, 1987a, 1987b).

When viewed in combination with Steele's (1997) work on the effects of racial stereotypes on academic performance, a compelling explanation for the identity–achievement paradox begins to emerge. Through his research on student attitudes toward testing, Steele has shown that students are highly susceptible to prevailing stereotypes related to intellectual ability. According to Steele, when "stereotype threats" are operative, they lower the confidence of vulnerable students and negatively affect their performance on standardized tests. Steele (1997) writes, "Ironically, their susceptibility to this threat derives not from internal doubts about their ability but from their identification with the domain and the resulting concern they have about being stereotyped in it" (p. 614). For Steele, the debilitating effects of stereotypes can extend beyond particular episodes of testing and can have an impact on overall academic performance. Yet, because he does not locate the problem in the culture of students, Steele suggests that schools and universities can adopt a number of strategies to reduce the stigma experienced by women and racial minorities and thereby reduce the effects of stereotype threats.

If we attempt to combine the arguments that have been made about immigrant students with those of Steele, we could extrapolate that recent immigrant students are less likely to be susceptible to the threat associated with negative racial stereotypes because their "newness" to the U.S. social landscape protects them. Not having been socialized to see themselves as inferior, immigrant students are less likely to see themselves that way. They are also less likely to "resist" aspects of schooling that require conformity and assimilation to values and norms that domestic minorities regard as White and middle class, and therefore inimical to their sense of identity (Solomon, 1992).

In contrast, because of the ways in which they are socialized and become racialized in school settings, middle-class Black students are more likely to identify with the styles and behaviors of lower-class members of their racial/ethnic group. This occurs in part because, unlike the White middle class, the Black middle class is closely connected through family ties, residence, and popular culture to the Black lower class (Portilla, 1999). Rather than risk being ostracized for differentiating themselves from their peers, middle-class Black students may adopt attitudes and behaviors that undermine their possibilities for achieving academic success. As I will describe later, they may avoid academically enriching activities and courses if these are perceived as "White," and they may adopt self-defeating behaviors that reduce their likelihood of success in school. These behaviors will occur unless decisive steps are taken in schools to prevent students from linking their racial identity to negative school performance. Several national studies have shown that Black students watch more hours of television than any other group, place greater priority on social acceptance and popularity, and are less likely to engage in leisure reading than White students (Clark, 1983; Ferguson, 2000). Undoubtedly, such tendencies also contribute to the underperformance of middle-class African American students.[5]

The experience of my eldest son is illustrative of the ways in which the construction of racial identities in school settings can undermine the academic performance of talented middle-class Black and Latino students. Until he entered tenth grade, Joaquin was an exemplary student. In addition to doing well in school, he was a talented musician (he played piano and percussion for several years) and an exceptional athlete (soccer, basketball, and wrestling). Not only was it rare for me to receive complaints about his behavior in school, but most of the adults that worked with him described him as courteous, respectful, and a leader among his peers.

However, when Joaquin entered tenth grade, his grades declined dramatically. Not only did he receive failing grades for the first time in math and science classes, but he began cutting classes and getting into trouble at school. As my wife and I struggled to figure out what was happening to Joaquin and how best we could support him, I gradually began to learn that much of the change in his performance was related to the expectations he had set for himself. By tenth grade, most of Joaquin's closest friends were failing in school. These were primarily African American kids from working-class families who had grown up in our neighborhood in south Berkeley, one of the poorest sections of the city. Although most of his friends seemed to be doing fine academically while they were in elementary and middle school, on entering high school their behavior and academic performance took a turn for the worse. Lacking sufficient guidance and support at home, distracted by less academically focused peers, and finding out that they could cut school with impunity due to the permissive culture at Berkeley High School, many of Joaquin's friends were in danger of dropping out of school entirely by tenth grade.

When we confronted Joaquin about the decline in his performance, he consistently made reference to how much better he was doing than his friends. When we encouraged him not to compare himself with them but to strive to do his best, he responded that we didn't understand what he was going through. Frustrated by my inability to help him change his performance in school, I struggled to understand. However, it was not until he reminded me to think about what it had been like for me to be in high school myself that I "got it." As a high school student I had coped with the isolation that came from being one of few students of color in my advanced classes by working hard to prove that I could do as well as or better than my White peers. However, outside of the classroom I also worked hard to prove to my less studious friends that I was cool. For me this primarily meant playing basketball, hanging out, fighting when necessary, and acting as though I was one of the "fellas." In fact, it also meant that I was forced to adopt a split persona: I behaved one way in class, another way with my friends, and yet another way at home.

During his tenth-grade year, Joaquin was in the midst of figuring out how to pull off a similar personality make-over. His failing grades and poor behavior were clear signs that he had not yet found a way to balance his desire to succeed academically and to be accepted by his friends. As a result, he was at risk of failing in school despite his abilities and despite the support and pressure to succeed he received at home.

Fortunately, during his junior year Joaquin did find his own way to achieve a balance between school success and social acceptance. By his senior year he distanced himself and became critical of his old friends and much more focused on preparing himself for college and for life after high school. Once again his grades improved and he returned to playing piano (and began producing music) and rejoined the soccer team. In fact, by his senior year he was associating with a more diverse group of young people and seemed far less concerned about how he would be judged by others for crossing borders related to race and class. Unlike his old friends who slipped through the cracks because they lacked support at home and school, Joaquin was able to recover academically. His lowered grades made him less attractive to the best colleges, but his relatively high test scores enabled him to be admitted to a reputable private liberal arts college.

Joaquin's brief bout with academic failure provided me with an important lesson on how a student's social frame of reference can profoundly influence his achievement in school. My own research on this topic suggests that the process through which racial identities are developed is not nearly as dichotomous as portrayed by researchers like Ogbu and Fordham (Noguera, 2001b). Rather than framing the identities adopted by students as either oppositional or conformist, we can understand that a range of possibilities for expressing one's racial identity exists. That high-achieving minority students will adopt a raceless persona (Fordham & Ogbu, 1986) or construe doing well in school as "acting White," is just one possibility.

There are also many examples of Black and Latino students who manage to do well in school while retaining a sense of pride in their racial and cultural identity. I was one of those students and I know many others. I did well in school and I never felt that I needed to "act White" in order to succeed, or to disassociate myself from my Black and Latino peers. During my high school and college years I was an activist. I was one of many students who became active in political movements in the 1970s and 1980s, such as the struggle for ethnic studies and the anti-apartheid movement. My political activism enhanced and furthered my intellectual development in that it provided me with motivation to read and write, to study with discipline and purpose, and to grapple seriously with ideas. My identity as a Black, working-class student of Caribbean and Latin heritage, grounded me and provided me with the fortitude to perform well in elite institutions, places that were often alienating and inhospitable to people from my background.

As a teacher in inner-city high schools and as a professor at the University of California, Berkeley, and Harvard University, the vast majority of talented students of color I have worked with have had a positive and clear sense of their racial identity. They often have been motivated to succeed out of a desire to help their families and give something back to their communities. I generally have taught very large courses, and I have had the pleasure of teaching and getting to know many students from diverse backgrounds. The vast majority of those I've come to know are people who managed to balance academic success and retain a sense of pride in their identity and heritage.

Typically, the ones I remember best are the ones who had to overcome the greatest obstacles to succeed. Students like Jerry Arriano, who grew up poor in a single-parent household in the Mission District of San Francisco. He attended Balboa High School—one of the worst schools in the city—and struggled through remedial courses in his first few years at UC Berkeley. Jerry went on to excel at Berkeley and is now preparing to graduate from the University of California, San Francisco Medical School. There are others like him. Dumilla Hewitt, Estella Mejia, Keenan Jackson, Javier Hernandez, Jesse DeLeon, and Eddie Javious all came from severely disadvantaged backgrounds and were not well prepared to handle the rigors of college. Yet, these individuals adjusted to the alien culture of college, defied the negative racial stereotypes, and performed exceptionally well, not only in college but in their professional careers. Although the individuals I've listed are in different fields—medicine, law, education, public policy—each has retained a strong sense of his or her racial/ethnic identity and has found a way to pursue a career that enables him or her to serve the needs of disadvantaged communities and constituencies.

In *Losing the Race* (2000), John McWhorter writes with shame and disappointment about the African American students at UC Berkeley who frequently missed his classes, arrived late, turned in poor work, or failed to turn in anything at all. He claims that the vast majority of the Black students he taught are individuals who live by excuses and display no serious interest in their education. How could it be that John McWhorter and I, both of whom were teaching at UC Berkeley, could have had such different experiences in teaching Black students? I don't limit my analysis to Black students because I have taught disadvantaged students from diverse backgrounds and found that they face similar obstacles. I can only postulate that our disagreement appears to be tied to the lessons we have drawn from our childhood experiences. McWhorter attributes his professional success to his talent and intelligence, and he uses himself as proof that racism is not an obstacle that prevents Black people from succeeding. In contrast, I regard the success I have experienced as evidence that many others could make it if given the opportunity. Some of my students have told me that, like John McWhorter, they occasionally were harassed by their peers in high school for acting White simply because they did well in school. However, unlike McWhorter, most of these students draw on this experience to think about what they can do to counter and redirect such self-destructive patterns of behavior.

My own research and experience suggest that high-performing students of color are more likely to be successful if they attend schools that support and affirm their racial and cultural identities (Noguera, 2001b). The three high schools previously identified in the Black Student Eligibility study for the University of California were places that actively encouraged students to feel pride in their race and culture even as they encouraged students to excel. Numerous other researchers have found that schools and classrooms that deliberately incorporate the culture of their students into the curriculum and pedagogy are more likely to be successful with students of color (Banks, 1981; Boykin, 1983; Ladson-Billings, 1994; Nieto, 1992).

The idea that schools can affirm the values, culture, and aspirations of the students they serve is a possibility that rarely is considered by scholars like Obgu, Fordham, or McWhorter. In fact, they accept the idea that minorities must assimilate and conform to the dominant culture, and place the onus for accommodation on students. While it is important to recognize that all students need to learn the normative codes that will enable them to succeed in mainstream U. S. society (Smitherman, 1977), I believe there is much that schools can do to increase student achievement. Improving teacher–student and school–parent relations, and adopting policies that actively encourage minority students to take rigorous courses, are just some of the measures that can be taken (Fashola & Slavin, 1997).

There are also a number of researchers who have shown that there are many adolescents who succeed academically by adopting multiple personas and identities. Such students adopt the cultural norms that are valued in school settings, while embracing the speech, style of dress, and larger identity construct associated with their racial group outside of school (Phelan, Davidson, & Yu, 1988). Such students may experience stress as they learn how to code switch, and on some occasions they may feel compelled to choose between one persona or another (Smitherman, 1977). However, many academically successful students of color learn to code switch effectively, and more often than not they learn to do this on their own without an adult explicitly teaching them the "culture of power" (Delpit, 1988).

Understanding the process through which racial identities are constructed in school is important in order to devise strategies that enable us to counter the insidious ways in which race and achievement become linked. In Chapter 4, I will draw on research from 4 years of work at Berkeley to demonstrate how the link between racial identity and student performance becomes operative within school settings. However, in departure from both Ogbu (1987b) and Steele (1997), I will describe how the structure and culture of school contributes to the creation of this linkage. Finally, I will describe how the concerted efforts of educators, parents, and students can make it possible to alter school conditions so that the link between racial identity and achievement can be broken. Such a break will make it more likely that minority students can be freed from the harmful effects of racial stereotypes as they pursue their education.

CHAPTER 4

Unequal Outcomes, Unequal Opportunities: Closing the Achievement Gap in Berkeley

To the outsider or uninformed observer, Berkeley might seem to possess all of the conditions necessary to have excellent public schools. Home to a world-class public university (the University of California, Berkeley), a national research center (Lawrence Berkeley Laboratory), and numerous independent bookstores and publishers, Berkeley is a place where education and the pursuit of knowledge are the vocation of many residents and much more than a casual pastime. It is an affluent and sophisticated city, a place where new ideas—both the innovative and the idiosyncratic—are born, and a place where civic participation in the affairs of the city is extensive and widespread.

With its liberal, highly educated population, Berkeley has long been in the forefront among cities that have embraced progressive social reforms. From integrated housing, to curbside recycling, to disability rights, to rent control, Berkeley has shown a willingness to enact experimental social reforms long before they were popular or embraced elsewhere (Nathan & Scott, 1978). Sometimes referred to by outsiders as "The Peoples' Republic" or more derisively as "Bezerkeley," the city consistently has been a leader in setting trends on matters related to social policy and has provided a safe haven for those who challenge conventional thinking. Free needle exchanges for intravenous drug users, access to marijuana for medicinal purposes, and provision of domestic partner benefits for municipal employees, are just some of the reforms embraced by Berkeley long before they were openly discussed or considered elsewhere.

As might be expected, Berkeley's commitment to progressive ideals and its willingness to act on them also have been evident in education. In 1968, Berkeley became one of the first school districts in the nation to voluntarily desegregate its schools (Kirp, 1982). Significantly, it did so not through passive acquiescence but through a bold assertion of public support and by adopting a plan that called for the burden of busing to be shared by Blacks and Whites.[1] When opponents of desegregation attempted to undo the reform by recalling the members of the school board, Berkeley voters, in a rare display of public support for racial desegregation, squelched the backlash and resoundingly affirmed their support for the new busing plan (Kirp, 1982).

Throughout the 1970s, Berkeley schools experimented with a variety of reforms that its leaders hoped would improve the education offered to its minority students. In 1969 Black students at Berkeley High School (BHS) demanded and were granted the first African American studies department established at a high school in the United States. The logic behind this concession was that separate and distinct approaches to educating Black and White students were necessary and desirable. Such thinking led to the creation of several smaller separate high schools in the mid-1970s, including the Umoja House for Black students seeking a culturally defined educational experience, and the Raza House for Chicano students seeking something analogous for themselves. Ultimately, these experiments in racial separation were brought to an end by the U.S. Department of Education, which determined that maintaining racially separate schools was a violation of several civil rights statutes and was therefore illegal (Kirp, 1982). Despite this reversal, the thinking that created these kinds of race-based policies continued to influence district policies (Noguera, 1993).

THE RACIAL ACHIEVEMENT GAP: FROM NOBLE GOALS TO TOUGH ISSUES

Despite this impressive track record of public support, Berkeley schools are characterized by extreme disparities in academic outcomes among students from different racial/ethnic backgrounds. At every school in the district, student achievement on most standardized tests follows a bimodal pattern with respect to the distribution of student scores (see Table 4.1). The majority of White students score at or above the 80th percentile on most norm-referenced tests, while the scores of Black and Latino students generally hover between the 30th and 40th percentiles (Berkeley Alliance, 1999; Noguera, 1995d). Similar patterns emerge when the composition of special and compensatory education programs is compared with the composition of gifted and talented and advanced placement courses: Black and Latino students overwhelmingly constitute enrollment in the former, while affluent White students populate the latter. Wide disparities in achieve-

Table 4.1. Berkeley Unified School District Academic Outcomes, 1999

	1999 BUSD Student Performance on Stanford 9		**Grade Point Averages for BUSD Eighth-Grade Students (by school)**		
	60th–90th NPR*	1st–30th NPR	ML King	Willard	Longfellow
Black	18.0	63.1	2.14	1.74	1.46
Asian	47.7	37.9	3.34	3.03	2.26
Hispanic	24.9	61.4	2.64	2.33	1.64
White	81.2	8.6	3.42	2.98	2.44

*National Percentile Ranking
Source: Berkeley Unified School District, 2001.

ment are also evident in the grades assigned to students, in attrition rates, and in suspension and expulsion rates at all schools in the district (Diversity Project, 2000).

Given its long history of liberalism and its reputation for embracing progressive causes, one might expect that Berkeley citizens eventually would have become outraged at the persistence of such glaring disparities. Yet, a careful analysis of the political dynamics that have shaped policy in Berkeley's schools reveals that the community actually has tolerated a degree of racial inequality in student academic outcomes that any objective analysis would indicate is quite extreme. In fact, until recently, there was surprisingly little effort to address this problem.

I became aware of what I came to regard as Berkeley's complacency on this issue shortly after I was elected to the School Board in November 1990. Toward the end of one very late meeting, the Board was presented the results of a battery of examinations that had been administered to students in the spring of the preceding year. The results showed once again that racial disparities in the scores and the bimodal pattern were firmly in place. Since I was new to the Board, I was unfamiliar with how such issues were to be addressed. Although it was already quite late (nearly midnight), and all of us were tired, I felt it necessary to query the district's senior administrators about how to interpret the test results. I asked, "What are we supposed to do with this depressing information?" I was told that because the exams were authorized by the State of California, the Board had to formally acknowledge receipt of the results. I pushed further to find out how the district intended to respond. With most of those present growing impatient due to the late hour of the meeting, I was told by the new superintendent that the district was committed to finding solutions to the problem and the matter would not be swept under the rug. I soon learned that this would not be the case.

Over time, I came to realize that Berkeley had grown accustomed to the idea that its African American and Latino students would always lag behind White students on most measures of achievement. I also came to understand that this complacency was not due to malicious neglect or overt racism. Rather, it was an issue that had come to be regarded as impossible to solve because sophisticated Berkeley citizens attributed its cause to class rather than race. It was widely assumed that because students of color disproportionately came from families with less income and education, it would not be possible to close the gap in achievement. I also learned that racial disparities in academic outcomes had come to be accepted as a "racial phenomenon" and thus only "racial" solutions had been considered (Noguera, 1993).

Over the years, the failure of Black and Brown students had given rise to a number of racial remedies—from Black and Latino studies programs, to a new ethnic studies requirement, to mentoring and tutoring programs targeted specifically at these groups. Many of these initiatives were championed and designed by educators and parents of color. Frustrated by what they regarded as indifference on the part of the district, many community advocates argued that racially and culturally relevant interventions were the only way to solve the problem. However, in the effort to solve what they regarded as racial problems with racial remedies, I perceived an inadvertent willingness to absolve the district of responsibility for addressing the problem. Defining the issue of student achievement in narrow racial terms contributed to a failure to consider how the resources of the entire district could address the failure of poor Black and Brown students. In a community known for its progressive ideals, there was a disturbing willingness to tolerate inferior educational opportunities for lower-performing African American and Latino students.

The most obvious example of Berkeley's willingness to tolerate blatant forms of racial disparities was evident at the continuation school known as East Campus (renamed Berkeley Alternative High School) where, as noted in Chapter 1, I had started teaching in 1988. Serving approximately 160 students, most of whom were sent there because of poor grades, poor attendance, or poor behavior, the school was comprised almost entirely of African American students. Through my conversations with guidance counselors at Berkeley High School, I learned that White students who failed or missed too many days of school were assigned to independent study and rarely sent to East Campus. When it was started as the McKinley School in the 1970s, it had a reputation as an alternative "hippie" school and was predominantly White. However, by the mid-1980s, the school had been moved to a new facility, and in almost every sense imaginable was marginal to the district, geographically and otherwise.

During my 3 years at East Campus, the academic performance of students at the school received so little attention that basic information such as graduation, drop-out, and college attendance rates of students were not even maintained. Although there was no evidence that the school served its students well, the district made little if any effort to improve the quality of education provided by the school. Tucked away on the margins, this small racially segregated school had been accepted as a dumping ground for students regarded as incorrigible and uneducable.

East Campus is only one example of disparate treatment accorded to students of different racial and socioeconomic backgrounds. Throughout the district, other forms of racial inequity can be found in the quality of programs such as special education and English as a Second Language (ESL) classes that cater primarily to minority students, and in the disciplinary practices of the schools. To understand how these disparities are rationalized and thereby tolerated and accepted, it is necessary to understand how efforts to address them have been politicized over the years. Educators and parents in Berkeley have been far more likely to criticize and blame each other for the persistence of poor achievement among minority students than to take constructive action to address the problem. Politicization in turn has contributed to paralysis, and finger pointing has contributed to a lack of clarity about the nature of the problem and limited the possibility that action could be taken to improve academic outcomes for failing students.

TWO SCHOOLS IN ONE: SORTING STUDENTS AT BERKELEY HIGH SCHOOL

Persistent racial disparities, finger pointing, and paralysis have been most clearly evident at Berkeley High School, the only comprehensive secondary school in the district. BHS is a relatively large school with approximately 3,000 students and nearly 200 teachers, counselors, and administrators. According to the district's data, approximately 40% of the students at BHS are White, 40% are African American, 10% are Latino, and 10% are Asian American (Berkeley Alliance, 1999). These percentages are undoubtedly inaccurate because approximately 10% of the students who responded to a survey administered by the Diversity Project to the Class of 2000 identified themselves as mixed race (Diversity Project, 2000). One-fifth of the student population is identified as limited in English language proficiency, and among these students over 50 languages are spoken.

As is true for the rest of Berkeley, racial differences tend to correspond closely to differences in socioeconomic status. The vast majority of White students reside in middle-class and affluent neighborhoods in the hills and north Berkeley, while the majority of African American and Latino students come from low-income communities in the flatlands of south and west Berkeley. Additionally, approximately 25% of BHS students do not reside in Berkeley at all. They enroll in BHS either through interdistrict transfer or by surreptitiously claiming Berkeley residence. The vast majority of these students are Black and reside in poorer neighborhoods in Oakland and Richmond (Diversity Project, 1999).

On the basis of almost every significant indicator, BHS is a school that does not serve its Black and Latino students well. Nearly 50% of Black and Latino students who enter BHS in ninth grade fail to graduate, and among those who do, few complete the course requirements necessary for admission to the University of California or the California State University systems (Berkeley Alliance, 1999). African American students constitute the overwhelming majority of students who are suspended or expelled from the school for disciplinary reasons (Diversity Project, *Final Report*, 2000), and they constitute the majority of students enrolled in special education classes. Finally, the ESL program functions as a separate and distinct school within the larger school, and its students, most of whom are Latino and Asian, are effectively denied access to college preparatory classes and other resources available at BHS.

In contrast, for most White students, BHS is a highly successful school offering a vast array of educational opportunities and enriching experiences. The vast majority of White students graduate and matriculate to 4-year colleges and universities, and a significant number are admitted to Ivy League colleges and the University of California (Report on College Admissions, 1996). BHS consistently produces several National Merit scholars, most of whom are White, and the jazz band, debating club, and school newspaper (all of which are almost exclusively White) have received several national awards. With its varied and innovative curriculum, BHS is one of few public schools that actually attract White students away from private schools.[2] Their parents, many of whom are professionals with advanced university degrees, know that BHS offers more honors and advanced placement courses than many private high schools. For this reason they have refused to abandon this urban public school. In fact, many White parents and students perceive the diversity of the school as an added benefit, and some regard their decision to send their children there as a progressive political act.[3]

To serve what many have perceived as the divergent needs of these two broad categories of students, BHS effectively has become two schools within one facility. For some, it is a college preparatory school as good as or even better than many elite private schools. For others, it is as bad as any other inner-city school serving economically disadvantaged Black and Latino students. Officially, BHS is only one school with one principal, faculty, and football team. But for students and anyone else who spends time there, divisions along racial and class lines are evident and present in nearly every aspect of the school.

Patterns of racial separation are most evident when one enters the school grounds at the beginning of the school day. Across the sprawling campus, students can be seen huddled in racially distinct groupings. Black students congregate in front of the administration building near a map of Africa that has been painted on the asphalt. White students gather in the center of the campus on the steps of the Community Theater. Along Martin Luther King Way on the periphery of the school, groups of Latino students generally can be found hanging out near and around a Mexican mural. Smaller groups of Asian students find their place along a wall adjacent to the science building. Each grouping is racially distinct, but the lines between them are permeable as can be seen from the significant number of students who mingle in mixed groups or who cross over to interact with individuals from another group.

This form of racial separation is the most noticeable, and because it appears to be voluntary and a matter of choice, there is a sense that this is what students prefer. Yet, racial separation is not limited to the clustering that occurs outside of the school. It shows up in classrooms and clubs throughout the school, and these forms of separation are not voluntary. Rather, they are products of the school's sorting practices and its structure and organization. Although the separations created by tracking—the practice of sorting students into courses based on some measure or estimate of their academic ability (Oakes, 1985)—are less visible, their impact on student outcomes is far more profound. Despite its obvious divergence from Berkeley's long-term commitment to racial integration, racial separation in all its forms, like racial disparities in academic achievement, is a social phenomenon that has come to be accepted as normal at BHS.

THE DIVERSITY PROJECT: CHALLENGING RACIAL INEQUALITY AT BERKELEY HIGH SCHOOL

In 1994, the school was jolted out of its passive acceptance of the status quo when a documentary on the school aired nationally on public television. Based on interviews with and profiles of students and teachers over the course of a school year, *School Colors* portrayed a school mired in deep racial separation and polarization. More than just a documentary on a particular high school, *School Colors* was used as evidence of the failure of racial integration in public schools 40 years after the *Brown* decision.

Reaction to the film within BHS was strikingly uniform. Teachers, students, and parents of all kinds angrily condemned the film as a distorted depiction of their school. They argued that the film lacked balance because it failed to show the positive aspects of the school and the many interracial relationships that exist there. They complained that the film makers omitted scenes that would have contradicted their pessimistic message, and they charged that the producers who had been given complete access to the school had abused their trust. Many at BHS believed the film makers knew, before they even arrived at the school, what story they wanted to tell. Now exposed before a national audience, the city that had given birth to voluntary racial integration of public schools was being used as living proof that the experiment had failed.

At the time of the film's airing, I was still serving on the Berkeley School Board. I felt particularly betrayed by the film makers because I had been instrumental in helping them to gain access to the school. However, unlike the others who quickly dismissed the film and its message, I watched the film over and over again, and even showed it to many of my classes at UC Berkeley. The more I saw the film, the more I recognized the extent to which it had captured accurately what was going on at BHS. I knew that while the issues at BHS were more complicated than had been conveyed in the film, it had succeeded in capturing some troubling truths about the school. Through their intensive examination of racial dynamics within the school, the producers created a medium through which the performance of racial identities could be observed clashing and interacting with the institution and the social conventions operative there. Although I still had criticisms about some of the ways in which racial issues were portrayed, I realized that the film did reveal some of the complex ways in which racial inequality is reproduced and the peculiar role of individual choice and agency in that process.

It was largely as a result of the film that I and others who had worked at and with the school for many years came together to create the Diversity Project as an organizational vehicle for addressing issues of racial inequality within BHS. Initiated by a BHS parent who was also a lecturer in the School of Education at Stanford University, the Diversity Project was created in Summer 1996 to address two questions/issues:

1. What are the factors that contribute to the disparity in academic achievement between students of different racial and class backgrounds at the school?

2. What are the factors that are responsible for the racial separation of students within the school?

Comprising more than 30 teachers, students, parents, school board members, and university researchers, the Diversity Project focused its initial year of work on research aimed at finding answers to these two questions. We purposefully created a team including the various constituencies that make up the school because we wanted to ensure that our work would not contribute to further polarization. Our plan was to use findings generated from our research to guide and influence changes at the school. We relied on research not because we believed that there was any magic in using data to analyze the school. Rather, we focused on research because we believed that the inquiry process could provide a new and different way to approach issues that had come to be seen as "natural" and unchangeable. From the start, we understood that we would have to do more than merely document patterns of racial disparity and separation that were already well established. We recognized that in order for our research to bring about a change in student outcomes, we would have to find ways to change the way in which people thought about racial patterns at the school.

To accomplish this goal, we devised research strategies that were designed to achieve the following objectives:

1. *Make the familiar seem strange and problematic*—By using research to enable teachers, students, and parents to question their assumptions about why students do or do not succeed academically, and to understand how these beliefs are linked to assumptions about the nature of racial identities.
2. *Critically examine the organization and structure of privilege*—By making the various constituencies within the school aware of the ways in which organizational practices harm the educational interests of some students while enhancing the opportunities of others.
3. *Empower the disadvantaged and marginalized*—By utilizing the inquiry process to make the needs and interests of those who historically have been most peripheral to the school, central to its operation and mission.

We recognized from the outset that school reform is an inherently political process, and thus there would have to be a constituency to actively push for greater equity in educational opportunities. Without such a force, we feared the parents of high-achieving White students, who were already well organized and who benefited from the status quo, might attempt to undermine equity efforts they perceived as harmful to their interests. For this reason, we sought to use the research process to create a degree of balance in the school that also would allow parents of students who were not well served to be heard.

MAKING THE FAMILIAR SEEM STRANGE AND PROBLEMATIC

As the Diversity Project attempted to find a way to respond to racial disparities in academic achievement at BHS, we understood that the biggest obstacle to be overcome involved the explanations and rationalizations of this phenomenon that already existed in the minds of most people. Data on the attrition of minority students and on their performance in academic classes had been publicized and made available to the entire school and community for many years. Leaders in the African American and Latino community were aware of this poor track record and had been highly critical of the school in the past. In fact, several community organizations, such as the local chapter of the NAACP and the Black Ministerial Alliance, had become increasingly outspoken in their condemnation of the school because of these persistent patterns of failure. In response to this outrage, the School Board and the district's administration expressed genuine concern but could offer little in the way of concrete strategies to address the problem. It was common knowledge that the majority of Black and Latino students were doing poorly at BHS, but there was little evidence that anything was being done to effectively address the problem.

Given this context, the Diversity Project set as its immediate goal the need to shift the focus of attention away from a search for blame to a search for solutions to the problem. To do this, the Project conducted a survey of entering ninth graders in the Class of 2000 (approximately 700 ninth graders who entered BHS in Fall 1996). We posed questions about their experiences in school and, as we analyzed their responses, we used student records to incorporate data such as grades, test scores, and course selections made by the students. The goal of this inquiry was to find out how students from different racial and socioeconomic backgrounds were sorted into different academic paths and trajectories within the school. In part, we wanted to know how much of this sorting was done by the school and how much by the students themselves. We also surveyed 85 sports teams and clubs to determine the make-up of extracurricular activities and to learn how these forms of voluntary association contributed to racial separation within the school.

By the end of the school year, we were ready to share our findings with the faculty and broader community. To facilitate discussion, the faculty was divided into four groups and assigned to rooms where large graphics illustrating the findings from our investigation were displayed. In the first room the charts illustrated how the assignment of students to math courses in ninth grade influenced their trajectory into other academic courses and electives within the school. For example, it showed that students who were placed in honors geometry, 87% of whom were White and who disproportionately had come to BHS from private schools, were on track to complete the advanced math and science courses needed for admission to the University of California. We also displayed graphics that showed these students were more likely to be enrolled in a higher-level foreign language course (e.g., second-year or above French or Spanish, or first-year German or Latin) and honors biology.

In contrast, another set of graphics showed that students who had been placed in the lowest-level pre-algebra class, 83% of whom were African American and Latino, were not on track to complete the University's science and math requirements (see Figure 4.1). With over 90% of the students failing the pre-algebra course in the Fall 1996 semester, it was clear that no more than a handful would be able to complete the math and science course sequence needed to fulfill the University's entrance requirements. Moreover, students placed in pre-algebra were not likely to be enrolled in a college prep science course, and if they had a foreign language class, it was most likely to be beginning Spanish or Swahili (Diversity Project, 1999). Most surprising of all was the fact that nearly all of the students who had entered BHS through interdistrict transfer or under "care giver status" (the vast majority of whom were from Oakland) had been assigned to pre-algebra.

The course enrollment charts were followed by the presentation of a map of the city of Berkeley broken down by zip code. Within each zip code, the average grade point average (GPA) for students residing within the area was indicated (see Table 4.2). As might be expected, the map revealed a clear and distinct pattern: Students from homes in the poorest sections of the city, with the highest African American and Latino populations, had the lowest GPAs, while students in north Berkeley and the affluent Berkeley hills, had the highest GPAs. Interestingly, although the map revealed patterns that anyone associated with the school would expect, reaction to the map was striking. Teachers were amazed by the consistency of the patterns and wondered aloud why such a pronounced trend existed. The comment of one veteran teacher captured the sentiment of many of the teachers: "I expected kids from the poorer sections of the city to do less well but I'm amazed that it's this blatant. Something must be going on" (personal interview, May 2, 1997). The map turned out to be such a powerful illustration of the relationship between social class and academic achievement that the June 16, 1997 issue of the *San Francisco Chronicle* fea-

Figure 4.1. The Paths Through Berkeley High School Class of 2000: Course Options by Ninth-Grade Math Placement

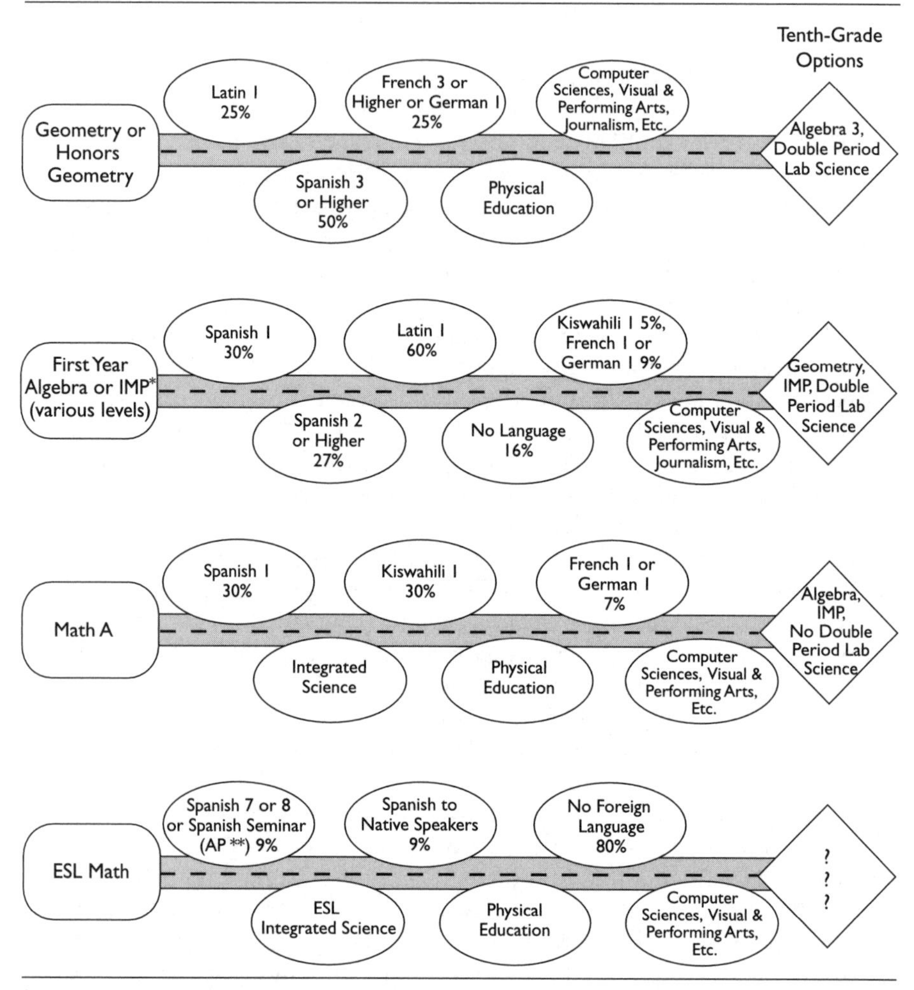

* Interactive Math Program
** Advanced Placement
Original Graphic by Jean Wing

Table 4.2. Ninth-Grade Class of 2000 Student Grade Point Average (GPA) by Zip Code of Residence and Median Household Income

Zip Code	*Median Household Income**	*Mean GPA for Ninth Graders*
94710	$22,866	2.19
94704	$17,930	2.44
94703	$24,499	2.46
94702	$25,389	2.49
94706	$34,522	3.02
94709	$27,105	3.17
94705	$46,689	3.25
94707	$62,567	3.30
94708	$68,911	3.37

* From 1990 U.S. Census data.

tured a copy of the map in a front page article describing the research that had been done by the Project.

Surprisingly, as teachers discussed the findings from the research, there was no argument about the accuracy of the data, nor did the conversation about the data deteriorate into a debate over who was to blame for these patterns. Instead, teachers wanted to know more about what could be learned from the data, and they asked questions to further probe the information that had been collected. For example, they wanted to know how the grades students obtained in math compared with those in English and history (subjects that had been de-tracked for several years already). Others wondered how the grades students received correlated with their attendance in school. Additionally, some wanted to know how effective the academic support programs were that had been set up to help students who were struggling academically.

There were similar reactions to the data derived from the survey that was presented in another classroom. The survey data provided information on what students liked and disliked about BHS, as well as information about how often they studied, whether or not they were employed and for how many hours a week, and where they went when they needed academic support. Many teachers reacted with surprise when they discovered that a majority of students indicated that the diversity of the student body was one of the things they liked best about their experience at BHS. There was a bit of irony in this finding because the vast majority of students also said that most of their friends were not from diverse backgrounds. Students also expressed considerable support for the "freedom" they enjoyed at BHS. For most, freedom was interpreted as the opportunity to set their own course schedule and the ease with which they were able to cut classes without being caught.

Discussion of the data generated from the student survey and course enrollment patterns opened the door to a more difficult discussion about the implications of the findings for students and the school as a whole. Confronted with evidence that course assignment in ninth grade would determine students' trajectory over the next 4 years, some teachers began to question the fairness of the course assignment process. Teachers learned that course assignments in math were made by counselors who based their decision on a review of student transcripts, without a formal assessment of student ability. They also learned that some of the support classes that had been set up for struggling students had higher failure rates than the classes they were designed to reinforce. Concerns about the lack of structure at BHS (e.g., the absence of a coherent tardy policy and the inconsistent application of penalties for cutting) led to a discussion about the permissive culture of the school. BHS was a place where the "freedom" granted to students effectively allowed large numbers of them to fail and slip through the cracks.

The presentations in the third and fourth rooms focused on how patterns of separation extend beyond the classroom and show up in those areas of the school where membership is based on voluntary association. Our data showed that nearly every club, sports team, and extracurricular activity offered by the school had a racially exclusive make-up. Even more disturbing was the fact that any activity that might be regarded as having the potential to enhance one's academic performance (e.g., academic clubs and the debating team) were comprised almost exclusively of White students.

In our discussions it became clear that because they had been in place for so long, such patterns of separation were rationalized as the product of choices made freely by the students. Some adults at the school condoned these practices as a way of accommodating the diverse cultures and interests present within the school, and they argued that these patterns of separation provided a form of cultural affirmation. However, others saw these voluntary forms of racial separation as a way of disguising the patterns that reinforced the racial disparities at the school. In its report, the Project cited several studies on extracurricular activities that show that students who are involved in sports, music, the arts, and other clubs, generally perform better in school than students who are uninvolved (Steinberg, 1996). Additionally, we used the survey data to show that students who were involved in extracurricular activities were more likely to feel connected to and to identify with the school. Studies have shown that the psychological effects of such a connection can positively influence academic performance (Steele, 1990).

Our discussions with teachers about the factors that produce racially distinct clubs and sports teams made it possible for the adults who had long come to accept these patterns as unavoidable and normal to consider actions that might be taken to alter them. In the discussions that ensued, teachers pondered whether with some encouragement Latino students, who frequently played soccer on their own time in unstructured pick-up games, could be recruited to the school's soccer team. The advisor for the school newspaper offered to initiate a concerted outreach plan to recruit minority student writers. Similar efforts were proposed to change the racial make-up of activities like football, basketball, and Afro-Haitian dance. Past experience had shown that relatively few students were willing to play the role of Jackie Robinson and cross the school's racial borders on their own. For this reason it was acknowledged that to diversify student participation in clubs and courses that historically had been perceived as racially exclusive, it might be necessary for adults to play an active role in recruiting students of color so that a critical mass in representation could be achieved.

After one year the Project seemed to have succeeded in shifting the focus of the conversation about student achievement away from a search for blame and toward a search for solutions. However, we fully realized that far more difficult work lay ahead as we moved forward in implementing change. We understood fully that those who benefited from the school as it was might not welcome efforts to change it. For this reason, pursuit of our second strategy was seen as essential.

EXPOSING THE ORGANIZATION AND STRUCTURE OF PRIVILEGE

As is true in society in general, racial inequality at BHS is accompanied by racial privilege. Just as certain institutional practices contribute to the concentration of African American and Latino students in lower-level classes, other policies and practices reward and privilege upper-middle-class White students. Of course, it must be kept in mind that the sorting of students into courses and placing them on different academic trajectories is not based on overtly racist behavior or harmful intentions on the part of counselors and administrators. Rather, these policies and practices appear on the surface to be benign and race neutral. Student placements presumably are based on "objective" measures of academic ability and not some form of racial preference. However, close analysis of the practices used to sort students and their impact on student learning opportunities suggests that the intentions of those making decisions are less relevant than how low-income students of color are affected by the decisions that are made.

Just as the persistent failure of large numbers of students of color is accepted as normal, so too is the academic success of many upper-middle-class White students. Both phenomena typically are explained on the basis of class rather than race. Given their highly educated parents and access to extensive private resources (e.g., private tutors and college advisors, therapists, computers, and travel opportunities), the outstanding academic performance of many White students is hardly surprising. Many White students at BHS leave elite private schools to enroll in BHS. In general, these students are better prepared and therefore are able to take full advantage of the many resources available at BHS. However, while it is clear that class privilege creates academic advantages, it is also clear that the school does not operate as a neutral and level playing field in the way it responds to the background differences of its students. In fact, there is considerable evidence that suggests that inequity actually is reinforced and exacerbated by the practices and biases of the school.

The prevailing expectation that White students will succeed and the disproportionate power wielded by their vigilant and ever-observant parents have prevented adults within the school from questioning practices that clearly reinforce the benefits these students enjoy. As we continued our research in the second year, members of Project Diversity felt that exposing these forms of privilege was important to create a more balanced discussion about the achievement gap at BHS. We felt that if the conversation about equity ignored the ways in which some students benefited from the organization of educational opportunities at the school, any effort to reform or alter these arrangements that required a reallocation of resources would be vigorously opposed. Our hope was that by showing how certain school practices favored high-achieving students, we might be able to point out the kinds of reforms that could bring about higher levels of achievement for others.

As we began our research, we soon realized that we faced a major challenge in attempting to expose the ways in which the structure of the school privileged high-achieving students. Whereas BHS had several activities that were designed to explicitly address the needs of minority students—separate graduation ceremonies, newspapers, clubs, and courses all designed specifically for Black or Latino students—there were no analogous activities for White students. This is not because there were no activities or courses that catered exclusively to White students; it simply reflected the fact that they were not labeled in that way. Advanced placement courses in English literature or calculus, sports such as lacrosse and golf, or clubs like Model United Nations are not set up to exclude students on the basis of race. But such activities have catered almost exclusively to White students for many years, and there has been little if any concern about their homogeneous make-up in this racially diverse school.

The survey and school record data generated by the Project showed these racial patterns quite clearly (see Table 4.1). In addition to these data collection activities, we sought to identify institutional practices that directly reward academically motivated students, or students whose parents are eager to ensure that their kids receive the best opportunities available at the school. It did not take long for us to identify examples of these practices because there are several of them at the school. They include the practice known as self-scheduling, which allows students to designate preference for a particular teacher when setting up their schedule for classes for the coming semester. The practice favors students who are prepared to make their selections early and who know which teachers are regarded as the best. As it turns out, most White students take advantage of self-scheduling, while most Black and Latino students do not. Students who do not choose classes on their own are placed in classes that still have space after self-scheduling is over. This means that those who fail to exercise choice are more likely to be placed in classes with teachers who for some reason are not held in high regard. Many White parents have the time and flexibility to come to the school during the day to guide their children through the course selection process. We also learned that there were e-mail lists used mainly by White, high-achieving parents to share information about teachers, courses, and other information relevant to the school. Minority parents are not excluded from these e-mail lists, but no outreach is done to ensure that they are included. Differences in the amount of time parents can spend at the school and in the quality of information they possess, reinforces existing differences in academic ability.

Another example is the practice of waiving the requirement that students in tenth grade take a course in social living. The social living course is designed to teach "life skills"—sex education, drug and alcohol abuse prevention—and generally is regarded as a valuable course. However, during our research we discovered that high-achieving White students systematically avoid the social living class. While they are not ideologically opposed to the subject matter covered, their parents regard the material as fluff and a waste of school time. The parents know that they are allowed to request waivers from the course for personal or religious reasons, and many choose to exercise this option. By avoiding the social living course, the students can enroll in more rigorous academic elective courses that provide them credit toward college (the social living course does not). It is not clear how the news about the right to waive the course spreads among

White parents and students, but the results are quite remarkable: A very small number of the students in this mandatory course are White.

The minimal graduation requirements at BHS provide another example of a practice that favors White students while limiting long-term opportunities for Black and Latino students. Despite its reputation as a school with high academic standards, BHS requires only 2 years of science and 2 years of math for its graduates. This is also the state's requirement for high school graduation, but several schools require more, since the University of California and the State University systems require at least 3 years of courses in both subjects. Most Black and Latino students meet the minimum requirement for graduation, while most White students at BHS exceed the state's requirement and graduate with 4 years of math and science. Their parents push them to take more than they are required to because the parents tend to have a greater understanding of the competitive college admissions process. They also know that advanced placement courses are weighted more heavily in college admissions decisions, and they make sure that their children take full advantage of these courses. The fact that fewer Black and Latino students exceed the minimal requirements in math and science courses allows those departments to offer a greater number of advanced courses to those students deemed qualified to enroll. There is no conspiracy to deny minority students access to higher-level courses, but without an explicit push to enroll them in these courses, they are at a disadvantage when they apply to college.

The relatively low graduation requirements of BHS also result in White students graduating with more units of credit on average than Black and Latino students. This occurs largely because students who are already turned off to school are less likely to take courses that are not required of them. It means that White students on average actually receive more minutes of instruction than most Black and Latino students. Parents who are familiar with the admissions requirements of elite universities understand the importance of enrolling their children in the broad array of elective courses available to students at BHS. Hence, courses such as Latin, computer science, and economics cater disproportionately to the most affluent and privileged students. By allowing students to choose whether or not to enroll in these courses, BHS rewards those who are most motivated and informed. Even minority students with high grades and demonstrated ability are less likely to enroll in these rigorous courses unless they are encouraged to do so by an adult. Without active recruitment from teachers and counselors, it is unlikely that patterns in course enrollment will change.

Finally, the most common form of racial preference involves the innumerable subtle ways in which differential treatment is accorded to White students in everyday interactions between adults and students within the school. Through focus group interviews, we learned that students of all kinds are very conscious of how differently they are treated by adults at the school. Black and Latino students walking in the halls are likely to evoke suspicion and even fear from the adults they encounter. In contrast, White students, even those who are cutting classes, are less likely to be stopped and questioned because it is assumed that they have a legitimate reason to move about. Even when students are caught cutting, differential sanctions often are applied for infractions of the school's discipline policies.[4] Black and Latino students frequently receive stiffer penalties than Whites for similar offenses, due in part to the greater ease with which White parents are able to serve as advocates for their children. When confronted with the possibility of punishment for the violation of a school rule, White parents frequently involve attorneys whose intervention often has the effect of intimidating school administrators.

Differential treatment is also present in the way teachers teach students who have been labeled as gifted and talented, versus the way they teach those considered ordinary or academically deficient. In part, this is because some teachers lack the skill or the rapport needed to teach low-achieving students effectively. However, expectations are also a factor because teaching low-achieving students often requires more work, at least in terms of classroom management, than teaching high-achieving students. It is not uncommon for teachers who are regarded as exceptional with high-achieving students to be perceived as boring and uninteresting by their low-achieving students.

Given the numerous examples of racial privilege within the organizational structure and culture of BHS, it was imperative for the Diversity Project to be strategic in the approach it took to address the issue. To avoid the fierce resistance of affluent White parents who we knew would oppose any effort to reduce the benefits their children enjoyed, members of the Project were extremely careful about the language they used when describing potential solutions to disparities in academic achievement. Rather than questioning the existence of advanced courses, we recommended that the school adopt strategies to increase the enrollment of African American and Latino students into these courses. The Project also suggested that the school increase its graduation requirements to 3 years of science and math courses. We also recommended that the school eliminate the awarding of "Ds" as passing grades, since a "D" signified that a student had not mastered the material covered in a course. Because we framed our recommendations as a call for higher academic standards for all students, it became very difficult for those who may have perceived these changes as contrary to their interests, to oppose them. We understood that in a liberal community like

Berkeley, it was not appropriate to defend low academic standards for minority students, or to openly express indifference to their plight.

EMPOWERING THE DISADVANTAGED AND MARGINALIZED

As might be expected, not only are African American students disadvantaged and marginal within the school community, but so are their parents. At most school activities that call for parental involvement and participation, African American and Latino parents are vastly underrepresented. This is also true on decision-making bodies where parents have a say in how resources are allocated, and it is most dramatically true on back-to-school nights when parents are invited to meet their children's teachers. Historically, the auditorium where several hundred parents gather prior to visiting the classrooms of their children's teachers is filled almost exclusively with White parents. Little more than a handful of Black and Latino parents can be seen sprinkled throughout the crowd. Their absence at these events generally has been interpreted as a lack of interest in their children's education.

The members of the Diversity Project decided that if we were going to be successful in our efforts to promote change within the school, we would have to take on this issue. We recognized that just as those who benefited in the present circumstances might attempt to defend the status quo, those who had been poorly served by the school might be most likely to support changes that led to greater equity. Moreover, since we had positioned ourselves as facilitators rather than as advocates for a particular reform agenda, we realized that something would have to be done to create a more balanced discussion about reform at the school. For this reason we consciously devised research strategies that, by increasing their ability to voice their concerns within the school, would enable African American and Latino parents to become empowered as actors and decision makers.

The parent outreach committee of the Project was created to facilitate change in who participated at the school. The committee decided to organize a series of focus group discussions for Latino and African American parents designed to elicit their views on the school. Specifically, we wanted to know what concerns they had about the education their children were receiving, what kinds of obstacles parents encountered when interacting with school officials on behalf of their children, and what kinds of changes they felt would help make BHS more receptive to their concerns.

Over the course of 6 months, more than 70 focus groups were conducted with over 400 parents. To ensure that maximum opportunity was provided for open communication, all of the sessions with Spanish-speaking parents were conducted in Spanish and held at a Catholic church in the community. Food and child care were provided as an added incentive to attract high levels of participation. Finally, the focus group sessions were tape recorded and transcribed so that a report summarizing the issues raised could be developed and presented to a strategic planning committee that was established in Spring 1998. The committee, which was comprised exclusively of teachers and administrators, was charged with developing a specific set of recommendations for changes at the school based on the findings from the Diversity Project's research.

The parent outreach committee of the Diversity Project also recruited parents to join in conducting the focus groups and carrying out the research. This was important because their participation in the research led this active core group of parents to take on leadership roles as the school moved forward in enacting reforms aimed at institutionalizing parental involvement at the school. Beginning in Fall 1999, the group succeeded in getting the BHS administration to designate a surplus office for use as a parent center. The center was created to provide parents with a place to go when they had concerns about how their children were being treated at the school. The center also provided training to teachers on how to conduct constructive meetings with parents. With grants from local foundations and the support of the BHS administration, the Diversity Project was able to hire two part-time parent organizers, one African American, the other Latino, to serve as staff for the new center.

In addition to creating the parent center, which was actually the first reform recommended by the Diversity Project to be implemented, the research contributed to other organizing efforts among Black and Latino parents that have had a significant impact on the school. Breaking the long-established pattern of nonparticipation, at a community forum in May 1998 that was held for the purpose of soliciting responses to the strategic plan, nearly half of the parents present were African American and Latino. Most were parents who had become active in the leadership of the parent outreach group. During the meeting several spoke openly and forcefully about their criticisms of the plan and freely offered suggestions on what they would like to see included in it. After the meeting several teachers commented that it was the first meeting that they had attended in which the composition of the parents matched that of the student body. In Fall 2000, a new organization called Parents of Children of African Descent (PCAD) was created. Drawing on the Project's research, which showed high rates of failure in ninth-grade math, PCAD called for and helped create a new course for students who failed math in the fall semester. Although PCAD's involvement was not welcomed by the school or the math department, the new course was very successful and the pattern of accepting the failure of large numbers of minority students was fundamentally challenged (Maran, 2001).

Another group comprising primarily Latino parents recently formed to advocate for the needs of Latino students, particularly those in the ESL program. Their efforts have focused on the large number of students who remain permanently confined to the ESL program and therefore are unable to gain access to advanced courses and other resources that are available to students at the school. With the parent center and groups like PCAD monitoring the school and its treatment of students of color, it is unlikely that complacency about disparities in student achievement will return. It is clear that pressure alone will not help BHS to improve. However, without active and ongoing effort to address all forms of racial inequality at the school, it is likely that complacency will return and that adults at the school once again will grow accustomed to the permanence of the achievement gap.

LIMITS AND POSSIBILITIES OF RESEARCH TO COUNTER INEQUALITY

The change process initiated by the Diversity Project has been slow and it is still not clear that our efforts will lead to increased minority student performance. Although some of the reforms that were introduced as a result of our work show promise, many of the factors that I regard as most important in influencing patterns of achievement (teacher expectations, tracking, and effective student support) have not been systematically addressed. For this reason, I readily admit that all of our work may have been for naught; there is no guarantee that patterns that have been in place for years will be permanently altered. However, the greatest asset of the Project has been our persistence. The fact that we committed ourselves to working on these issues for 4 years made it impossible for the school to lapse back into passively accepting the failure of large numbers of African American and Latino students. Even after my work with the Project ended when I left Berkeley and moved to the east coast, the work continued and the focus on creating greater equity at the school has been kept alive by teachers and parents who worked closely with the Project.

Unfortunately, the pace of change has been hindered by dysfunction within the organization of the school and by constant changes in leadership. From 1996 to 2002, four different principals led the school (during 2001–02 the school was led by two co-principals). Although change at the school is needed, each change in leadership has resulted in significant setbacks for reform initiatives. During the 1999–2000 academic year, 13 fires were reported at the school, one of which was so severe that the central administration building was destroyed (Maran, 2000). Amidst so much turmoil and upheaval, it has been very difficult to keep the school focused on efforts to address equity. However, these setbacks have not deterred a number of parents and teachers from pursuing reforms that they hope will lead to greater equity and higher achievement for all students.

Like many other schools, BHS has seen more than its share of research projects and reform initiatives. Too often, such efforts start with great fanfare but fade and lose momentum as the inertia of tradition and prevailing norms reclaim advantage. To counter this tendency, the Project transferred leadership of the work over to teachers, parents, and administrators who have a long-term investment in the school. This has ensured that the work continued long after the university researchers left. BHS also has received support from the Bay Area Coalition for Equitable Schools, a community-based school reform organization, which has helped to sustain these efforts. Time will tell if the vigilance of these groups will result in lasting change.

CHAPTER 5

Segregation, Poverty, and Limits of Local Control: Oakland as a Case Study

With the adoption of the Public School Accountability Act (PSAA) in 1999, schools in the four Bay Area school districts, like public schools elsewhere in California, came under increased pressure. All four districts had struggled in the past with efforts to raise student achievement, but with the passage of PSAA the districts were faced with the ominous prospect of having some of their lowest-performing schools taken over by the state if progress in achievement could not be demonstrated. Additionally, PSAA called for the state to publicly release the results of test scores for each school and district on the mandated assessments and to end the practice commonly referred to as social promotion. The goal, according to Governor Gray Davis, was to set higher expectations for all of the key constituencies associated with education. He explained his goals in his first State of the State speech after being elected governor.

> Accountability must not be just a buzzword. It must have real meaning in the real world. Our children deserve no less. . . . No one gets a free ride. Students will be tested. Teachers will be reviewed. Principals will be held to account. And parents will be urged to take greater responsibility. (Johnson, 1997)

For district leaders in San Francisco, Oakland, Richmond, and Berkeley, the governor's new emphasis on accountability represented a significant challenge. With several failing schools and students, the release of data related to academic performance was likely to mean intense local scrutiny and criticism of the districts. Low student achievement had been a problem for years, but for the first time the districts were faced with the prospect that the state would intervene to take over schools that were not improving. PSAA also called for schools to be ranked on the basis of aggregate test scores and for the rankings to be published in local newspapers. The release of such reports would increase significantly the pressure on district leaders in that it would serve as a blunt reminder to the communities served that large numbers of children were not being well educated in their schools.

As it turned out, concerns about the impact of PSAA were warranted. Each year since the state began releasing the academic performance index (API) rankings, a consistent pattern has emerged: Poor academic performance is most common in school districts serving low-income populations, particularly in racially isolated urban and rural areas where poverty is concentrated (Ed Data, 2002). Several of the schools in Oakland, San Francisco, and Richmond received the lowest possible ratings, but even in Berkeley, which had some highly ranked schools, there were striking and disturbing disparities in achievement when the scores were disaggregated by the race and class backgrounds of students.

The State of California claimed that PSAA would enable the public to hold local school districts accountable for the academic performance of students. However, the policy was not accompanied by measures that would ensure that schools could meet the conditions necessary to provide adequate educational opportunities for all students. In high-poverty neighborhoods this meant that it would be up to the community to find ways to improve schools on its own. Numerous studies have shown that poverty and racial isolation contribute significantly to school failure (Coleman et al., 1966; Jencks, 1972), but the state does very little to mitigate the effects of these external conditions. Instead, responsibility for monitoring educational quality is delegated to superintendents and elected school boards in keeping with the long-standing practice of allowing local communities to manage and operate public schools (Blasi, 2001).

There is a vast body of research and evidence that shows that this approach does not work. In most cases, poor communities lack the resources necessary to monitor the quality of education provided to students. Concentrated poverty and racial segregation limit the ability of parents to exert control over the schools that serve their children, and educational leaders in such communities often lack the resources to take on the task themselves. For a variety of reasons that have been discussed in earlier chapters, conditions external to schools, such as poverty, crime, housing affordability, and health care access, exert considerable influence over conditions within schools (Coleman et al., 1966; Noguera, 1996). Unless the state or federal government intervenes decisively to support schools in low-income communities, it is unlikely that such schools will ever improve.

To analyze the limitations of local control and to show why it is not an effective way to hold schools accountable, this chapter will draw on research and work that I have carried out in schools and community organizations in Oakland, California, over a 20-year period. I use Oakland because I believe a careful examination of the case shows clearly how poverty and racial isolation have contributed to the problems that have plagued schools in the district. Again, I make use of the concept of social capital in developing this analysis because it serves as a useful means to show how social relationships and networks are related to the quality of civic life (Sampson, 1998; Wacquant, 1998). Through an analysis of the factors that have hindered the development of social capital in low-income communities in Oakland, I will describe why local control is inadequate as a mechanism for holding schools accountable in high-poverty areas. Drawing on focus group interviews conducted with Oakland students, I also will show how students have been affected by attending failing schools. Finally, I will make the case for developing social capital and civic capacity: two strategies that can be used to transform inner-city schools into genuine assets for the communities they serve.

RACE, CLASS, AND SCHOOL ACCOUNTABILITY

Although there is considerable variation among local school districts in the United States with respect to the demographic composition of the students and communities they serve, the policies used to regulate U.S. public schools are amazingly consistent. This is the case with respect to the application of federal statutes (e.g., special and compensatory education) that are used to regulate the provision of educational services to specially designated populations. It is also the case with respect to the strategies employed by states to hold school districts accountable. In the past 5 years most state governments have implemented academic standards and assessments to monitor student achievement (Elmore, 1996). With few exceptions, there is also a high level of consistency in the policies that provide the legal parameters for school governance through a practice commonly referred to as "local control."

Throughout the United States, communities of all kinds elect individuals to school boards who have primary responsibility for managing the affairs of public schools. Local control is a unique form of governance that is a product of the decentralized and largely unplanned historical process that gave birth to public education in the United States (Katznelson & Weir, 1985). Unlike most other nations that have centrally planned and managed educational systems, the United States has a highly decentralized system in which primary responsibility for the affairs of schools is delegated to local school boards. Local control continues to be widely practiced even during periods of intense criticism over the quality of public education, largely because it is perceived as inherently more democratic than a centralized federal or state-managed system (Linn, 2000).

Local governance of public schools ostensibly serves as a means to ensure that schools are responsive and accountable to the communities they serve. Locally elected school board members are typically responsible for overseeing matters pertaining to financial management and personnel (e.g., collective bargaining agreements), while the education professionals they hire have primary responsibility for managing the provision of educational services. The system is designed so that those with a vested interest in the affairs of public schools—parents and the local community—are well positioned to monitor conditions in their schools.

Yet, inequities among school districts and the communities they serve are rampant and extreme, and local control does not make it easier for schools to address the academic needs of poor students. Academic performance outcomes generally reflect broader patterns of inequality that are evident elsewhere in U.S. society (Kozol, 1991; Noguera & Akom, 2000). Local control and financing of public education exacerbate educational inequality because there is wide variation in the ability of communities to generate revenue and support for schools at the local level (Cibulka, 2001). As a result of local control, affluent communities with a higher tax base generally are able to provide more funding for schools than are poor communities. Even in states such as California, where as a result of *Serano* v. *Priest*[1] the formula used to finance schools is more equitable, there is wide variation in the ability of communities to generate supplemental resources.

Differences in per pupil spending often mirror differences in the abilities of school districts to generate and sustain civic engagement in various activities and affairs related to the management and operation of public schools. While affluent communities generally have little difficulty eliciting community participation in school board elections, site decision-making councils, and other avenues for civic involvement, low-income communities often encounter obstacles in enlisting and sustaining the involvement of parents and a diverse cross-section of community members in such activities (Epstein, 1993).

Low levels of parental and community participation in public schools frequently are interpreted as an indication of disinterest in education. Yet, these patterns follow trends that are common to other forms of civic engagement (e.g., voting, participation within political parties and community organizations) in low-income communities (Putnam, 1995). The reasons that have been suggested for lower involvement vary, ranging from lack of time and information (Gold, 2001), to feelings of powerlessness and a low sense of individual and collective efficacy (Lareau, 1989). Whatever the explanation, it is clear that in urban areas like Oakland, where poverty is concentrated and poor people are socially isolated, the parents of the children who experience the greatest difficulty in school also tend to be the least involved.

POVERTY, RACIAL ISOLATION, AND OAKLAND'S FAILING SCHOOLS

As is true for most other school districts in the United States that cater to poor children and their families, on most measures of academic performance the Oakland Unified School District demonstrates little evidence of success in educating its students. For example, data from the California Department of Education show that 43 of Oakland's 56 elementary schools received a ranking of 5 or less on the API.[2] This means that according to the state's performance measure, two-thirds of Oakland's elementary schools are considered "low performing." Under the 1999 Public School Accountability Act, low-performing schools are to be subject to various sanctions and possible state takeover if they show no improvement over 3 years.

The challenge confronting the district as a result of the new policy is daunting. More than half of Oakland's elementary schools received an API rating of 1 or 2 (the lowest possible score) from the state. Prospects for change appear even more remote among secondary schools. All but one of the 16 middle schools and all seven of the district's high schools received API ratings below 5. The API ratings for Oakland's schools are consistent with a broader set of academic indicators such as the drop-out rate (25.2%), the suspension and expulsion rate, student grade point averages, and college eligibility rates (19.6%). All of these indicators serve to reinforce the widespread impression that Oakland public schools are failing and that enrollment in them should be avoided by those who can.

Yet, despite the public embarrassment engendered by the publication of the school rankings, the threat of state takeover actually may do little to prod the district to improve. With hundreds of failing schools and districts across California, the ability of the state to intervene is likely to be limited. Moreover, the state's own track record in managing failing districts suggests that it may be no better than local school districts at improving failing schools.[3]

Oakland has received more than its share of ridicule and blame for the failure of its schools. In 1996 national attention was focused on the district as a result of the controversy created by the district's adoption of a policy that called for Ebonics (also known as Black vernacular English) to be treated as a legitimate second language. As news and confusion spread about the school board's new language policy, Oakland immediately was subjected to ridicule and scorn for promoting what critics referred to in the media as "bad English" and "slang" (Perry & Delpit, 1997). Within a few weeks of the board's resolution, the California legislature and the U.S. Congress moved quickly to prohibit the use of state or federal funds to support implementation of the policy. The district even came under attack from several prominent African American leaders who charged the district with damaging the education of Black children through its poorly conceived policy.

RESPONDING TO THE NONACADEMIC NEEDS OF STUDENTS AND THE "CAPTURED MARKET" PROBLEM

Interestingly, even as Oakland's schools were castigated over the Ebonics resolution, few of those who engaged in the attack offered any recommendations for actions the district might take to solve the problem it was attempting to address. The widely misunderstood policy had been adopted by the school board in response to a recommendation from a task force on African American student achievement. The task force had been formed for the purpose of devising a strategy to address widespread academic failure among African American students (the grade point average for Black students in Oakland in 1996 was 1.8). While it might be fair to question the district's emphasis on Ebonics as a strategy for raising student achievement, the absence of alternative suggestions served as the strongest indication that the critics had no idea themselves of what should be done to respond the problem.

Yet, as disturbing as the outlook for schools in Oakland might appear, a closer look at the characteristics of the students it serves reveals that the situation is more complex than it seems. According to the state's data, nearly two-thirds of students in the district qualify for free or reduced-price lunch based on household income (Education Data Partnership, 2001), and over 40% of students come from families served by the CalWORKS program (formerly Aid to Families with Dependent Children). The concentration of poverty is even more intense when one considers that all of the schools that received an API rating of 1 or 2, and have been designated "low performing," serve student populations where over 90% of the children qualify for free or reduced lunch. Additionally, more than a third of the district's students are from families that recently immigrated to the United States and whose first language is not English (Education Data Partnership, 2001).

The school district is also responsible for providing adequate educational opportunities for these students, who speak over 70 different languages.

Oakland students also come to school with a wide array of unmet social, material, and emotional needs that affect their ability to learn. For example, because their families are often uninsured, many poor children lack access to adequate health and dental care (Perkins & Chen, 1998). This means that they are less likely to receive preventative treatment and more likely to rely on hospital emergency rooms when they become ill. As is true for poor children elsewhere in the United States, Oakland students are more likely to suffer from asthma and tooth decay and less likely to receive eye glasses when they need them (Perkins & Chen, 1998). As a result of poverty and the high cost of housing in the Bay Area, many Oakland students experience a high level of transience and are forced to change schools frequently when their families move into new housing. Finally, although data on these issues are less reliable, anecdotal evidence from teachers suggests that large numbers of Oakland's students come to school hungry, without adequate clothing, and suffering from stress as a result of domestic conflict in their families (Noguera, 1996).

At Lowell Middle School in west Oakland where I conducted research in the early 1990s, over 40% of the students suffered from some form of chronic respiratory condition, and two-thirds of all students lived in a household with someone other than a biological parent (Noguera, 1996). District officials applied considerable pressure on the school's leadership to raise test scores (which were among the lowest for middle schools in the district), but they did little to address the health and welfare needs of students at Lowell, even though they were well aware of the obstacles these created. District administrators adopt a narrow focus on raising student achievement, not because they do not understand that a broad array of social and economic factors influence academic outcomes, but because they lack the resources to address the external conditions that have an impact on student learning.

District administrators are not the only ones who ignore the health and welfare needs of poor children as they press schools that serve them to improve. State and federal policy makers collect data on some of the needs of poor children, but do little to ensure that districts like Oakland receive additional resources to address these needs. Instead, even though more affluent children in neighboring school districts such as Piedmont, Moraga, and Orinda arrive at school better prepared academically and generally have fewer unmet needs, significantly more money is spent on their education than is spent on children in Oakland (Ed Data, 2002). Even as the state moves forward with its effort to hold all schools accountable for the academic performance of students, it continues to ignore the fact that poor and affluent students have vastly different needs and generally are educated under very different conditions. Moreover, the state's accountability policies, like the idea of local control, ignore the fact that low-income communities such as those served by public schools in Oakland lack the resources to hold schools accountable for the service they provide to students.

Despite the severity of the problems facing children in school districts like Oakland, such matters generally have not resulted in state or national intervention. Rather, under the pretense of local control Oakland's educational problems are treated as local matters to be addressed by locally elected officials and the community itself. Although the state and federal governments allocate a variety of supplemental funds to serve the special needs of particular populations of students (e.g., special education, bilingual education, and compensatory education), authority for managing the affairs of schools in Oakland is delegated to the locally elected school board. With seven elected and three appointed members, the board of education has responsibility for managing a district comprising 55,000 students, with an annual operating budget of approximately $370 million. Although the per pupil expenditure in Oakland is greater than the state average ($6,334 vs. $7,120 in Oakland), the funds available are largely insufficient to meet the health and welfare needs of Oakland's impoverished students.

Yet, lack of financial resources is only one of the reasons why so many of the needs of Oakland's children are unaddressed. Despite the severity of the education and welfare challenges facing Oakland's schools, matters related to financial management often have taken precedence over these issues. The Oakland Unified School District is the largest employer in the city. Given the high levels of poverty and unemployment, economic considerations, such as the letting of contracts for construction, maintenance, and educational consulting, and collective bargaining issues generally, often take on greater importance and receive more attention than educational issues. Conflicts over how to allocate the resources controlled by the school district is of such great importance to the economy of the city that providing quality education to all students often has not been treated as a priority.

Finally, there is another important reason why educational issues often have been neglected in Oakland, and in many other school districts located in impoverished communities throughout the United States. Public schools in Oakland serve a captured market. The student population is largely poor, immigrant, and non-White, and completely dependent on the school system. Private schools are not accessible to most poor families due to cost, and leaving the system typically is not possible even if one is dissatisfied with the quality of school services provided. With a majority of the students served by Oakland's schools trapped by economic circumstances, dependent, and unable to leave, affairs of the district can be managed with little concern for whether or not those served are satisfied with the quality of education provided. With the exception of the superintendent and principals, who are removed easily and frequently, employees in the district can be confident that their positions are secure, even though the system they work for largely fails to fulfill the mission for which it was created. In common with other school districts in California, state funding to Oakland's public schools is determined by the average daily attendance of its students. As long as parents continue to enroll their children in the district's failing schools, the miserable status quo can be sustained indefinitely.

ROLE OF SOCIAL CAPITAL IN IMPROVING SCHOOL QUALITY

Several researchers have suggested that the quality of education children receive is directly related to the ability of parents to generate social capital (Coleman, 1988; Lareau, 1989; Noguera, 2001a). Social capital is a concept that has been used by social scientists to describe benefits individuals derive from their association with and participation in social networks and organizations (Putnam, 1995; Sampson, 1998; Woolcock, 1998). Like economic capital, social capital can provide concrete benefits to those who have access to it, such as jobs, loans, educational opportunities, and a variety of services. The more connected one is to groups or individuals that have access to resources, the greater the possibility that one can obtain concrete material and social benefits.

However, becoming connected to influential social networks is not easy. Access to some networks may be based on family ties, income, religious affiliations, or association with powerful groups that has been cultivated over time. It generally is not possible to simply join an exclusive social network. In addition to having less economic capital, the poor often have less social capital than the affluent because their connections tend to be limited to other poor people or to organizations with fewer resources (Saegert, Thompson, & Warren, 2001).

In cities such as Oakland, poverty and racial isolation constitute significant barriers to acquiring social capital, particularly "bridging" and "bonding" forms of social capital that have been identified as most important for community development (Woolcock, 1998). Bridging social capital refers to the connections that link poor people to institutions and individuals that have access to money and power. In Oakland, poor people of color generally lack bridging social capital because they often are excluded from influential social networks as a result of race and class barriers, and social isolation. For example, although Oakland has several powerful and influential Black churches, their membership is more likely to be drawn from middle-class residents who reside in more affluent neighborhoods and the suburbs than from the lower-class communities in which the churches are located (Commission for Positive Change, 1990). The same is true of many African American political clubs in Oakland, such as the NAACP, the Niagra Democratic Club, and the East Oakland Democratic Club. Influential churches and civic associations play important roles in the political life of the city and often provide important services to the poor. But most poor people in Oakland do not participate in these organizations, and their absence further exacerbates their marginalization and social isolation.

Bonding social capital that provides connections among and between poor people (Woolcock, 1998), and that serves as a basis for solidarity and collective action, is also in short supply in Oakland. Over the past 15 years, Oakland has attracted large numbers of Mexican and Asian immigrants who have moved into neighborhoods in east and west Oakland that traditionally were African American (Clark, 1998). This demographic shift has had the effect of diminishing community cohesion as language and cultural differences have contributed to fragmentation and distrust between new and older residents (League of Cities, 2002). Aside from the fact that they reside on the same streets and even in the same apartment buildings, the people in these rapidly changing communities are strangers who perceive themselves as having little if anything in common and do not work together in pursuit of common community interests. Instead, growing diversity has increased the level of competition over community resources, which in turn has heightened tensions and fueled intergroup conflict. Tensions and occasionally violent outbursts related to demographic change have been manifest most frequently in Oakland's public schools, one of the few sites where different groups come into direct contact with each other (Noguera & Bliss, 2001).

Finally, poor people in Oakland tend to be concentrated in neighborhoods that lack strong social institutions, public services, and businesses. The census tracts where poor people reside in greatest numbers also have the highest rates of crime and therefore are regarded as less desirable places to live by the middle class (City of Oakland, 1994). In east and west Oakland, the poorest sections of the city, there are few banks, pharmacies, or grocery stores. Libraries, parks, and recreational centers are present in these neighborhoods, but residents frequently complain that drug trafficking and crime have rendered these potential community assets unusable (Office of Economic Development, 1994). Sociologist Loic Wacquant (1998) has argued that public institutions in inner-city neighborhoods actually may generate negative social capital (i.e., undermine social cohesion) because their unresponsiveness to the needs of residents undermines and erodes the social well-being of the community. Furthermore, in addition to possessing few social assets, the poorer neighborhoods of east and west Oakland have a disproportionate number of vacant, abandoned, and derelict sites. Undesirable land use facilities such as solid waste transfer stations, drug treatment centers, and industrial plants that emit toxic pollutants (Office of Economic Development, 1994) are also plentiful in these areas.

Throughout the United States, close examination of residential patterns reveals a high level of racial segregation and class isolation (Clark, 1998; Massey & Denton, 1993). This is also the case in Oakland where since the 1960s race and class boundaries have tended to correspond to fairly distinct geographic patterns and census tracts (U.S. Census Bureau, 2000). Reflecting a pattern common to cities throughout the United States, Oakland's flatland neighborhoods disproportionately comprise lower-class racial minorities, while White middle-class and affluent residents of a variety of backgrounds reside in the hills and outer-ring suburbs. Following a trend evident in other parts of the United States, formerly White suburbs to the south and east of Oakland are now more racially diverse, but data from the 2000 Census suggest that race and class segregation remains firmly intact there as well (U.S. Census Bureau, 2000). Unlike in the pre-civil rights period, when racial boundaries were enforced by legally sanctioned segregation, restrictive covenants, and occasionally violence, in the post-civil rights era property values and social networks play a similar role (Massey & Denton, 1993).

SOCIAL CAPITAL AND INSTITUTIONAL RESPONSIVENESS

The prevalence of race and class isolation often has direct bearing on the quality of schools children attend. In Oakland, children tend to enroll in schools located in neighborhoods where they live. As a result of this practice, the poorest children generally enroll in the lowest-performing schools, while middle-class children from more affluent neighborhoods attend better schools. As Table 5.1 reveals, differences between schools in different neighborhoods are striking. Although the district does not prevent low-income parents from enrolling their children in higher-performing schools, lack of transportation and limited space make this an option that few can exercise.

The relationship between poverty and school quality requires further elaboration. Research shows that poor children generally are less well pre-

Table 5.1. Selection of Oakland Schools by Neighborhood and Academic Performance Index Rating

Poor			Affluent		
School	*Neighborhood*	*API Rating*	*School*	*Neighborhood*	*API Rating*
Golden Gate	West Oakland	1	Chabot	Claremont	9
ML King	West Oakland	2	Hillcrest	Montclair	10
Sobrante Park	East Oakland	1	Joaquin Miller	Hills	10
Brookfield	East Oakland	1			

Source: Ed Data, 2002.

pared than middle-class children with respect to their academic skills at the time they enroll in school (Jencks & Phillips, 1998). Rather than adopting measures that might reduce the effects of differences in prior academic preparation, schools often exacerbate pre-existing differences in ability by providing poor children with an inferior education.

In this respect, Oakland is no exception. The schools where a majority of poor children are enrolled not only have lower test scores, but also tend to have inferior facilities and generally are more disorganized. They also have fewer certified teachers and higher turnover among principals (*District Profile*, 2001). Some of the schools, such as Lowell Middle and McClymonds High School in west Oakland, tend to have lower enrollment because they have difficulty attracting students, while several of the schools in the San Antonio and Fruitvale sections of east Oakland are overcrowded and literally bursting at the seams.

Despite the consistency of this pattern, there is no evidence that the condition of schools in low-income neighborhoods in Oakland is a product of intentional policy or a conspiracy aimed at depriving poor children of a quality education. At least part of the problem lies with the lack of social capital in Oakland's low-income communities, and the disproportionate social capital possessed by others. The leadership of Oakland's public schools is more likely to be pressured with demands from its unions and the small but influential number of middle-class parents it serves than by advocates and parents of poor children. The first two constituencies are well organized, politically savvy, and have access to financial and legal resources. Occasionally, poor parents also organize themselves to apply pressure on the school district, but their efforts are rarely sustained. Even when they are, the demands of poor parents can be ignored more easily because such parents typically lack the ability to exert leverage on school officials.

Yet, differences in political influence explain only part of the reason why the needs of poor children receive less attention. Research on social capital in schools shows that poor children of color and their parents also tend to be treated differently in schools (Lareau, 1989; Noguera, 2001a). While middle-class parents often have access to resources (e.g., education, time, transportation, etc.) and networks (contacts with elected officials, Parent Teacher Associations, and, if necessary, attorneys) that enable them to exert influence over schools that serve their children, poor parents typically have no such resources (Epstein, 1993; Noguera, 2001a). Even if they lack these sources of support, middle-class parents possess the ultimate tool for exercising leverage on schools: They generally can withdraw their children if they are not satisfied with the schools. Poor parents typically lack this option, and for this reason the degree of their satisfaction with the schools their children attend has little bearing on the quality of education that is provided.

For all of these reasons, poor parents are less able to hold the schools their children attend accountable for the quality of education they provide. They have less time to attend meetings related to school governance, fewer personal resources to contribute to schools financially, and fewer options to exercise if they are dissatisfied with the treatment they or their children receive. As a "captured market" they are a group of consumers who are compelled to accept the quality of educational services provided to them, whether they like it or not.

A DREAM DEFERRED: RACIAL POLITICS AND THE UNFULFILLED PROMISE OF BLACK POWER

With academic failure so persistent and widespread, one might wonder why a community with a reputation and history for political activism would not have acted long ago to radically reform its schools. Oakland was the birthplace of the Black Panther Party, an organization that took on another public institution that was perceived as failing to serve community needs, namely, the police department, which it accused of engaging in rampant harassment and brutality. Oakland's history of Black leadership and political activism goes back to the 1920s when Oakland had one of the most active chapters on the west coast of the Universal Negro Improvement Association—the largest Black political organization in U.S. history—headed by Marcus Garvey. In the 1930s it served as the national headquarters of the powerful Sleeping Car Porters Union (Franklin & Moss,

1988). In the 1970s Oakland voters transformed the city from a company town dominated by Kaiser Aluminum and controlled by White Republicans, into a city where all of the major public officials (mayor, city manager, superintendent of schools, police chief, state assemblyman and congressman) were African American (Bush, 1984).

However, political activism and racial succession in politics have not made it possible for those served by the Oakland public schools to exert influence and control over them. Unlike unions and political organizations, which typically have been comprised of individuals from middle- and stable working-class backgrounds, since the advent of school desegregation public schools in Oakland have catered primarily to children from lower-class families. Poor people in Oakland have not had the power or resources to effectively exercise influence over their public schools. Middle-class residents have been less likely to take on this challenge because their children are less likely to be enrolled in failing schools with poor children or in the district at all. Poor parents and community activists have organized at various times to call for reform and improvement in the city's schools, but for the most part such efforts have not resulted in significant or sustained improvements. Moreover, the fact that Black middle-class administrators have held important positions throughout the district for over 30 years has done little to bring about greater accountability and responsiveness to the needs and aspirations of those who rely on the public schools.

For the past 10 years there have been renewed attempts to mobilize grassroots pressure for school improvement. The Oakland Citizens Organizations (OCO), a broad multiracial, faith-based coalition, has mounted considerable pressure on the district for meaningful improvement and reform. At large public gatherings it has organized, OCO has pressured public officials to pledge their support for changes in the operation and management of the schools. Yet, while their efforts have led to the adoption of significant policy changes, such as site-based decision making and an initiative to create several new, smaller schools (Thompson, 2001), general academic improvement remains unattained.

The election of Jerry Brown as Mayor of Oakland in 1999 also has brought increased pressure and attention on the schools. Brown raised the need to reform Oakland's public schools prominently in his mayoral campaign and pledged to use his office to bring about a complete overhaul of the school district. Brown's efforts to improve Oakland's schools have consisted primarily of attempts to obtain greater control over the leadership of the district. He has attempted to do this by pressuring the school board to appoint his ally, George Musgrove, as interim superintendent. He was also successful in getting voters to amend the city charter so that he could appoint three members to the board. However, after a year in office,

Musgrove was not selected by the board to serve as permanent superintendent. By all accounts, the Mayor's relationship with the new superintendent, Dennis Chaconas, has not been good, and thus far the only concrete change that can be attributed to the Mayor's influence is the opening of a new military academy charter school (Brown, 2001).

Part of the problem with the approach that has been taken by OCO, Mayor Jerry Brown, and the State of California, is that more than just pressure is needed for Oakland's schools to improve. While a great deal needs to be done to increase the administrative efficiency of the district and to generally improve the quality of teaching, the simple fact is that the schools cannot serve the needs of Oakland's poorest children without greater support. Other public agencies must provide additional resources and services to address the health, welfare, and safety needs of students so that the schools can concentrate their attention on serving their educational needs.

Dennis Chaconas has made concerted efforts over the past 2 years to address the problems plaguing the school district. He has shaken up the central administration by replacing several long-term managers with younger professionals recruited from outside the district. He also has applied greater pressure on the principals of low-performing schools and removed several principals from schools where there was little evidence of progress in raising achievement. It is undoubtedly too early to know whether the superintendent's efforts will produce meaningful improvements in Oakland's schools. However, past experience suggests that placing greater demands on the district administration, the school board, or the schools themselves is unlikely to lead to change. Unless increased pressure is accompanied by systemic changes in the way schools respond to the needs of students and parents, and genuine assistance is provided to the schools serving the neediest children, it is unlikely that lasting, significant change will be made.

CHANGING SCHOOLS FROM THE OUTSIDE-IN: POTENTIAL ROLE OF SOCIAL CAPITAL AND CIVIC CAPACITY

Given the failure of past reform efforts in Oakland and in other large urban school districts, there is a growing consensus that alternative strategies to improve the quality of public education must be considered. Although by no means popular among policy makers and reform advocates, strategies that attempt to develop the social capital of parents and to cultivate the civic capacity of communities may be the most important steps that can be taken to further educational reform in cities like Oakland. If carried out in a coordinated manner, the two strategies could bring about several significant changes in the way public schools in Oakland have functioned and produce lasting changes in school systems.

Developing Social Capital

There are several reasons for one to be optimistic about the potential of such an approach. First, developing the social capital of parents may be the only way to address the captured market problem. It is generally true that any organization that is able to function as a monopoly over a segment of a market, can afford to operate without regard for the quality of service it provides to its clientele (Gormley, 1991). It is often difficult to improve such organizations because there is no incentive for good service or penalty for poor service. This is true whether the organization in question is a public hospital, an airline, or a police department. If the quality of service provided has no bearing on the ability of an organization to continue to operate, and if those who receive the service have no way to effectively register their concerns, self-initiated change is less likely.

Unlike many defenders of public education, proponents of vouchers and various other school choice schemes have understood the importance of addressing the captured market problem. Voucher advocates have argued that the solution to the problem lies in allowing parents to change schools by "voting with their feet"—to leave a school when they are not satisfied with the quality of education offered to their children. They argue that such a strategy will force bad schools to close when they lose students, and that competition is the best way to promote reform (Chubb & Moe, 1990; Gormley, 1991). Not surprisingly, polling data show high levels of support for vouchers among low-income, minority voters in urban areas where the worst schools tend to be located (Wilgoren, 1997).

Despite the understandable appeal, voucher advocates generally ignore the fact that schools rather than parents retain the ultimate choice over who will be admitted to a school, and the supply of good schools is limited. Vouchers will not provide parents with access to selective private schools both because of the prohibitive cost of tuition and because the selectivity of such schools is designed to favor an elite and privileged population of students. Moreover, the few high-performing public schools in Oakland have limited space and enrollment, and cannot easily accommodate increased demand for access. Finally, research on voucher programs shows no clear evidence that private schools are better than public schools at educating low-income students (Rouce, 1999). There is even less evidence that private and parochial schools are clamoring for an opportunity to educate poor children if and when they flee from failing public schools.

Efforts aimed at developing the social capital of parents can address the captured market problem when combined with policies that empower parents and make schools accountable to those they serve. In Chicago, this has been done through the development of elected local site councils (LCS) that are comprised of parents and community representatives (G. A. Hess, 1999). The LCS has responsibility for hiring and monitoring the performance of the school principal, reviewing and approving the school's budget, and receiving reports on academic plans. Under such an arrangement, how parents feel about the education their children receive is more likely to be taken into consideration because parents are empowered as decision makers at school sites (Fine, 1993).

To be effective, such a strategy also must be combined with ongoing efforts to organize parents and keep them informed about their rights and responsibilities so that the LCS does not come under the control of a small number of well-organized people or become manipulated by a savvy administrator. For this to happen, efforts to develop the social capital of parents must be accompanied by technical assistance, translation services, child care, and active support from community-based organizations. Churches and community groups that possess strong ties with poor communities, especially those with recent immigrants, are often well positioned to provide training and to facilitate contact and communication between parents and schools.

Many new charter schools have been designed with these goals in mind. At several new charter schools parents are asked to serve on the site council or expected to provide services to their school voluntarily (Clinchy, 2000). In some of these schools, such an approach creates conditions for a genuine partnership between parents and educators. Unlike many public schools that do not actively encourage parents to be involved in the education of their children, many new charters require active participation and have a clearly enunciated approach for promoting parents' rights and responsibilities.

Strategies such as these represent significant investments in the social capital of parents because they fundamentally change the relationship between parents and schools. Unlike traditional schools where parents most often interact with school personnel as individuals, the approach used in Chicago and several charter schools provides a basis for collective empowerment. Acting on their common interest in quality education, organized parents are better positioned to demand good service from schools and to hold them accountable when expectations are not met.

Developing Civic Capacity

Like social capital, civic capacity building also occurs outside of schools but can have a direct impact on what happens within them. Civic capacity building requires organizations and institutions that may not have any direct relationship to education to play an active role in supporting schools in their efforts to provide services to students (Stone, 2001). It compels the leaders of public and private organizations to think creatively about how to bring the resources they control to bear on the goal of educating students. Most important, civic capacity building forces the members of a community to cease blaming schools for their failures and to focus instead on how to help them improve.

In a city like Oakland, civic capacity building could involve at least four different kinds of activities. First, it could entail the use of community volunteers in roles as tutors and mentors for students. Several school districts have been very successful at getting public and private organizations to provide release time to their employees so that they can provide services in schools. In San Francisco, a private nonprofit corporation coordinates the recruiting and training of volunteers who provide a variety of services in schools. Several other school districts have taken advantage of the Americorp Program to get university students to provide college counseling, tutoring, and other services to students. Strategies such as these enable schools to reduce the adult–to–student ratio and make it possible to address the needs of students who have fallen behind academically.

Second, civic capacity can involve the formation of school–community partnerships to provide work-related internships and to support the development of career academies. Research on high schools has shown that career academies are possibly the most successful means for increasing student engagement in school (Conchas, 2001). Several Oakland high schools already have career academies, some of which perform quite well; however, involvement by community-based organizations and businesses has been minimal. To obtain the maximum benefit from these partnerships, on-site learning opportunities through internships need to be created so that the partnerships can produce genuine career opportunities for students. The biotech academy established by the Bayer Corporation at Berkeley High School and now in place at five other high schools in the Bay Area is a model of what can be accomplished. Students in the program receive advanced training in science and math, and through the participation of local community colleges and California State University at Hayward, students have the opportunity to pursue related studies in biotechnology so that they do not get stuck in entry-level jobs. When done successfully, school–community partnerships can provide students with meaningful learning opportunities outside of school, enhance the relevance of what they learn in school, and in the process transform education from an activity that is strictly school-based to one that is embraced by the entire community.

Third, school–community partnerships that lead to enhanced civic capacity also can focus on the provision of professional development services to school personnel. Given the high turnover among teachers and administrators in a district like Oakland, there is an ongoing need for professional development and training. Partnerships with local universities may be the most effective way to provide support to teachers in pedagogy and curriculum content. However, public and private organizations also can play a role in supporting administrators, particularly school principals, who increasingly are required to take responsibility for a broad array of activities beyond traditional school management. Given the work demands that school personnel must contend with, most professional development activities need to be site-based. It is also important for those who provide the training and support to have a genuine knowledge of the work performed by educators.

Finally and most important, the area where civic capacity development is needed most urgently is in the provision of health and welfare services to students and their families. Throughout the United States, there are several effective models for providing a range of services to students at schools. In all cases, the best programs are based on a partnership between schools and community agencies. For example, the Children's Aid Society in New York City operates eight community schools that offer health, dental, recreational, and employment training services to students and their families (Dryfoos, 2001). A number of Beacon and Full Service schools operate throughout the United States and often remain open 12 hours a day by drawing on a second shift of community professionals to run after-school programs. While many of these programs are exceptional, the number of students served by them is miniscule. Most of the best programs operate at individual school sites, and not a single one operates throughout an entire school district.

Given the high levels of poverty among schoolchildren in Oakland, a comprehensive, city-wide strategy for providing social services at school sites is needed. For the sake of cost efficiency, this necessarily will involve improved cooperation between the school district, city government (which funds recreational and youth services), and county government (which funds health and social services). Private organizations (e.g., YMCA, Girls and Boys Clubs) as well as churches and nonprofits also can play important roles in developing systems of support for students, but the large public agencies undoubtedly will have to take the lead since they control the bulk of resources for social services.

Given that all three public agencies provide services to the same population of families, improved coordination in service delivery actually could reduce redundancy and increase cost efficiency. However, interagency cooperation is difficult to accomplish on a large scale because the individuals staffing these organizations generally have no prior history of co-operating, and bureaucratic narrow-mindedness is not a small hurdle to overcome. For this reason, leadership and support from the mayor, superintendent, school board, and county board of supervisors will be needed so that those who carry out coordination activities have the backing to overcome the obstacles they inevitably will encounter.

LIMITS AND POSSIBILITIES OF COMMUNITY SUPPORT FOR SCHOOLS

In contrast to many analyses of urban school systems in the United States (Kozol, 1991; Maeroff, 1988), it is my hope that the one presented here is relatively optimistic. I genuinely believe that it should be possible for Oakland public schools to effectively serve the educational needs of their students. Further, by creating conditions that enable schools to be held accountable by those they serve, and drawing on the active support and participation of the numerous assets and resources present in the city, Oakland should be able to significantly improve its schools. This is not to suggest that the obstacles to bringing this transformation about are not formidable, but clearly the conditions and possibility for change do exist.

The same may not be true for other poor communities that have less money and fewer community assets. Strategies that develop the social capital of parents and civic capacity of communities in socially isolated areas where poverty is concentrated, are less likely to produce lasting improvements in public schools. Small cities like East Palo Alto or Compton, California; North Chicago; or Poughkeepsie, New York, simply cannot be expected to elevate the quality of their schools on their own. In such places, the array of social and economic hardships besetting the community are so vast, and the availability of resources so limited, that outside assistance will be needed if change is to be made. In such places, the limitations of local control of schools and the inequities it tends to reinforce are most evident.

Rather than presuming that all schools can be treated the same, state and federal officials must recognize that socioeconomic conditions within the local context can act as significant constraints limiting possibilities for local control of schools. Put more simply, without the power and resources to exert control over schools, low-income communities cannot be expected to hold their schools accountable. Nor is it reasonable to expect that schools in such communities will be able to solve the vast array of problems confronting students and their families on their own. Unless states enact measures to mitigate the effects of poverty and racial isolation, local control will remain little more than a guise through which the state can shirk its responsibility for ensuring that all students have access to quality education.

The fractured nature of civil society in the United States may make it unlikely that policy makers will enact the kinds of far-reaching changes in social policy that are needed. Ideology, racism, and divisions related to class, national origin, and even geography historically have prevented politicians and vast segments of the general public from considering problems affecting the poor as a matter of national concern. The Leave No Child Behind Act, which will increase significantly the federal government's role in failing local school districts, is unlikely to provide the help that is needed. The measure does nothing to address the horrid conditions present in many failing schools, and it does not even begin to attempt to ameliorate the social inequities that affect schooling.

Although reforming public schools will not eliminate poverty or racial discrimination, education continues to be the only legitimate source of opportunity available to the poor. Beyond the skills and job opportunities that education can make possible, it also can serve as a means for the poor and oppressed to imagine a more just social order (Freire, 1972). Social movements that lead to greater societal change often are born from the ability to imagine alternative possibilities (Horton & Freire, 1990). For communities struggling to meet basic needs, improvements in education can be an effective means to obtain tangible benefits even without other more far-reaching social reforms.

Public education historically has occupied a special place within American civil society because it often has been the birthplace of democratic reform (Tyack, 1980). For African Americans, education has long been recognized as vital to collective improvement because "it is the one thing they can never take away" (Anderson, 1988, p. 67). Education is also the only social entitlement available to all children in the United States regardless of race, class or national origin (Carnoy & Levin, 1985). In the past 10 years, support for improving public education also has been the only domestic issue that has generated broad bipartisan consensus among policy makers. Given its unique status, it makes sense for those interested in finding ways to reduce poverty and racial inequality to focus at least some of their energies on efforts to improve the quality and character of public education in the United States.

CHAPTER 6

The Culture of Violence and the Need for Safety in Schools

The threat of violence is pervasive and omnipresent in urban areas across the United States. This is especially the case in economically depressed inner-city neighborhoods where jobs are scarce and poverty is highly concentrated (Wilson, 1987). In fact, along with poverty, racial segregation, and crime in general, violence is one of the features that distinguishes the urban from the nonurban (Skolnick & Currie, 1994). Per capita homicide rates in the United States significantly surpass those of other industrialized nations (Hebert, 2002), and in many American cities the rates frequently rival and occasionally exceed those of nations at war.[1] The fear of violence serves as justification for the heavy police presence in many American cities. It also operates as an invisible social boundary that separates areas regarded as "safe" for business and middle-class residents, from areas where the poor are confined and that unofficially have been designated "no-man's lands."[2]

The threat of violence has become a major issue of concern for schools in recent years, and consequently it has become a top priority on the national education agenda.[3] Mass shootings in Littleton, Colorado; Jonesboro, Arkansas; Paducah, Kentucky; and elsewhere have heightened the public's fears and added significantly to the level of concern. Although available data and evidence show that the incidence of violence in schools is not rising (Schiraldi & Ziedenberg, 2001), there is a growing perception that schools are more violent and dangerous than ever before. Despite the public's fears, relatively few schools actually have experienced mass killings, and children are safer in school than they are on the streets, in parks, and even in their homes. In polls and surveys, students, teachers, and parents report a greater degree of fear of violent assault at school, and greater concern about safety and student discipline generally, than they did 10 years ago (Pollack, 1999). Once more, fear drives public policy more than data or research.

As might be expected, schools in urban areas like the Bay Area also have been affected by growing concerns related to the threat of violence. In recent years, all four districts—San Francisco, Oakland, Richmond, and

Berkeley—have adopted tougher policies and security measures in an effort to assure the public and parents that schools can be made safe. Following the national trend, zero tolerance policies have been enacted and some schools have been transformed into fortress-like facilities, fully equipped with metal detectors, surveillance cameras, security guards, and police officers.[4] Costly expenditures on security have been made even when the districts have been under severe fiscal constraints (Applebome, 1995). To cover the costs of increased security, the districts at times have made significant reductions in their operating budgets and cut deeply into academic programs. For example, Richmond Unified School District (now called West Contra Costa) spent thousands of dollars to install metal detectors at all of its high schools during the early 1990s, even as it was dismantling important academic programs due to multimillion dollar budget deficits.[5]

More often than not, the fortification of schools has been pursued with little thought to how those who spend their time there—students, teachers, and administrators—are affected by the increased emphasis on security and its impact on school climate. Along with parents, these typically have been the constituencies that have called for actions to be taken to ensure school safety. However, the presence of guards and metal detectors actually can create a false sense of security. For example, shortly after the installation of metal detectors at Richmond High School, two students were shot in the building (Asimov, 1994). Somehow, those responsible for security at the school failed to consider that a determined armed assailant might not enter through the front door.

I became aware of the tendency of schools to overemphasize security during a visit to McClymonds High School in west Oakland in 1991. During a visit to a program for teenage mothers, I asked the security guard who escorted me how they managed to keep the walls free of graffiti. The guard laughed and responded, "This is a lock-down facility. Any student caught out of the classroom during class time is stopped immediately." I pointed out to the guard that most of the classes I observed had very few students in them. He responded by pointing out the irony of his job. "My job is to keep the building safe. It don't really matter if the kids come or not, so long as the school is safe. But sometimes it do feel like I'm protecting a building that's mostly empty." I then asked if the teachers and staff at the school felt safer as a result of the emphasis on security. Again, his response conveyed a degree of irony one might not expect from someone in charge of security: "A lot of them are still scared. It's really the neighborhood they're afraid of 'cause west Oakland has a bad reputation. It don't matter how many guards you have up here, some of these folks is just plain scared. If you asked me, it might be better if there were more people in the halls. Some parts of the school are more dangerous 'cause ain't no one else around. But they don't ask my opinion on these things so I just do my job" (September 16, 1991).

There is substantial evidence that implementation of the most common forms of security (i.e., guards, metal detectors, and cameras) does not guarantee that schools will be safe (Devine, 1996; Noguera, 1995b). I believe that many of the measures taken to secure schools are largely symbolic. They are intended to send the message that those in authority can maintain order and security. But schools that rely on guards and metal detectors rarely feel like safe places, and when teachers are removed from the disciplinary process and replaced by guards, safety and order actually may decrease. Nonetheless, district leaders have uncritically embraced such policies in an attempt to reassure the public that something is being done to respond to the threat of violence. Given the current climate, they may have no other choice. However, we should not confuse security with a school environment that is safe, nurturing, and supportive of teaching and learning.

FIGHTING VIOLENCE, TARGETING KIDS

In the 1990s, youth crime, like adult crime, declined substantially across the United States and throughout the Bay Area (Donziger, 1996). Despite this reduction, calls for increased penalties against juvenile offenders and the construction of new corrections facilities actually have increased. In Alameda, San Francisco, and Contra Cost Counties, the arrest rate for every category of juvenile crime, particularly violent crime, dropped significantly from 1992 to 2000 (see Table 6.1). However, in Spring 2001, members of the Alameda County Board of Supervisors were actively debating whether to construct a new detention center that would become the largest juvenile corrections facility in the nation. Some members of the board justified the new facility by arguing that even if it could not be filled with local offenders, it could generate revenue for the county by taking in inmates from other areas and states.

Several scholars have noted that crime rates have little bearing on the politics of crime prevention (Currie, 1985; Donziger, 1996). Polls showing that the public is worried about the threat of violent crime carry more weight and are far more persuasive than data showing that crime rates are actually down. Moreover, it is rare to find a politician who will openly suggest that there is a need to find alternatives to incarceration or to support prevention policies that actually have been shown to reduce juvenile crime.

Table 6.1. Crime Rate per 100,000 in Alameda County

Offense	1992	1994	1996	1998	2000
Violent offense	769.3	892.4	746.0	599.0	420.0
Property offense	1,804.0	1,442.0	1,447.0	1,057.0	869.5
Drug offense	781.0	710.5	451.9	388.3	356.2
Sex offense	78.7	54.2	47.0	49.9	56.9

Interestingly, although the schools where the mass shootings occurred largely have been located in middle-class, suburban communities comprising primarily White residents (Gottfredson, 2001), inner-city schools have captured the public's imagination as the bastions of carnage. Similarly, although the perpetrators of the shootings most often have been middle-class White males who were subjected to harassment by their peers (Perlstein, 1998), low-income students of color, especially African American males, have been targeted disproportionately for punishment (Ayers, Klonsky, & Lyon, 2000).

This is not to say that violence is not an important issue in large inner-city schools; however, it is not a new issue. The threat of violence has plagued several of the high schools and middle schools in low-income neighborhoods in the Bay Area for many years. Gang rivalries, interracial conflict, and interpersonal violence have been a problem at schools such as Castlemont and Fremont in Oakland, and Mission and Balboa in San Francisco for many years. Even Berkeley High School, which serves large numbers of middle-class White students from well-educated families, periodically has experienced outbreaks of violence.[6] While I was serving as an elected member of the school board in Berkeley during the early 1990s, the board was called into emergency session on several occasions to consider requests for additional expenditures for security at the high school. Fortunately, there have been no mass shootings at any of the schools in the Bay Area, but long before Columbine the threat of violence was an issue with which many schools were coping.

Given the conditions present in many of the low-income neighborhoods where schools are located, it is not surprising that school violence is an issue. Many schools are in neighborhoods that are regarded as dangerous, and where the incidence of street crime and violence are quite high. Children walking to and from schools in the San Antonio neighborhood of east Oakland, the Iron Triangle in Richmond, or the Tenderloin in San Francisco, must negotiate streets where crime and violence are pervasive and where drug dealers openly ply their dangerous trade. Having grown accustomed to hearing the staccato of gunfire on a regular basis, many children learn to distinguish between the types of firearms used most often in their neighborhoods. They also learn when ducking for cover rather than gawking at the carnage is the best course of action to take following a shooting. In order to survive, children in such neighborhoods are forced to learn at relatively young ages how to contend with dangers that lurk in alleys, passing cars, and the eyes of strangers.

LOWELL MIDDLE SCHOOL AND THE CLIMATE OF VIOLENCE

My own understanding of how the constant presence of violence in children's lives influences their attitudes and behavior has been shaped to a large degree by my experience working with Lowell Middle School in west Oakland. From 1992 to 1995, I worked closely with the school as a researcher and supporter of efforts to develop partnerships between the school and community agencies that would provide social services to students (Noguera, 1995b). Located in one of the poorest and most crime-ridden neighborhoods in Oakland, Lowell is not regarded as one of Oakland's better schools. In fact, during the 3 years that I worked there, its enrollment was less than half of what the school could accommodate, while other schools in central Oakland were literally overflowing with students.

Compared with many schools serving middle-class children, the academic offerings at Lowell were quite sparse. Science courses were offered to seventh and eighth graders, but there was no modern equipment in the science laboratories. During one of my early visits to the school, I actually found a room full of science materials that were not being used. The teacher informed me that she had chosen not to use the equipment because she was sure that the students would break it. Lowell had a school library, but according to the librarian, no new books had been ordered or received in the past 10 years. Algebra was offered to eighth graders, but only 15 students were considered sufficiently prepared to take the course during the year I started this study. There was also a computer laboratory, but access was limited to students enrolled in the computer course. The only other elective course available was Spanish, which was limited to eighth graders, although a variety of ESL, special education, and remedial reading classes were offered.

Lowell is located in a community with high concentrations of poverty, and the effects of poverty are manifest within the school. In 1993, 95% of the students qualified, on the basis of parental income, for free or reduced-price lunch. Through a conversation with the school nurse, I learned that 43% of the students were identified as either asthmatic or having some form of chronic respiratory condition, a problem she attributed to the freeways and heavy industry that surround the school and community. Finally, and most surprising to me, 68% of the students lived in a household with an adult who was someone other than one of their biological parents (e.g., grandparents, relatives, foster care). The nurse explained this situation to me in the following way: "Most of these kids don't have what people think of as a 'normal' home. They live with their grandmothers or in foster care because their parents are missing—in jail, on drugs, or just plain gone. When you think about what they deal with everyday, you understand why some of them are so angry at the world" (interview, February 18, 1993).

During my 3 years of work at Lowell, I met many angry children: kids who would explode into an uncontrollable rage over what appeared to be a minor affront from a teacher or another student, and others who on certain days seemed to simmer with a quiet anger that they kept inside and to themselves. It was commonly understood among adults at Lowell that sometimes kids needed to be left alone, and not forced to work or participate in classroom activities if they didn't want to. The vice principal explained the school's approach to me in this way:

> Sometimes these kids are hurting inside. They may have just gotten a whippin' at home. Or maybe somebody they know got shot or put away. You just don't know what it could be, and sometimes you can't force them to talk to you or to do work like everybody else. On those days you just let them be. The fact that they made it to school on a day when they're carrying so much hurt, it tells you that they care about school. It also tells you that this is where they get to be away from the pressure at home. So we try not to add to the pressure. We let them know that sometimes they can just go sleep in the nurse's office if they need to or come cry in my office if it will help. These little people carry more pressure with them than most adults do, and we have to be patient with them.

During the time I spent at Lowell there were actually far more light moments of playfulness and levity than occasions when the mood seemed tense or dangerous. When I would observe kids interacting during nonstructured times such as recess, or in the minutes before or after school, they seemed as light-hearted as any group of young adolescents. There were many heated arguments, and quite a bit of name calling, but relatively few fights. I could see lots of evidence of posturing and outward appearances of toughness, but there were far more moments of silliness and exuberant play. The occasional outburst of rage served as a reminder that the potential for violence was never far away, but even the threat could not overshadow the joy and happiness that most of the children seemed to experience each day.

As one might expect, Lowell is a school where the threat of violence is constant and palpable. In my interviews with teachers and administrators, concerns about safety came up frequently, although most often outsiders and the surrounding neighborhood were perceived as the primary source of danger to the school. During the 1992–93 school year, 14 weapons were confiscated from students at school (one toy gun, five knives, three baseball bats, and five sticks or clubs). Within the school district, Lowell ranked tenth among 32 middle schools for the number of weapons confiscated. During the same period, eight students were expelled for violent behavior (mostly fighting) at school, 76 were suspended, and the police were called to campus on 21 separate occasions to respond to violent incidents involving students or outsiders. Many teachers admitted that the increase in police presence was attributable to a growing tendency to involve law enforcement in matters that previously would have been handled by the school administration. As one veteran physical education teacher explained, "Nowadays they call the police for every little thing. It don't make no sense. These kids ain't bad. They may be hardheaded, but they ain't bad. But some of these folks are really scared of them and as soon as there's a little fight or something they wanna rush off and call the police. It ain't right but I understand it" (interview, April 5, 1993).

The school principal attributed most of the problems related to violence to outsiders and a small number of difficult and disruptive students, who "lack sufficient guidance at home and act out at school in an effort to get attention" (interview, March 16, 1993). Although there was only one instance of a student striking a teacher over a 10-year period, several teachers expressed concern for their personal safety because of crime in the neighborhood and because they perceived there to be an increase in violent and aggressive behavior of students. This fear was expressed in the following statement by a veteran social studies teacher at Lowell:

> In the past the kids would respect you just because you were the teacher. You were a person in authority and they knew they had to do as you said. Nowadays the kids are different. They have their own rules, and just because you're a teacher it doesn't mean that they're going to treat you any different than anybody else. On the wrong day, any of us could be the victim of attack. (interview, March 18, 1993)

"KILLING THE MAN WITH THE BALL": STUDENT PERCEPTIONS OF VIOLENCE AND AGGRESSION

Shortly after I started working with the school in Fall 1992, I learned at a faculty meeting that students were playing a particularly violent game of "Kill the Man with the Ball" during the lunch recess. This is a game that I was familiar with, having played it as a child while growing up in New York. The rules of the game require participants to chase, physically apprehend, and pile on top of the person running with the ball until it is released and picked up by another person who starts the chase over again. Students at Lowell had modified the rules such that anyone caught carrying the ball could be beaten quite severely. The principal brought the matter to the attention of the faculty because several students had been seriously injured as a result of the game. She wanted suggestions from the faculty about what should be done to address the problem. As might be expected, most teachers responded by calling for an immediate ban on the game. One suggested that the ball should be taken away, while several others added that the leaders of the game should be punished and perhaps suspended.

After listening to the conversation as it progressed over half an hour, I reluctantly intervened to pose the following question: "What is there about this game that kids find so attractive that they are willing to risk playing it despite the possibility that they might experience a serious injury?" Interestingly, none of the adults in the room could answer the question. I then pointed out that they would have difficulty enforcing a ban on the game because there were only two security guards monitoring over 350 students during lunch recess (teachers were on lunch break during recess). As they pondered the difficulty entailed in implementing a ban on the game, I suggested that they allow me to speak with a small group of the most active participants so that we could learn more about their motivations for engaging in such a dangerous activity.

Before the group discussion, I went out during recess to see if I could observe the game. As I expected, although the two security guards had been instructed to prevent students from playing the game, I found a group of kids off in one corner of the asphalt-covered playground actively engaged. Of the 15 to 20 kids involved, most were boys, but four girls hung around the periphery of the game, occasionally entering the fray to chase down and hit an unlucky participant carrying the ball. While I watched the game, what struck me most was how happy the children seemed to be even as they or one of their playmates was being pummeled. I looked on with some degree of bewilderment as I saw kids compete enthusiastically over who would carry the ball and run with it, even though it was understood that doing so meant one was fair game for collective abuse.

The following day, I sat down to meet with a group of seventh- and eighth-grade students who had been picked out by the security guards as the most regular players of the game. I started by explaining the concerns that their teachers had raised about the game and I told them that I had observed them playing myself and also felt concerned that someone could be seriously hurt. The students readily acknowledged that the game was dangerous, and several showed me bruises and scars they had received from playing. However, when I asked why they played such a violent game, the students responded with laughter. They explained that it was only a game, and even though some people did get hurt, no one became angry because they understood the rules: Any form of punishment is allowed if you catch the person with the ball. They also informed me that they had changed the name from "Kill the Man with the Ball" to "Nigger Ball." When I asked why the name had been changed, I was told by one of the few girls who played, "Because this is how niggers get beat."

I then probed for further elaboration about the appeal of the game. Most said they played simply because it was fun. Another offered that they learned valuable skills from the game such as how to cover vital body parts when attacked. When I asked if they had been attacked before, they laughed. One student explained that most sixth graders get jumped at the start of school by older seventh- and eighth-grade students. He added that next year he expected to be jumped when he entered ninth grade at the high school nearby because "that's the way it is—the new kids get jumped." Another student explained that he had been beaten once by the police. He pointed out that the police "beat you a lot worse than what you get out here on the playground. They have sticks, guns, and mace."

Unwilling to accept their answers at face value, I pushed further. I pointed out that even though bad things such as car accidents could happen to anyone, it didn't make sense to prepare for such an occurrence by deliberately allowing oneself to be hit by a car. My logic was compelling and seemed to effectively undermine the arguments they had used to defend the game. Finally one of the students explained that the main reason why he played the game was for the excitement. Nodding their heads in agreement, the other students made it clear that the thrill of being chased was ultimately the main attraction of the game. One boy offered, "When you got a bunch of people chasing you down and you know that if they catch you they gonna whip your ass, that shit is exciting."

As I reflected on what I was hearing, I was forced to acknowledge that I too could see the excitement of such a game. As a college student I had played rugby, a game that is not too different from the one they were playing, and as a youngster I too had enjoyed rough play that involved tackling people and being chased. However, knowing that some of the students were being hurt and that the school eventually would find a way to ban the game, I asked the group whether there weren't other games they could play that would be exciting but less dangerous. This question opened up a discussion about how bored the kids were during recess because there was nothing to do on the asphalt lot that posed as a playground. I asked if they would play nonviolent athletic games (e.g., soccer, touch football, basketball, etc.) if provided with equipment, and the students enthusiastically said that they would.

Perhaps even more important than the practical solutions it offered, our discussion about the game provided students with an opportunity to reflect on their own behavior and actions. As we talked about the game and the very real threat of violence that many of them confronted each day, I became increasingly aware of the fact that many adults at this school had no idea of how kids experience violence in their everyday lives. Our conversation prompted me to try to learn more about their perceptions and the feelings that motivate aggressive behavior. Specifically, I wanted to know when they considered violence to be an appropriate and legitimate form of behavior. At the time I thought that finding the answer to this question would be the key to finding ways to counter the threat of violence that many of them were forced to contend with.

NORMALIZATION OF VIOLENCE AND THE ROLE OF THE MEDIA

I cite this example at length because it represents in a small but significant way the insights that may be revealed when students are engaged in critical discussions of violence and aggression. For many students living in tough inner-city neighborhoods, violence is a fact of life, a central feature of the social fabric that is ubiquitous and key to the experience of growing up. As Elijah Anderson (1990) observed through his ethnographic research in neighborhoods in west Philadelphia, violence is often unavoidable for many young people. One learns to cope with the threat of violence or one runs the risk of becoming a victim.

As a youngster growing up in Brooklyn and Long Island, I learned how to defend myself at a fairly young age because there were many times when my parents or an adult would not be present to protect me from danger. I also learned that the best way to prevent violence was to be prepared for it. You could prepare either by learning to read a situation quickly—to know who posed a threat and to map out a plan for escape—or by knowing how to defend yourself. For me and for many of the children that I grew up with, fighting was a fact of life and an integral part of our socialization into adolescence. You learned how to fight just as you learned how to ride a bicycle or how to dance. If you were a good fighter, you earned the respect and praise of your peers, but if you were a poor fighter or someone who was afraid to fight, you ran the risk of being harassed, bullied, and victimized.

However, I also learned at a relatively young age that violence was a serious matter, and that there were dangerous people out there on the streets who were quite willing to hurt or even kill. When I was 14, my cousin of the same age was murdered for refusing to yield his leather jacket to a couple of muggers who were only slightly older than he. At the time, this was an uncommon event and the community was shocked. There is still a youth recreation center in the Bronx named after my cousin, Ronald Frazier. The following year, an acquaintance at my school, a bully with a reputation for athletic prowess and a bad temper, was arrested for kidnap and rape.

My own background gave me the sense that I understood the reality of the students attending Lowell Middle School. I assumed that their experience with violence was like mine, but I also had doubts. My doubts came from my sense that things had changed. I knew that the crack epidemic of the 1980s had escalated the degree and extent of violence in many inner-city neighborhoods, and I knew from my experience working in the mayor's office in Berkeley that many young people in neighborhoods like west Oakland were heavily involved in the trade. I also knew that guns were now more available than they were when I was growing up, and that drive-by shootings and car jackings had become more common. My awareness of these changes left me wondering whether the attitudes of children toward violence had changed. I wanted to find out because I had the hunch that by learning how young people perceived violence in their environment, I might gain a better sense of what could be done to prevent violence.

To begin to understand how students perceived the threat of violence within the context of their everyday experiences at school, I undertook a study of student attitudes, utilizing the grounded theory approach developed by Glaser and Strauss (1967).[7] As is typical for most inquiries that are premised on grounded theory, I drew on my prior knowledge about the subject matter to formulate a research strategy. An inductive approach to my inquiry made most sense to me because despite my familiarity with the subject, I had no compelling hypothesis or explanation for the questions that motivated my research.

I wanted to understand how students perceived the threat of violence in their environment and how this perception influenced their attitudes toward violent behavior. I was also interested in understanding the ethical judgments they made regarding the manifestations of violence they observed and/or experienced in their daily lives. Specifically, I wanted to know if there were circumstances in which students might regard violent behavior as legitimate or appropriate. I also wanted to know what connection, if any, their responses might have to their personal stance toward violence.

Working in collaboration with one of the teachers at the school, I started this research by viewing parts of films containing violent images with a classroom of 22 eighth-grade students. I started with media images of violence because a growing body of research suggests that exposure to violence in the media has an effect on the attitudes of young people toward violence (Barry, 1993). I wanted to understand how students perceived depictions of violence in film and which forms they found to be entertaining, and to learn about the ethical judgments they made in connection with the violence they saw. I also wanted to know whether they identified with the victim or the perpetrator of violence when they observed it on film.

We started the project by viewing the opening scene from the film *Raiders of the Lost Ark*, the first in a series of movies starring the character Indiana Jones. The scene followed Indiana as he entered a dark cave in search of a special indigenous artifact. Upon collecting the artifact, Indiana narrowly escapes as the cave collapses and the natives, who ostensibly own the artifact, chase him with spears and poison blow darts. Interestingly, as I queried the students about the 8-minute segment of the film, initially no one could recall observing any violence. I found this interesting because during the opening scene two people are killed. I attributed this oversight to the suspense in the scene and the fast pace of the action. Before we watched the scene a second time, I instructed the students to look closely and keep track of when a person was killed. This time all of the students were able to recall the instances of violence that were depicted. When I asked what they felt about the violence, they unanimously reported that they enjoyed it immensely. They described the scene as "cool" and exciting, and they all agreed that the two characters that were killed during the opening segment deserved to meet their ends because they had been disloyal to Indiana.

We then viewed a scene from the movie *The Untouchables* starring Kevin Costner as Eliot Ness. I chose the scene in which Al Capone, played by Robert De Niro, chastises the members of his gang, as they are seated around a dinner table for a meeting, for allowing Ness to disrupt their illegal liquor sales. Capone paces around the table with a baseball bat in his hands as he explains that organized crime, like baseball, is a team sport, and when one person makes a mistake they let the whole team down. To demonstrate just how unhappy he is about such poor performance, Capone proceeds to pummel one of his associates to death with the bat. Interestingly, rather than focusing on the beating itself, the camera focuses on the blood that slowly oozes out onto the table and the shocked faces of the other mobsters.

In the discussion that followed, a clear gender pattern emerged with respect to the students' reactions. All of the boys asserted that they loved the scene, while most of the girls stated that they were repulsed by it. Several of the boys explained that they liked it because they felt it depicted how gangsters really are. One boy explained, "If you're gonna be a gangster you've got to be ready to take your punishment." In contrast, the girls were more likely to express sympathy for the victim. Articulating the sentiments of most of the girls in the class, one girl remarked, "He was just sitting at the table listening, and then his boss, who was supposed to be his friend, starts whacking him upside the head with a bat? Now that ain't right." At the time I felt it was possible that the reactions of the boys may have been influenced by the group dynamics in the classroom. They were unanimous in saying that they identified with the assailant, Capone, because they admired his toughness.

For the final exercise I used a short segment from the film *Straight out of Brooklyn* by Mattie Rich. This critically acclaimed film, produced by a 19-year-old on a shoestring budget, is about a family grappling with the hardships of life in the crime-ridden Red Hook housing projects. In the opening segment the camera focuses on the reactions of a brother and a sister, as they are awakened from their sleep by the sound of their father beating their mother in an adjacent room. Although the camera moves briefly away from the two kids to follow the father chasing the mother across the living room, throwing furniture as he moves violently toward her, at no point in the scene is any actual violence portrayed. Instead, what the viewer hears is the cries of the mother and the angry assault of the father, while what the viewer sees is the anguish and anger of the children who remain locked in their room unable to intervene.

Interestingly, although this film actually contained the least violence of all three films—no one was killed and no actual violence was shown—the students had the strongest reaction to it. This time no one said they were entertained by the scene, nor was there any evidence of excitement and pleasure among the students. Instead, the students were visibly disturbed. One of the boys started the conversation by demanding to know, "Why did you show us that? I hate to see stuff like that. It makes me sick." Another girl said, "Seeing a mother get beat isn't funny or entertaining." When I pointed out that they did not actually see the father hitting the mother, another girl responded, "It don't matter. You can hear it and you can see the kids' faces. I can just imagine what they must be feeling." There was no debate when I asked whether they identified with the victim or the perpetrator, and no need to probe deeply about the ethics involved in the scene because the students were united in their repulsion toward the father who perpetrated the violence.

As we discussed their reactions to the three scenes, the conversation shifted from an uncritical acceptance of violence as entertainment, to a more detached and reflective analysis of violence and film making. During the course of our conversation it became clear that a number of students were aware of the ways in which film makers manipulate their feelings about violence. One boy offered that "movies like *The Untouchables* and Indiana Jones are fun to watch because you know it ain't real." I pointed out that the beating scene in *The Untouchables* was much more graphic than the violence shown in *Straight out of Brooklyn*. A girl who had been quiet for most of the class discussion seemed to speak for the entire group when she explained, "The last film might be less violent but it's real to us. A lot of us have seen stuff like that, and that makes it different. I don't know about no archeologists or gangsters, but I do know about men hitting on women. Stuff like that happens for real, and it ain't fun to watch in a movie."

VIOLENCE IN EVERYDAY LIFE

The violence in film project left me questioning some studies that suggest a strong link between exposure to violence in film and violent behavior among teenagers (Barry, 1993). While it was clear that depictions of violence, particularly when they are part of a story filled with action and suspense, are highly entertaining, it was not clear that exposure to such films would result in any direct link to violent behavior. In fact, I was heartened to learn that students drew a clear distinction between what they regarded as realism and fantasy in portrayals of violence. However, even after watching and discussing the films with this group of students, I realized that I knew very little about the factors that conditioned their attitudes toward violence in everyday life. I suspected that because of where they lived, many of these young people were forced to learn how to deal with the threat of violence at a fairly young age. I wanted to probe deeper to know when and in what circumstances they regarded violence as a necessary and legitimate way to respond to a threat.

To find answers to these questions, I surveyed and conducted interviews with 48 students at two middle schools in the Bay Area—Lowell and Willard Middle School in Berkeley—during the 1992–93 school year. I chose the two schools because they provided a striking contrast along the dimensions of race, class, and environmental context. I surmised that such a contrast might illuminate the ways in which social context—the community, neighborhood economy, and physical environment—influenced the attitudes and perceptions of young people toward violence. Additionally, I suspected that while students at the two schools seemed to exist in completely separate worlds, a closer examination might reveal ways in which their perceptions were similar as a result of their exposure to television and other media, and the more diffuse influences of popular youth culture. Understanding how these factors—the cultural and the environmental—influenced the attitudes and perceptions of students toward violence, was a primary goal of this inquiry.

Willard is a medium-sized middle school—812 students, 36 teachers, a principal, two assistant principals, and three counselors. It is located in a park-like setting on 12 acres of land, with large athletic fields, a swimming pool, and tennis courts. It is surrounded by the homes, the average value of which exceeded $300,000 in 1992–93, of middle-class families in a predominantly White community. The community is made up largely of college-educated professionals, although there is a working-class side of town where most non-White families live.

While the hallways at Lowell are dark and dank, the hallways at Willard are bright with natural illumination from skylights in the ceilings, and grass and trees cover the campus. Similarly, the way these schools relate to the surrounding community is also a telling feature of comparison. While Lowell is enclosed by a fence approximately 15 feet high that borders the perimeter of the campus, Willard and its facilities—pool, playing fields, tennis and basketball courts—are accessible to its neighbors and the general public. The design of the two schools suggests that whereas Lowell regards its community with suspicion and fear, Willard perceives the community as an ally and its facilities are regarded by residents as a public resource and asset. In fact, the beautiful garden in front of Willard was created and maintained by the school's neighbors.

The contrasts between Lowell and Willard are striking in other ways as well. An analysis of test scores at Willard revealed that 17% of students were identified as gifted and talented, and 26% had scores low enough to be eligible for compensatory education. Eighteen percent of the students entered seventh grade below grade level in reading, with a corresponding 12% in math, and less than 7% were identified as being in need of some form of special education. Willard students have access to a variety of elective courses, including Spanish, French, computer science, art, music, dance, and health education. Four sections of algebra and one course in honors geometry are offered to students who are deemed qualified. Only 15% of the students at Willard were qualified to receive free or reduced-price lunch, and according to the principal, the Parent Teacher Student Association raised over $100,000 during the previous year to support field trips and other educational activities at the school.

Unlike Lowell, Willard is a racially integrated school. There are roughly equal numbers of African American (42%) and White (38%) students, and Latino (9%) and Asian (11%) students are present as well. Test scores reveal a racial achievement gap at Willard, but most of the teachers I spoke to asserted that differences in achievement were more likely attributable to socioeconomic factors than to race. None of the adults I spoke to mentioned that there were any racial problems at the school, and several cited the integrated clubs and sports teams as evidence of racial harmony among students. "Kids get along here," reported one of the security guards. "We're like a family at Willard. We have problems just like any other school, but race ain't one of them" (interview, March 17, 1993).

Despite the relative affluence of the school, the families it serves, and the community in which it is located, concerns about the threat of violence were high. In interviews with teachers and administrators, several expressed concerns and uncertainty about what they described as a "climate of violence." While the source of this threat was difficult to pin down, the sentiments expressed by one eighth-grade English teacher captured some of the anxiety that was conveyed to me.

> The attitudes of the children have changed. They use harsher language with each other when they argue, and when they fight, you'd think they wanted to kill each other. It's not a place where kids are carrying guns or anything, but something's different about kids today, and to me it's a lot more scary. (interview, April 7, 1993)

Mirroring the national trends previously described, the teachers' concerns about violence were not matched by empirical evidence. Only two weapons (one knife and one club) were confiscated from students at Willard over a 3-year period. During the 1992–93 school year 36 students were suspended and four students were expelled. The police were called to the school on two occasions for violent incidents during the same period (both incidents involved students from other schools). There were five security guards at Willard, an additional guard having been hired in the 1991–92 school year in response to heightened concerns about security. Interestingly, all five of the security guards were African American males, and they were the only African American males other than the three custodians who were employed at the school.

My access to both schools was made possible by prior relationships with the faculty and administration. To get started, I approached each principal with an offer of assistance in devising a violence prevention strategy for their schools that would be informed by concrete knowledge about the views and perceptions of students. Like many other schools, both were faced with growing concerns from parents and teachers related to the threat of violence. Although neither school had experienced any major incidents of violence in the past few years, heightened awareness about violence at other schools throughout the country prompted both principals to readily agree to participate in the study and welcome my offer of assistance.

The design called for surveys and interviews with students to be conducted in eighth-grade social studies classes, with the support and cooperation of the classroom teachers. Twenty-two students were surveyed and interviewed at Lowell, and 28 students at Willard. In both classes the study was introduced as part of a unit on violence prevention that I taught as a guest teacher over a 2-week period. The unit began with a lecture/presentation on the forms of violence in American society—violent crime, interpersonal and domestic violence, police and military violence, and violent acts carried out by hate and terror groups. This was followed by a discussion of how these forms of violence are represented in the media. Following a brief interactive discussion to clarify the focus of the study and definition of terms, a survey was administered that consisted of 10 true/false statements, four multiple choice questions, and one open-ended question (see Figure 6.1). Once the surveys were completed and collected, I engaged the students in a whole group discussion of their responses in an effort to understand why they responded as they did. This enabled me to get a better understanding of the logic behind the responses and also provided an opportunity for open discussion of related issues.

Following completion of the survey, I conducted individual interviews with the students over the course of the week, using the four multiple choice and one open-ended question from the survey as the basis for our conversations. Each interview lasted approximately 30 minutes. All of the questions were designed to solicit the students' views and perceptions of violence and to ascertain the extent to which they perceived violence as a threat within the school environment. In the following section, I present an analysis of the students' responses.

LEARNING ABOUT VIOLENCE FROM STUDENTS

Among the students at the two schools, the responses to both the survey and the interviews revealed dramatic differences, and some unexpected similarities. This was revealed in responses to the true/false statements, discussion of the survey that followed, and individual interviews. For ex-

Figure 6.1. Survey of Student Experiences with and Perceptions of Violence

	Lowell		Willard	
True/False Statements	*True*	*False*	*True*	*False*
1. In the last year, someone that I know was a victim of violence and was either hurt or killed.	18	4	6	22
2. I sometimes carry a weapon for protection.	8	14	4	24
3. I have been in a fight in the last month.	9	13	4	24
4. I have been in a fight in the last two months.	13	9	4	24
5. I hardly ever fight if I can avoid it.	21	1	24	4
6. Using violence to get what you want is never the right thing to do.	7	15	16	12
7. I enjoy watching violent movies.	18	4	23	5
8. I often worry about being hurt by someone when I am at school.	19	3	3	25
9. I often worry about being hurt by someone when I am at home or in my neighborhood.	19	3	2	26
10. I respect and look up to people who know how to fight well.	11	11	2	26

Multiple-Choice Questions	**Lowell**	**Willard**
11. If you know that someone wants to fight with you, the best thing to do is:		
a. Tell an adult.	3	21
b. Tell your friends or family members so that you have some back-up.	15	3
c. Carry a weapon for protection.	3	0
d. Try to resolve the conflict peacefully.	0	2
e. Other ___________	1	2

Multiple-Choice Questions	Lowell	Willard
12. If you knew that another student brought a weapon to school you would:		
a. Tell a teacher or the principal.	0	15
b. Mind your own business and not tell anyone.	16	7
c. Talk to the person to find out what was going on.	2	1
d. Talk to your friends about it.	4	5
13. If you know that two people are going to fight after school the best thing to do is:		
a. Watch the fight.	16	17
b. Help the person that is losing.	0	0
c. Tell an adult.	2	7
d. Go home and mind your own business.	4	4
14. Which of the following is a legitimate reason for fighting:		
a. Someone looks at you the wrong way or says something bad about you.	6	2
b. Someone threatens you, a family member, or a friend.	15	12
c. Someone hits you, a family member, or a friend.	19	21
d. Someone says something bad about your mother.	9	7
e. Other ____________	8	5
15. Are there any occasions when violence may be appropriate? (Open-ended)		

Note: Respondents could choose more than one answer to any given multiple-choice question.

ample, whereas 18 of the 22 students at Lowell responded "true" to statement 1, "In the last year, someone that I know was a victim of violence and was either killed or hurt," only 6 of the 28 students at Willard responded affirmatively. Similarly, in response to statements 8 and 9, "I often worry about being hurt by someone when I am at school," and ". . . when I am at home or in my neighborhood," the vast majority of students at Lowell (19 of the 22) selected true, while at Willard only two or three students chose true.

Other items revealed similar patterns of difference. In response to statement 2, "I sometimes carry a weapon for protection," students at Lowell were twice as likely to respond affirmatively (8 of 22) as students at Willard (4 of 28). Similarly, students at Lowell were far more likely to respond "true" to statements 3 and 4, "I have been in a fight in the last month," and ". . . in the last two months." Nine of the students at Lowell responded affirmatively to statement 3, and 13 to statement 4, compared with four students at Willard who answered true to both. The vast majority of students at both schools responded true to statement 5, "I hardly ever fight if I can avoid it" (21 at Lowell, 24 at Willard). However, more students at Lowell than at Willard responded "true" to statement 10, "I respect and look up to people who know how to fight well" (11 at Lowell, 2 at Willard).

Differences in the attitudes and perceptions of these two groups of students were even more dramatic in the interviews and whole group discussions of the survey. For example, in response to question 11, "If you know that someone wants to fight with you, the best thing to do is . . . ," the majority of students (15) at Lowell chose response b—"Tell your friends or family members so that you have some back-you." In contrast, the overwhelming majority of students (21) at Willard chose response a—"Tell an adult," as the preferred method for handling a threat from another student.

In the discussions that followed their responses to this question, students at Lowell overwhelmingly felt that telling an adult if a person wants to fight with you is not a viable option because it can provide only temporary relief. According to one female student:

> If you tell a teacher that somebody wants to fight with you, it's not like they're gonna walk you home. The most they can do is get the person sent to the office, but if the fight didn't happen yet, the person ain't even gonna get in trouble.

For these students, telling a friend or family member was a better solution because it might enable the student to avoid the fight altogether in that a show of force could neutralize the threat of violence. Another student explained the logic behind such a response in this way:

> When they see that you got back-up if your partners are with you, they know it ain't gonna be like they can just beat you down. Somebody is gonna get hurt and it ain't gonna just be on one side. Then they know they better just leave you unless they want some real action to jump off.

In contrast, the majority of students at Willard considered telling an adult to be the most reasonable and effective way of handling a threat from another student. For these students there was no doubt that once such a matter was brought to the attention of a responsible adult, a violent conflict could be avoided. Adults at the school site were perceived as capable of protecting and supervising students, and these students believed that any individual threatening to use violence against a peer was likely to be punished severely. This certainty was conveyed in the following way by a male student at Willard:

> . . . the campus monitors at our school are really tough. If anyone wants to fight somebody they usually get caught right away by one of these guys. And they are really big. You'd have to be crazy to think that you could get away with fighting at this school, and if you tried to get someone after school, the principal or somebody will get you the next day, and kids who fight usually get suspended. You can't get away with any fighting around here, not even play fighting.

It is significant that at both schools in the study, conflict resolution programs had been in place for several years, and many students, including some who participated in the study (four students at Lowell, three at Willard), had been trained to serve as mediators at their school. However, despite this training, it is particularly noteworthy that not many of the students at either of the schools chose response c, "Try to resolve the conflict peacefully." In each interview, after discussing the student's response to question 11, I also probed to find out why he or she had not chosen the other possible responses. At both schools, the most consistent explanation given by students for not attempting to resolve a conflict peacefully was that students perceived such an approach to be unrealistic and impractical. When confronted with the prospect of an actual fight with another student, peaceful students did not see resolution through dialogue as a viable option. The following quotes from students at Lowell and Willard provide some insight into their reasoning:

> (Male student from Lowell)
> When someone wants to fight you, they usually don't give you a chance to do any talking. That stuff [conflict resolution] only works if the principal or somebody is around. If it's just you and the other person, you got to let your fists do the talking otherwise you could get hurt. I usually try to get the first punch in. That usually works better than trying to talk about it.

> (Female student from Willard)
> Conflict resolution is OK if you're in class, or PE, or even during recess at lunch time. If you know that adults are around, it's smarter to try to talk it out than to fight. I don't fight anyway, but I was one of the people that was trained to be a school mediator, and I know that it only works during school, not after.

While it is difficult to discern whether students were being completely honest in their responses, it is important to point out that only three of the students at either school chose response c, "Carry a weapon for protection." Most of the students expressed the view that introducing weapons into a conflict increased the likelihood of escalation and the penalties that might be imposed on those who were caught. In the view of one female student from Lowell:

> If you bring a knife or something then the other kid is gonna probably bring something, then it just gets too crazy. It's better to fight and get your butt kicked than to make it worse by bringing a weapon. Somebody could get killed.

The three students from Lowell (all male) who felt bringing a weapon might be an appropriate way to handle a confrontation, stated that the use of a weapon was the best way to neutralize and prevent violence from a group of people who intended to do them harm. They also explained that acquiring a weapon, including a hand gun, would not be very difficult given that they each knew friends and family members who possessed firearms.

Similar patterns were revealed in the responses of students to question 12, "If you knew that another student brought a weapon to school you would . . ." Students at Lowell were far more likely to choose response b—"Mind your own business and not tell anyone"(16 of 22 students), while students at Willard were more likely to choose response a—"Tell a teacher or the principal" (15 of 28 students). Two female students from Lowell said that they would attempt to talk to the person about why he or she was carrying a weapon if they knew the individual (response c). Four students at Lowell and five students at Willard said that they would warn their friends that a student was in possession of a weapon so that they could avoid the individual (response d). However, none of these students stated that they would also tell an adult about the matter, either because they feared there might be retaliation at some point in the future from the student with the weapon, or because they felt this was the best way to avoid trouble.

Once again, the reasons for the differences in the students' responses to this question were rooted in their perceptions of security within and outside of school. Repeatedly, students at Lowell stated that they were afraid that any attempt to report an armed student to school authorities would make it more likely that they would become the target of aggression. These students had no confidence in the ability of school administrators to provide them with protection. Moreover, several of the students expressed an unwillingness to violate school and community norms related to "snitching." This sentiment was summed up aptly by the following female student at Lowell:

> Why would you report someone for carrying a weapon in school? They probably need it for protection on their way home from school 'cause usually people don't use no weapons at school. Anyone who rats out somebody to the principal or the police deserves to get hurt. If they don't like it they should mind their own business. That's the best way to stay out of trouble.

In contrast, the views articulated by many of the students at Willard again revealed a higher degree of personal security. For these students, reporting another student to an adult was perceived as the most responsible way to deal with a student in possession of a weapon. Willard students had no doubt school authorities would be able to protect them, and few even mentioned the possibility of reprisals from the reported student. Some of these students expressed the view that by telling an adult about an armed peer, they actually were helping the armed individual because their actions could prevent the student from hurting him- or herself or someone else. According to one female student: "I would let one of the security guards know because they know how to deal with kids that have problems, and any kid who brings a weapon to school has problems."

In the interviews, students also were asked what they would do if they knew that two people were going to fight after school (question 13). In response to this question, similarities emerged. At both schools most students (16 at Lowell, 17 at Willard) said that they would want to watch the fight (response a). Students at both schools expressed some pleasure in watching other students fight, describing it as "fun," "exciting," "good action," and "heck'a cool." What is interesting about this reaction is that it shows an important contradiction related to student and, I believe, societal attitudes toward violence: While many are afraid of becoming victims of violence, they (we) may still derive vicarious pleasure from observing others engage in it.

Perhaps the most striking contrast between students at the two schools concerned their perception of safety in their neighborhood (statement 9). While only three students at Lowell said they felt safe when walking in their neighborhood, nearly all (26) of the students at Willard reported feeling safe. In fact, students at Lowell said repeatedly that they felt safer at school than anywhere else in their neighborhood. There was no similar split in the perception of students at Willard with respect to school and neighborhood safety. Students at Willard consistently reported feeling unafraid to walk home from school, or to play in parks or on the streets in their neighborhoods. Hence, while both groups of students might find some aspects of violence entertaining, the perception of the threat it posed to them varied significantly.

An examination of student attitudes and perceptions toward violence in school provides insight into how environmental factors influence students' sense of vulnerability and safety. In this study, students at both schools—the middle-class, suburban school and the low-income, inner-city school—shared important similarities with respect to their attitudes toward violence. For example, the majority of students at both schools thought of fights between students as exciting and entertaining. Also, the majority of students at both schools did not regard conflict resolution as an effective means to prevent fights when adults were not present.

Differences were evident among students at the two schools with respect to the taboo against snitching. Although most of the students seemed reluctant to report classmates who broke school rules, students at Willard were much more willing to report an armed student to an adult than were students at Lowell, who said they were more likely to mind their own business. The unwillingness to communicate with adults about a matter so important to the well-being and safety of students at Lowell suggests that the inability of the school to ensure the safety of its students makes them less likely to risk reporting their peers. Given the threat posed by the increased accessibility of weapons, the continuation of a taboo against snitching among young people adds considerably to the dangers schools and students face.

The difference in attitudes among students at the two schools also is directly related to their perception of the threat they face within the school and the environmental context. Students who believe that adults can and will protect them if they are threatened, are much more likely to call on adults to intervene and to prevent conflicts. They believe that fights can be avoided and their safety ensured by adults who are charged with securing the school environment. In contrast, if students feel vulnerable outside of school, they are likely to feel afraid within school as well because they may believe that there is no way for adults at school to protect them once they leave, and therefore no way to avoid the threat of violence. The most telling evidence of the inevitability of violence among students at Lowell came from the fact that none of the students thought that telling an adult was a viable strategy for avoiding a fight. This was true among both males and females, and even among students regarded by teachers as nonaggressive and nonviolent.

"AMERICA FEARS ITS YOUNG": THE EXAGGERATED FEAR OF VIOLENCE

In 1970, the rhythm and blues group Funkadelic released an album entitled "America Eats Its Young." Like many other young people at that time, I studied the psychedelic album cover and listened to the words to the songs over and over. I understood that the group wanted to draw attention to the young lives that were being devoured by the Vietnam War, by drug abuse and rampant violence, and by a growing alienation that was rooted in a rejection of the materialism of American society. It was also clear that rather than accepting responsibility for what was happening to its youth, Funkadelic wanted to call attention to the fact that America was blaming young people for problems they had not created.

If I were a songwriter, and if I were to write a song that captured public sentiment toward young people in America today, it would be called "America Fears Its Young." Increasingly, young people in American society are perceived as violent, dangerous, insolent, and uncontrollable (Russell, 1998). They are increasingly the object of paranoia and fear, even though it is far more likely for young people to be victimized by adults than the other way around (Donziger, 1996). Fear is greatest toward Black and Latino youth in the inner city. With media reports about gangs of youth engaging in unprovoked attacks against innocent bystanders, young people have come to embody the public's fears about uncontrolled violence in the inner city: fears that are used to justify extreme measures by police. Increasingly, America's fear of youth extends well beyond young people in the inner city. Skateboarders, punks, and even straight-laced, suburban teenagers can evoke anxiety among adults just by congregating in large numbers at shopping malls or in places deemed off limits to youth. Although this fear is often unfounded and irrational, there is considerable evidence that it is growing (Donziger, 1996).

The most obvious impact of this fear can be seen in the growing willingness of policy makers to lower the age at which youth offenders are prosecuted as adults (Hebert, 2002). In several states, juveniles as young as 13 can be prosecuted as adults for certain crimes (Blumstein & Wallman,

2000), and nearly half of the states have no exemption for juveniles in cases for which the death penalty can be invoked. Not long ago it was common for juveniles to be treated differently than adults on matters related to crime and punishment. Throughout much of the twentieth century, the prevailing wisdom was that delinquent adolescents should not be incarcerated with adults to prevent them from being both victimized and socialized into hardened criminals. Youth offenders were treated differently because we held onto the hope that, with moral guidance and education, some wayward youth could be rehabilitated (Ayers, 1997).

The fear of violence that is increasingly directed toward young people reflects a broader tendency in the United States to blame youth for problems that they did not create. For example, they are blamed for poor academic performance, and held accountable in numerous states by high-stakes exams that are being used as a requirement for graduation (Blasi, 2001). This is done even though it is widely known that most poor students attend schools that are unable to provide them with a quality education. Young people are blamed for drug abuse even though the vast majority of drug traffickers are adults, and they receive a disproportionate share of the blame for violence even though they have no control over the violence depicted in the media or the guns that circulate freely in their communities.

Because of their age and status as minors, young people, especially those who are poor and of color, are far more likely than any other segment of society to be victims of violence. Some, particularly Black and Latino males, are also more likely to be perpetrators of violence. The two phenomena—victimization and perpetration—are not unrelated; they reflect the fact that violence, like health, wealth, and political power, continues to be a central feature of the persistent inequality between racial groups in U.S. society (Earls, 1991).

When asked, the young people I've interviewed tell me that they learn about violence naturally: from fighting with siblings at home, from watching it on television or in the streets, or from experiencing it in skirmishes with classmates at school. When I speak to young people and encourage them to think about the roots and origins of violence, frequently they tell me that it is just part of American history. As one eighth grader at Willard put it, "I think the United States has won every war we've been in. We're good at violence. We're the strongest country in the world. I guess that's why we have so much of it here" (interview, March 14, 1993). Exposed to violence from the time they begin watching television, and inundated with rationalizations of violence by those with power and authority, it should come as no surprise that youth would be counted among its perpetrators and casualties (Gilligan, 1996).

I was reminded of how America's legacy of violence influences present-day issues when I took my family to see an exhibit called "Without Sanctuary: 100 years of Lynching." The exhibit was on display at the New York Historical Society and it featured photographs, newspaper articles, postcards, and "artifacts" (these included pieces of clothing, hair, and body parts) from lynchings that had occurred in various towns across the United States throughout the late nineteenth and early twentieth centuries. Aside from the physical cruelty meted out at these public executions—the quartering, tarring and feathering, and burning of Black corpses—the most disturbing aspects of the exhibit were the photos that captured the faces of spectators. While some depicted angry crowds enthusiastically engaged in vigilante justice, others showed what appeared to be family outings at which well-dressed observers casually gathered to observe and show support for these public displays of torture and carnage.

As I discussed these images with my children and tried to explain how the practice of lynching could have been tolerated for so long, I realized that at least some of the participants in the photos dated in the 1940s and 1950s probably were still alive. When I pointed this out, my 9-year-old son Antonio asked how those who participated in the lynchings had been affected by the experience. It was a good question, but one I could not answer. It was hard to imagine that one could partake in such brutal acts of violence and not be affected in some way. But as I tried to explain how the perpetrators of these acts of brutality had been affected, I could say neither that they were punished for their acts of violence nor that they were necessarily remorseful for their misdeeds.

There is a logic to violent behavior, but violence itself is often senseless. For example, since moving to Cambridge 2 years ago, I have had to contend with the fact that my eldest daughter Amaya frequently was subjected to harassment and physical attack from students at her new school, Cambridge Ringe and Latin High School. Despite my efforts to speak to adults about the matter to get them to intervene, I was unable to get school officials to protect her, especially since most of the fights occurred on her way home from school. Profoundly distraught over our decision to leave Berkeley and move to Cambridge, my daughter pleaded with me to allow her to return. She explained that as an outsider she would remain vulnerable because she had no friends to back her up. When I asked her to explain why the students did not like her, she explained, "These girls don't even know me and I don't know them. All they know is that I'm new, light skinned, and the boys think I'm cute. That's enough of a reason for them to hate me."

My daughter's vulnerability disturbs me, and my inability to protect her frustrates me. I have learned that dialogue with young people on issues like violence can provide a unique window through which to understand how they interpret and experience violence. Dialogue also can provide an opportunity for them to critique expressions of violence and become aware of the many ways in which it is sanctioned and glorified in our society. It is my hope that encouraging students to adopt a critical stance toward violence will enable more young people to reject the idea that violence is a legitimate means of resolving conflicts or dealing with declared enemies. A critical perspective may not protect young people from violence, but perhaps it can start to break the cycle of violence by undermining the logic that produces its normalization. As the ones who frequently embody our fears and concerns, I have found that young people have much to tell about their experience with violence and the lessons they learn about it from adults charged with protecting them.

One of my discoveries as I listened to young people express their thoughts on violence, safety, schools, and criminal justice, is that their views are often more honest and forthright than those of adults. The students at Lowell explained to me that adults either can't or won't protect them, so they learn to contend with it on their own. One girl at Lowell explained to me why she thought adults who urge kids to be nonviolent were hypocrites.

> Say if you was a teacher and you knew someone was after you and wanted to hurt you. And say you knew this person was serious because they had hurt other people before. And say no one believes you or they just tell you don't worry about it and to just stay out of trouble. Do you think the teacher is going to just put it out of her mind? Uh, huh. She's going to do something to make sure she don't get hurt, and if she can't find no one to protect her she's gonna protect herself. I don't care who you are, if you know people is trying to hurt you you're going to do what you can to protect yourself. That's the way it is for us, and that's the way it would be for them too.

IMPLICATIONS FOR PUBLIC POLICY AND DECISION MAKING

Given the ways in which many young people experience violence in their everyday lives, what should be the form and content of a reasonable set of policies created for the purpose of responding to their need for safety? Furthermore, how should such a policy take youth perspectives into account?

These are important but difficult questions. Their importance is derived both from the pressing nature of the problem and from the clear failure of traditional policy strategies. The question of how to respond creatively with policy is difficult because violence is not an isolated phenomenon that can be treated without consideration of the various factors that contribute to its occurrence. To devise policies that are effective in promoting public safety and that succeed in curtailing expressions of violence, would require policy makers to think comprehensively about the nature of the problem. While the cause of violence cannot be reduced simply to poverty, neglect, substance abuse, alienation, or uncontrolled aggression, any of these may operate as attendant factors shaping particular acts of aggression (Garbarino, 1999).

Our society has a poor track record of devising creative public policies on complex social issues. The current debate about violence, like the debate about crime in general, is framed largely by an escalating competition among politicians over how tough and how punitive laws should be. The idea that we also might need to devise policies that respond to the factors that contribute to violent behavior, is largely ignored. Creativity and deep thinking tend to be in short supply among policy makers on matters like these. In the short term at least, it seems as though we are more likely to continue to see policy shaped by the tendency to scapegoat and target the most vulnerable sectors of our society than we are to see visionary ideas.

Those who decry the current emphasis on punitive approaches to violence have a responsibility to enter the policy debate with reasonable ideas and viable alternatives. Protesting police brutality or the construction of new prisons and criticizing the thoughtlessness of zero tolerance policies in schools have done little to alter the present course of policy on these issues. It is also a mistake to allow concern for the excessive punishments meted out against perpetrators of violence to overshadow concern about the victims of it.

In order to be taken seriously, those who object to current policy must move beyond critique and take the step of putting forward alternative policies that address both the need for safety and the need to address the threat of violence. Educators must even go a step further. As the ones charged with ensuring the safety of children, we must find ways to make schools safe even as we work to implement alternative disciplinary policies that are more humane and less punitive. This requires that we enter the murky waters of partial solutions, dealing with a criminal justice system that too often metes out unequal justice. Although the courts may never be capable of administering "blind justice," and although schools are a long way from becoming truly equitable, these are the arenas we must work within. To seriously contemplate policies that can be adopted to support nonviolence, we must figure out how to work within the limits of what is possible at this historical moment, even as we also push and prod to extend even further the limits of what is possible. The challenge is to figure out how to be heard and taken seriously within debates over policy, rather than being content with the irrelevance that comes from being comfortably planted on the margins with other critics.

Once we have entered the fray of policy debates and started to work toward the development of enlightened policies and practices, then we confront the difficulty involved in educating public officials, the media, and the general public on the need to rethink assumptions about the nature of the problem. This is no small challenge. Prevailing assumptions about the nature of violence (that it is perpetrated by bad people) and the widely held beliefs about what it takes to curtail it (locking up more people) are formidable obstacles. Unless such views can be challenged effectively, it is unlikely that creative alternatives will ever be considered.

As hard as this kind of educational work may be, it is not impossible. In fact, it is the failure of current policy approaches to adequately address the public's desire for safety that actually creates the opportunity for alternatives to be considered. An example from the Oakland public schools reveals how this can work. During the late 1990s several schools in Oakland experienced interracial violence between African American and Latino students, some of which resulted in significant injuries as students began arming themselves. As might be expected, the school district responded by calling on the police department to quell disturbances when they occurred. Eventually, the police department began to express frustration with these tactics and openly acknowledged that focusing exclusively on security to respond to the problem was not effective and would not prevent future disturbances.

Recognizing the opportunity created by the frustration of the police and the unimaginative response of the school district, Youth Together (YT), a newly created youth advocacy organization, stepped into the policy void. Pointing out that many of the young people involved in interracial violence had no knowledge of the history or culture of the groups they were fighting against, YT called for the development of student-led, multiracial teams that would be trained to conduct educational workshops for their peers. As YT began working with students to address interracial violence, it also organized students to lead school change campaigns, based on the assumption that greater multiracial cooperation could be achieved by providing students with the opportunity to work together in pursuit of their common interests.

Faced with the failure of its own reactive policies, the district supported the YT strategy, which, given the policy void, proved to be relatively successful. For example, at Castlemont High School in east Oakland, the site that had experienced the greatest number of incidents of racial violence, students organized several successful teach-ins under the banner "One Land, One People." These student-led events provided an opportunity for students to learn about the history and culture of their peers and to openly discuss issues that had been the source of conflict. Out of these discussions, YT initiated a school change campaign focused on the need for a health center and cafeteria. This initiative brought a larger number of students from different backgrounds together over a sustained period in an effort that required frequent meetings, protests against district and county officials, and lobbying of other public officials.

The experience of groups like Youth Together shows that under the right conditions it may be possible to influence the direction and nature of public policy. The YT experience is significant because the solutions that were developed were conceived by students themselves, and although YT received support from adults, the efforts were led and organized by students. This kind of approach is a clear example of how the perspectives of young people can be incorporated and put into action. In the final section of this chapter I will draw from my work with schools and youth organizations in the San Francisco Bay Area to put forward six basic principles that I believe should be reflected in policy positions on issues related to violence.

1. Develop strategies that address the underlying causes of violence.

While it may not be possible to isolate the causes of particular incidents of violence and to devise interventions for each of them, it should be possible to develop strategies that address the most salient factors that contribute to patterns of violent behavior. Such an approach is more likely to be effective at preventing violent behavior than is mere reliance on the threat of punishment. Adolescents generally, and low-income youth especially, often have an ambiguous conception of their future (Garbarino, 1999), and for this reason the threat of a long prison sentence or a life in poverty may not be enough to positively influence behavior. Research on teen pregnancy and college attendance has shown that helping young people to cultivate a realistic sense of how they can improve their lives in the future can be an effective means of helping them to change their behavior in the present (Luker, 1996; Steinberg, 1996).

A number of very successful youth development programs take such an approach. For example, the Real Alternative Program based in San Francisco and Oakland, and the Omega Boys Club located at the Portrero Hills housing projects in San Francisco provide comprehensive services to young people whose living circumstances have placed them at risk of violence and other hardships. These nationally recognized programs provide tutoring, mentoring, job training and placement, counseling, college tours and advising, and field trips that increase the exposure of the young people they serve. Evaluations of both programs have shown that young people who participate are less likely to engage in violence and more likely to graduate from high school and attend college than young people from similar backgrounds who do not participate in such programs (Noguera, 1995a). Given the small number of young people served by such programs, there is a pressing need for policy makers to provide funding for replication and expansion of these kinds of services and to actively support such strategies as a central element of any violence prevention policy initiative.

2. Involve youth directly in the development of short-term and long-term solutions.

When urgent violent situations arise that require an immediate response, young people should be provided, if possible, the opportunity to engage in the process of thinking through temporary and long-term solutions. Although such efforts at inclusion require additional time, the ideas that are produced are more likely to be supported by young people and therefore more likely to be effective when implemented. Young people often have insights that differ substantially from those of adults. If young people are encouraged to share their views regarding how to respond to violent incidents, there is greater likelihood that more creative and effective strategies will be developed.

For example, following a stabbing at Castlemont High School in Oakland in 1993, students were invited to participate in a discussion with district officials over what should be done to restore a sense of order and safety at the school. One of the recommendations that most surprised the adults was the suggestion that all students wear temporary identification badges during school hours (the assailant was a nonstudent who entered the school illegally). In Oakland, the idea that students wear ID badges was loaded with a history of controversy because the last time such a proposal had been made it led to the assassination of former superintendent Marcus Foster by the Symbionese Liberation Army (SLA) in 1974. In addition to calling for ID badges, students also suggested that security officers be instructed not to harass students wearing badges when they were walking through the halls. As a longer-term solution, students called for meetings among Black and Latino parents because they believed that unless adults had the opportunity to get to know one another, students would continue to act on the distrust they learned at home and the fighting would not cease.

As it turned out, the short-term strategy succeeded in restoring a climate of safety at the school. Students willingly wore their ID badges and there were no confrontations created by increased security at the school. However, no action was taken to promote communication among parents. Even though it was generally known that the steady growth of the Mexican population was producing tensions in what traditionally had been an African American neighborhood, no efforts were made to find ways to increase contact between adults from these two communities. Once the immediate crisis was over, city and school district officials went back to ignoring the tensions that were building in east Oakland, and not surprisingly violence between Black and Mexican students continued to plague schools there in subsequent years.

3. Provide students with a genuine role in school reform processes.

Efforts to promote school safety should not be divorced from overall efforts to improve the quality of education provided. Although many urban schools have undertaken some sort of reform, it is very uncommon for students to be provided with the opportunity to become involved in meaningful ways as changes are discussed and considered. The failure of most reforms to improve the academic outcomes of students is widely recognized (Fine, 1993; Payne, 2001). However, in most cases, failure is attributed to some weakness on the part of the adults leading the initiative, inconsistency in the implementation of reforms, or an amorphous claim that schools lack the capacity to implement change. The fact that student perspectives on school are rarely incorporated into the reform process generally does not even show up in most analyses of reform failure.

Sarason (1971) wrote that any effort to alter the structure or organization of schools without consideration of the culture of schools would be doomed to failure. Although Sarason's remarks were focused primarily on the need for reforms to change the beliefs, attitudes, and practices of adults–teachers, parents, administrators—the same point could be made with regard to students. As the recipients of schooling, students often perceive conditions in school differently than the adults who work there. While they may be less attuned to the complexities of curriculum reform or educational policy, they often have very clear perspectives on issues such as school discipline, grading, teacher–student relations, and other issues that are central to everyday life in schools.

While students may not immediately question the more subtle aspects of the socialization they experience in schools, they can be encouraged to do so when conditions for open discussion are created. If we are genuinely interested in finding ways to increase student achievement and engagement in school, then student input and involvement must be recognized as legitimate and important. Especially in relation to issues such as school safety, sexual harassment, or disciplinary policies, the voices of students must be heard if those who see themselves as responsible for monitoring such issues genuinely hope to succeed in their efforts.

One brief example may be useful for illustrating how student participation can be effectively incorporated into the school change process. In the early 1990s, administrators and faculty at East Campus, a continuation high school in Berkeley, were considering whether they should close the campus during the lunch period. Discussion over the issue had been sparked by a growing awareness that large numbers of students were not returning to school after lunch each day. As the staff discussed what could be done to keep kids in school, they were mindful of the fact that efforts to create closed campuses at other schools in the Bay Area had sparked heated conflicts from students who resented the imposed confinement.

To avoid this possibility, the principal came up with the novel idea of discussing the issue openly in a forum with students. The school's relatively small size (enrollment of 150) made it possible for a school-wide forum to be held. During the forum, the staff learned that there were two primary reasons why students left school during lunch and never returned. The first was that students felt that the food sold at the school was terrible, and they preferred food that could be purchased at nearby stores. Additionally, because school ended at 1:30, by the time lunch was over, only an hour of class time remained. Given that many of the students worked after school, returning for an hour made little sense since they were already off campus and their classes were hardly compelling enough to provide a reason to return.

In response to the issues raised by the students, the principal came up with another novel idea: The campus would be closed but no fence would be erected. This meant that students would no longer be permitted to leave campus at lunch, but enforcement of the rule would be based on voluntary compliance. In addition, he recruited a group of volunteers to plan the development of a new school diner that would serve meals that students found attractive. The most radical feature of the plan called for the creation of a new dining area on the campus, where in a complete break with most school traditions, students and staff would eat together during the lunch period.

The most significant thing about the success of this exercise in collaboration is that East Campus was a school for "bad" students: a site designated to serve students who had been dismissed from other schools due to poor attendance or disciplinary problems. If it was possible to collaborate with students like those at East Campus on issues pertaining to school governance, it should be possible to risk greater student involvement in reform at other schools as well.

4. Promote a climate of respect by responding quickly and consistently to minor infractions.

Advocates of community-based policing have suggested that the presence of abandoned cars and graffiti, public consumption of alcohol, and street-level drug dealing all contribute to an environment in which major crimes are more likely (Currie, 1985). They argue that by responding aggressively to relatively minor infractions, police officers can reduce the likelihood that major crimes will be perpetrated. Similarly, the highly acclaimed Ten Point program that was created to reduce youth homicides in Boston is based on a collaboration between police and probation officers, church leaders, and community residents. Together, members of this coalition have reduced incidents of violence among juveniles by proactively responding to minor offenses such as marijuana possession and curfew violations committed by juveniles on probation (Patterson, 1998).

Researchers argue that these methods of policing are effective because they create a climate in which more serious crimes are less likely to occur.[8] Sampson (1998) has argued that community policing methods also can facilitate the generation of social capital, which can be instrumental in deterring crime. He suggests that communities where residents are connected to one another by overlapping social networks and local participation in formal and informal organizations "are better able to realize common values and maintain effective social controls" (p. 15).

Strategies similar to those utilized for the purpose of promoting neighborhood safety also can be applied in schools to prevent disruptive or violent behavior. Many of the schools that succeed in creating a safe environment without excessive emphasis on security (Sandler, 2000) take an aggressive stance toward discipline that is similar to the approach described here. However, what distinguishes the approach of these schools from that typically taken in public schools is that their disciplinary policies are not merely punitive, but are also preventive. Rather than suspending students with poor attendance and poor academic performance, these schools utilize other measures to address misbehavior. Preventive approaches to punishment are further enhanced when they are combined with counseling and regular communication with parents.

When schools respond rapidly, effectively, and consistently to offenses that often are treated as minor infractions, such as cutting class, sexual harassment, vandalism, graffiti, and hateful and disrespectful language, major offenses will be less likely to occur. This is because responding to minor offenses sends the strong message that any attempt to undermine the values of a school community will be addressed immediately. In this way assertive responses to minor infractions can serve as a means of reinforcing the values and mission of a school and help to create a climate where respect for learning and the rights of others are maintained as prevailing community norms.

5. Adopt a preventive approach to discipline utilizing strategies that encourage students to take responsibility for their behavior and learn from their mistakes.

The most common form of punishments used by schools to control behavior rely on various forms of exclusion, humiliation, and, when resources permit, individualized therapy. With the advent of zero tolerance, the overall direction of school disciplinary policies has been toward increasingly severe forms of punishment. A study conducted by Sandler (2000) identified a number of school districts where suspensions of kindergarten-aged children were not uncommon. In most school districts there is also a high correlation between academic performance and the students who most frequently are targeted for discipline. Throughout the United States a distinct pattern emerges: A disproportionate number of those disciplined are Black, male, from low-income families, and identified as either low achievers or developmentally disabled (Johnson, Boyden, & Pitts, 2000).

Although there is little if any evidence that the kinds of punishment most frequently used by schools have the effect of deterring or modifying behavior, these methods of punishment continue to be the only approaches used by most schools. In fact, with the advent of zero tolerance policies, the number of students suspended and expelled from schools actually has increased in several school districts in the past few years (Johnson, Boyden, & Pitts, 2000). In the current political climate the efficacy of suspending truant and low-achieving students is hardly ever questioned, nor are many people challenging the merits of dispatching expelled students unsupervised to the streets.

In place of traditional disciplinary measures, a number of psychologists have called for the use of different methods to prevent classroom disruptions and to modify student behavior (Garbarino, 1999). Some of the strategies that have been recommended include various forms of community service, mandatory after-school tutoring, Saturday school, public apologies, and retribution for victims. The basic idea underlying these methods is that discipline should not be used to exacerbate poor attendance or academic performance. Rather, whenever possible, students should be encouraged to learn from mistakes, and punishment should be designed to encourage reflection on their behavior. Finally, for those students whose personality or family circumstance require greater intervention, counselors and case workers should be utilized to provide individual attention and, if necessary, placement in alternative learning environments.

Such approaches strengthen the social capital of a community because they reinforce its values and the sense of mutual accountability. Of course, assertive discipline alone does not reduce the likelihood of violence or disruptions in the school environment. More important, it is an overarching climate of respect that permeates the culture of a school and guides social interactions that ultimately is the most important element of a safe and orderly environment.

6. Provide numerous opportunities for students to become more deeply engaged in school and in activities that further their development.

Several studies have shown that students who are actively involved in school activities are more likely to do well academically and less likely to get into trouble (Steinberg, 1996). This is also the case for students who are involved in extracurricular activities such as sports, music, theater, clubs, or student government. Similarly, teachers who are able to intellectually engage their students are less likely to experience disruptions and other behavior problems. As one veteran teacher told me when I asked how she managed to maintain such an orderly classroom in a school that had a reputation for being "out of control":

> My students know I don't play. When they're with me it's all about the work and they respond. They have to, because they know I ain't even gonna send them to the office. If they act out in my classroom they're gonna answer to me. And they don't want that. No, in my classroom work is not optional. That's the key: Keep them busy learning and you'll never have any problems with behavior. (interview, November 5, 1993)

There are several reasons why deepening student engagement in school is an effective strategy for promoting safety. The most obvious reason is that when students are busy with schoolwork or extracurricular activities, they simply have less time to get into trouble. Several clubs, especially most sports, require students to maintain minimal grades and to participate in tutorial programs. Students also may be required to spend a great deal of time after school and on weekends participating in an activity or club. With less idle time, students have fewer opportunities to engage in behavior that may be harmful to themselves or others.

Deepening student engagement in school also works as a strategy for promoting safety because it taps into students' intrinsic motivations to learn and achieve. Most research on learning shows that schools typically rely most heavily on extrinsic motivation (e.g., grades, awards, recognition, etc.) to enlist students to become academically engaged. Such strategies are generally most effective with middle-class, college-oriented students who perceive the external rewards as valuable and desirable. Lower-class students tend to be less motivated by external rewards because they are less likely to obtain them. Schools and programs that manage to tap into the intrinsic interests and desires of students tend to be successful with all kinds of students because the acquisition of knowledge, skills, and experience is perceived as meaningful by the students.

RESEARCH AND SCHOOL SAFETY

The complexity of the factors influencing manifestations of violence in schools compels educators to devise policy solutions to avoid the simplistic thinking that tends to characterize mainstream discourse on these issues. The challenge for activists and academics who seek to radically alter the direction of policy is to find ways to ensure that our perspectives, like those of the youth, are heard and taken seriously.

Research can play a major role in this regard, because if empirical evidence can be used to support particular policy positions, there is greater likelihood that they will be considered. Although traditional methods may be employed in carrying out this research, the need to challenge and problematize prevailing assumptions about the nature of violence should make this research different from what academicians typically produce. That difference should show up not just in the orientation of the work, but, more important, in its presentation and dissemination. Academic journals and conferences certainly should not be the only venues at which this kind of work is presented and discussed. School board and city council meetings, community centers, and school assemblies are just some of the places where research on youth violence should be heard, analyzed, and critiqued.

The challenge before us is great. The fear of violence and actual manifestations of it are transforming our society into one grand penal colony. In this prison, the inmates are not the only captives. Those who barricade themselves in their homes behind bars, security systems, and pit bulls also experience a loss of freedom. So too do those who are no longer able to walk on the streets at night or who fear allowing their children to play in the park, ride their bicycles on the street, or walk to the store on their own.

We need not accept this situation as our fate. However, if we truly seek to create a different future, one that is more peaceful and nonviolent than the present, we must actively go about creating it. That is a challenge for researchers, activists, young people, and everyone else who still has the ability to imagine and envision another reality.

CHAPTER 7

Conclusion: What It Will Take to Improve America's Urban Public Schools

Throughout this book I have tried to make it clear that it will not be possible to improve urban public schools until our society is willing to address the issues and problems confronting the children and families in the communities where schools are located. Even though there are a small number of schools that manage to serve children well despite the harshness of conditions in inner-city neighborhoods (Education Trust, 2002; Sizemore, 1988), these will continue to be the rare exceptions. Unless concerted action is taken to alleviate the hardships and suffering related to poverty and to spur development that can lead to economic and social stability for communities and families, little change in the character and quality of urban schools in the United States will occur. Given the long history of failure in urban public schools, this point should be obvious. Yet, despite the track record of failure, we continue to hear slogans from the federal government like "Leave No Child Behind" without the political will needed to realize this goal.

Stating this obvious fact does not really help in furthering the development of solutions. The action required—generating capital to bring economic development and social stability to urban areas—is relatively clear and straightforward, but the challenge of doing so is more complicated than it might seem. Local problems are frequently manifestations of larger societal problems, and as I've shown in Chapter 5, concentrated poverty severely limits the ability of communities to control and improve the quality of their schools. Larger issues such as the availability of housing and jobs, the location of industry, or the state of the regional or national economy have an impact on local conditions. Often, the effects of these larger forces cannot be mitigated at the local level. For example, because of the closure of several General Motors manufacturing plants in the 1970s and 1980s, the city of Flint, Michigan, is now bankrupt and its local government has been taken over by the state of Michigan (Casey, 2002). All observers acknowledge that there is little that local government or the state's intervention can do to reverse downward trends in the city unless action is taken to address the economic roots of the problem. Unemployment rates in Flint are three times higher than the state average, and not surprisingly, Flint's schools are ranked among the worst in the state. Undoubtedly, it will be nearly impossible to improve the quality of public schools in Flint unless help is provided in restoring the viability of the local economy and bringing stability to the community.

I learned about the limitations of local government firsthand while working as assistant to the Mayor of Berkeley during the 1980s and while serving as an elected member of the school board in the early 1990s. Through direct experience I learned that even with a relatively progressive local government in an affluent city, it was nearly impossible to solve problems such as chronic unemployment, drug trafficking, or homelessness. Although these were Berkeley's problems, their origin did not lie in the city but elsewhere—in a porous national border, in failed state and national policies for the mentally ill, in the lack of affordable housing, and in the flight of blue-collar jobs from the region. The situation was just as difficult in the school district, where declining revenue from the state required the school board to make deep and painful cuts in academic programs in order to balance the budget. At times we were able to rally the community around efforts to generate local funding for schools: through a bond measure and parcel tax, an initiative to save music programs,[1] or an innovative approach to address juvenile crime.[2] However, even when we could muster the will and the resources to address an issue, it was difficult to develop these into long-term solutions because of a variety of factors that could not be controlled at the local level.

The most disturbing fact about the persistence of failure is that the wealth and resources needed to support the work of schools are there. In an affluent region like the Bay Area, prospects for generating resources to address social and economic problems should be greater, even in high-poverty cities like Oakland and Richmond, than in less prosperous areas of the United States. As an international center for biotechnology, communications, semiconductors, and finance, and with two of the largest research universities (UC Berkeley and Stanford) in the United States located there, it should be possible for schools to receive the technical and financial support they need. Schools in such an affluent region should never lack qualified teachers or suffer from a shortage of paper, textbooks, or computers. The fact that these shortages exist in Bay Area schools is a clear indication that the ties between schools and public and private institutions are not well developed. In the Bay Area and throughout the United States, we must stop pretending that public schools can solve the problems they face on their own. As I argued in Chapter 5, building civic capacity in support of public education is essential if the potential of the region is to be realized.

The problems I've analyzed in this book—racial inequality, poverty, and violence—certainly are not unique to the four cities of the Bay Area. Nor are they problems that typically are thought of as educational issues. These are societal issues for which a national strategy is needed if conditions in schools and communities in urban areas are to significantly improve. There is a vast body of research in education that has shown the importance of addressing environmental issues to solve educational problems (Coleman et al., 1966; Dryfoos, 2001; Kozol, 1991), but rarely have we seen a concerted effort made to do so. Instead, policy makers and occasionally educators have tended to treat these environmental issues as though they were beyond the realm of education and have acted as if it were possible to improve schools without taking them on. Given the dismal record of failure in efforts to improve urban schools across the United States, it makes sense to try something new.

A new approach must be based on a framework that links educational issues to environmental issues, one that responds to the problems confronting schools in concert with those facing the local community. A small number of schools across the United States are doing this already by offering a broad range of services to students and their families on site (Dryfoos, 2001). There are also a small but growing number of Beacon schools that remain open 10–12 hours a day and provide a safe haven for children (McLaughlin, 2000). Such approaches are showing signs of promise but they need to be significantly expanded so that larger numbers of children can be served. Anything less is unlikely to bring about the changes that are so desperately needed. We must stop pretending that we can avoid confronting and addressing urban conditions as we try to devise strategies for improving urban schools.

The call for a more comprehensive approach to addressing the issues confronting urban public schools is based on more than just wishful thinking. There is a vast body of research that shows that addressing basic human needs is essential to furthering other forms of development (National Research Council, 2002). Psychologist Abraham Maslow (1962) has shown through his research that unless basic human needs are met (e.g., security, housing, nutrition), it is difficult for children to develop and grow up to be healthy, well-adjusted adults. Similar arguments have been made for developing societies, such as those in the Sub-Saharan Africa that are besieged by civil war, food shortages, and debilitating diseases. Without assistance in bringing relief from these pressing concerns, it is unlikely that such societies will succeed in improving their economies, developing democratic institutions, and meeting the needs of their citizens (Sachs, 1989). The same arguments have been made for children and schools in economically depressed areas in the United States (Schorr, 1997).

Although they are located within the wealthiest nation on earth, many inner-city communities have not been able to attract the capital needed to bring about economic growth and social stability. In fact, on a number of indicators—infant mortality, homicide, and the rate of HIV infection—conditions in economically depressed urban areas of the United States often rival conditions in the Third World. For example, the infant mortality rate of Oakland surpasses that of Kingston, Jamaica, and the rate of HIV infection in New York City and Los Angeles is higher than that of Sao Paolo and Mexico City (Andrews & Fonseca, 1995). Proximity to wealth does not ensure access to wealth, resources, technology, or services. Even when impoverished communities are surrounded by wealth, as is the case in small cities like Poughkeepsie, New York, North Chicago, or East Palo Alto and Marin City, California, it has still not been possible to attract capital that might lead to development.

The economic empowerment zones created by the federal government in the 1980s, which remains the primary strategy for addressing urban poverty today, have largely not succeeded in luring private industry and jobs to the inner city. Although there are a few isolated examples of successful projects, the policy has had a very poor track record in revitalizing and bringing sustained improvements to the poorest communities (Gittel & Thompson, 2001). Even in Los Angeles where promises to rebuild the city were made following the devastation caused by the riots of 1991, there is little evidence of improvement in the neighborhoods with the highest levels of poverty (Valle & Torres, 2000). The track record of public and private efforts to improve the quality of life in impoverished urban areas is poor, and increasingly this is not even an issue that politicians raise during campaigns for public office. Urban poverty, like congested highways, homelessness, drug abuse, and the depletion of the ozone layer, increasingly are accepted as major problems that simply cannot be solved.

This was not always the case. In the 1960s and early 1970s both Republicans and Democrats campaigned on promises to eliminate poverty and joblessness (Phillips, 1983). Although the most ambitious and far-reaching social programs were created during the Johnson administration as part of his Great Society initiative, even the more conservative Nixon administration promised to create full employment through enlightened private-sector initiatives (Heyman, 2000; Phillips, 1983). Speaking in an address to the nation in the wake of several race riots that were raging in cities throughout the country in 1967, President Lyndon B. Johnson made the following call for reform:

> The only genuine, long-range solution for what has happened lies in an attack—mounted at every level—upon the conditions that breed despair and violence. All of us know what those conditions are: ignorance, discrimination, slums, poverty, disease, not enough jobs. We should attack these conditions—not just because we are frightened by conflict, but because we are fired by conscience. We should attack them simply because there is no other way to achieve a decent and orderly society in America. (Harris & Wicker, 1988, p. 484)

These were the promises and the connections that were made during an earlier era. It was an era characterized by a sense of optimism that a great nation could solve even the most pressing problems. Since the early 1980s, there has been no similar vision or commitment to fighting poverty or reviving America's urban centers. Surprisingly, although for the past 10 to 15 years there has been a sustained interest in improving the quality of education, this interest has not prompted policy makers to rethink the approach taken to address the issues and problems confronting economically depressed inner-city communities. It is widely known that these are the areas where educational problems are most acute and the conditions in schools most severe. Yet, policy makers continue to pretend that it is possible to improve the quality of education provided in these communities without simultaneously responding to the social and economic issues within the local environment, or that a policy gimmick like vouchers or charter schools will solve this problem. For children who are poorly nourished, sick, neglected, and abused, neither vouchers, charters, nor increased academic standards and accountability will provide the educational opportunities and support that they need and deserve.

To a large degree, the retreat from more comprehensive approaches to addressing urban problems is ideological and reflects the low priority assigned to addressing the needs of the poor in the United States. The movement away from the interventionist policies of the 1960s began during the Carter administration at a time when cutbacks in social programs were rationalized as necessary because the economy was in recession and the federal government was faced with large budget deficits (Katz, 1989; Pinkney, 1984). Although it acted reluctantly, the Carter administration began cutting social programs like the Comprehensive Employment Training Act and enacted the first reductions in food stamps and housing assistance. Such programs could be treated as expendable and easily trimmed partially because they served constituencies that wielded little influence over government, and because increasingly social programs were regarded as "hand-outs" to the undeserving poor (Block, Cloward, Ehrenreich, & Piven, 1987).

With the election of Ronald Reagan in 1980, retrenchment in social services supported by the federal government accelerated. Eliminating social programs that served the "undeserving poor" and wiping out all other vestiges of liberalism became a central feature of the administration (Katz, 1989). During the 1980s, the Reagan and Bush administrations drew on the support of conservative scholars (Loury, 1995; Murray, 1984) who argued that social programs contributed to dependency among the poor and actually served to maintain poverty. Castigating welfare queens and poverty pimps who were accused of cheating the system, and liberals who made excuses for the pathological behavior of the poor, conservatives demanded an end to the policies of indulgence, and called on the poor to help themselves.

The legacy of the Reagan Revolution has endured even during periods such as the 1990s when the prosperity of the national economy produced a budgetary surplus and the United States was led by President Clinton, who claimed to be genuinely interested in fighting poverty. Instead of a new set of Great Society programs, the Clinton administration enacted welfare reform—"ending welfare as we know it"—a political feat that even the Reagan and Bush administrations were unable to accomplish. Under Clinton, the idea that poverty could be eliminated by reducing federal subsidies to the poor and extolling the virtues of hard work and self-help became the essence of federal social welfare policy once again.

For all of these reasons, our society is less willing to tackle the broad array of problems related to poverty in urban areas today. Even as indicators of policy failure in urban areas have become more apparent—with crime, unemployment, poverty, and incarceration rates still extremely high or rising in many urban areas (Heyman, 2000)—a change of course in federal policy appears unlikely. Thus far President George W. Bush's proclaimed commitment to "compassionate conservatism" has not produced any new, comprehensive national initiatives to address urban poverty. Although he has pledged to "Leave No Child Behind," the needs of many children continue to be neglected and child poverty rates in the United States continue to be the highest among Western industrialized nations (Terry, 1995). Only one out of seven children in the United States has access to quality preschool programs, and over 30% lack medical insurance coverage (Schorr, 1997). Even Head Start, which has been acclaimed as one of the most successful federal programs (Andrews & Fonseca, 1995), has not been significantly expanded. We know from research that the cognitive and neurological development that occurs during infancy plays a crucial role in long-term developmental outcomes for children (Diamond, 1999). Yet, we continue to treat child care workers as babysitters and provide minimal training and abysmally low wages to those who do this vital work.

The sad fact about the lack of interest in and commitment to social welfare policies is that some members of the current administration clearly know that more is needed. Prior to being appointed, Secretary of Education Rod Paige endorsed a call for the federal government to address the problems confronting urban public schools as part of a national urban policy.[3] Mr. Paige was widely regarded as an effective superintendent in the Houston Independent School District, and his leadership has been credited for the significant gains in student achievement that occurred there during the 1990s (Council of Great City Schools, 2001). However, Mr. Paige no longer endorses a call for a comprehensive urban policy, and there is no indication that anything like it will emerge from the current administration. Instead, voucher programs that promise to enable poor parents to escape struggling schools and testing to hold schools accountable are held out as the primary policy initiatives of the administration (No Child Left Behind Act, 2002). Failure to undertake a more ambitious effort to improve conditions in impoverished urban areas means that schools serving poor children will continue to suffer. They will suffer because the children and families they serve suffer, and schools cannot alleviate the suffering by themselves.

WORKING WITHIN THE LIMITS AND POSSIBILITIES OF CHANGE

In Chapter 1, I suggested that those who have not given up hope in the possibility of improving urban schools could benefit by adopting Paulo Freire's (1972) approach to viewing the problems confronting these institutions as "limit situations." Such an approach requires that our hopes in the possibility for change be tempered by a strong dose of pragmatism, given how formidable the problems that need to be addressed are. It starts with the recognition that while sweeping solutions to the problems confronting urban schools and communities are needed, they are not likely to be enacted at this time. Instead, partial solutions that alleviate the most severe hardships must be devised based on an understanding of the limits and possibilities of the historic period we are living in. This is not the same as working for piecemeal reforms or introducing palliative treatments to make poverty less painful.[4] Rather, even as we attempt to figure out how to take action in particular urban schools and communities, we must never lose sight of the need to work toward more ambitious goals—justice, equality, and genuine empowerment of the most downtrodden and marginalized citizens. For this to occur, each act of gradualism must be based on a willingness to engage in a process of change that aims at transforming relationships between those who have power and those who do not. Unless this transformation occurs, it is unlikely that even ambitious reforms will lead to lasting change.

Let me offer a few examples to explain how this might work by citing cases that demonstrate how it is working already on small (interpersonal) and even not so small (community) levels. My friend and colleague, Paul Kurose, an exceptional math teacher and a committed educator, described a situation he encountered with a student while working at Castlemont High School in east Oakland. One of his tenth-grade students, a quiet girl named Jamila, showed considerable academic promise based on her performance in his class.[5] However, she rarely turned in her homework and frequently missed several days of school. As a caring teacher, Paul pressed her, insisting that she turn in her work and attend class regularly. He did so out of concern for her education and welfare, and he did so persistently, thinking that his constant pressure would produce the change in behavior that he hoped for. Finally, exasperated by Paul's urgings, Jamila explained why she failed to turn in so many assignments: "Do you think that you would be able to do your work if every night your mother was bringing a different man into your house to have sex and smoke crack?"

Jamila's clarification of her situation shocked him. He had no idea that this student was coping with such a difficult situation at home and his initial response was to back off. Repulsed by what he heard and having difficulty imagining how he would have put up with such a circumstance, he gained new respect and appreciation for the fact that she made it to school at all. However, rather than pulling back altogether out of fear that deeper involvement would entangle him in this student's difficult life, Paul thought about how he could serve as a source of support to this needy student. To address the fact that Jamila was unable to work at home, he offered to provide her tutoring after school in his classroom so that she would have a place to complete assignments. Then he helped her to enroll in the Mathematics, Engineering, and Science Achievement program (MESA), a program sponsored by the University of California that provides minority students with extra counseling and academic enrichment to help them gain admission to 4-year colleges. MESA offered Saturday classes and a residential summer program that would give Jamila a chance to get away from her home. Finally, Paul told Jamila that if she ever needed help, she should call him and he would do what he could to assist her. His efforts on behalf of this student paid off. Despite the tremendous obstacles she faced, Jamila graduated from high school and was admitted to a local public university.

The actions taken by my friend Paul Kurose are illustrative of what it means to work within the limits and possibilities of the current situation in urban schools and communities. Although he could not save Jamila from the depressing situation she was in, Paul took steps to help her to eventually find a way to get out of it herself. Instead of retreating when he heard about the terrible situation she faced in her home, Paul extended himself and offered to be a source of support. He could not offer an immediate solution to the situation she faced at home, but he thought long and hard about partial solutions that could bring hope and long-term relief to the student.

Another example of acting within the limits and possibilities of the urban condition, comes from the Duddley neighborhood of Roxbury in Boston (Medoff & Sklar, 1994). For years, Duddley had been one of the most depressed and crime-ridden sections of the city. Although it once served as the summer home of the Governor of Massachussets, by the 1970s Duddley had become a neighborhood better known for drug dealing, illegal dumping, and drive-by shootings. Duddley was home to a diverse population of African Americans, Cape Verdeans, Dominicans, and Puerto Rican immigrants, and elderly Irish Americans who had never left the neighborhood. Despite their differences, all of the residents shared one thing in common: They were poor and lacked the ability to do anything about the continued deterioration of their neighborhood.

In 1980, the Riley Foundation, a local charitable organization, decided that it wanted to take the initiative to help improve conditions in the Duddley neighborhood. The foundation sponsored a community meeting at which it announced its intention to spend $3 million developing a plan for the community to address some of its most pressing problems—crime, housing deterioration, and the lack of social services. To the foundation's surprise, rather than being welcomed with open arms, the community responded with anger and rejected the offer of assistance. For the residents who attended the meeting, the foundation's offer represented yet another attempt by outsiders to take advantage of their powerlessness through a paternalistic display of charity. There was uniform agreement among the residents that any effort to improve the community must be led by the residents themselves.

To its credit, the Riley Foundation did not leave with hurt feelings and abandon the neighborhood. Instead, it decided that rather than trying to lead the revitalization effort, it would take a backseat role and allow the residents to lead. The foundation worked with residents to create a community development corporation, the Duddley Street Neighborhood Initiative (DSNI), that would lead the improvement effort. Over the next 20 years, DSNI worked with the foundation, city government, and several private corporations to address the chronic problems facing the Duddley neighborhood. Because of DSNI's commitment to a democratic, grassroots initiative, progress was slow but steady. By all accounts, DSNI's efforts have succeeded remarkably in transforming and revitalizing the community (Gratz & Mintz, 1998). Hundreds of new affordable houses have been constructed in the area, parks and neighborhood services have been restored, and several small businesses, including banks, have returned. Not only is the Duddley neighborhood a healthier, safer, and more vibrant community today than it was 20 years ago, but it represents one of only a few cases in the United States of an economically depressed area that has been significantly improved without displacing the poor people who live there. Most importantly, these improvements have been made under the leadership and direction of the residents.

The case of DSNI and the Duddley neighborhood represents another example of how working within the limits and possibilities can produce meaningful change in urban areas. Like my friend Paul Kurose, the Riley Foundation refused to back off when its initial offer of aid was rejected. Instead, the foundation learned how to work with residents to provide concrete assistance to alleviate hardships and ultimately to empower those it sought to help. Both examples represent partial solutions: Paul's student still had a drug-abusing mother who could not help her daughter, and Duddley is still a poor neighborhood faced with many social problems. However, because of Paul's willingness to help, the student was able to escape her home and go to college, and because of the sustained efforts on the part of DSNI to address the social and economic problems that have plagued the area, Duddley is now a stable community.

Most important, the process of change in both cases has been transformative. As a college graduate, Jamila is now in a better position to help herself and her family. She has decided to become a teacher and eventually she will be in a position to help other young people who face difficult situations like her own. Similarly, the residents of Duddley have been empowered through the community development process. Each fall elections for the community board of directors of DSNI attract hundreds of residents. In a community that historically was racially polarized, DSNI has created a vehicle through which a diverse cross-section of residents can work together in pursuit of their common interests. The helplessness that once permeated the area has been replaced by a genuine sense of hope and optimism.

It is important to note that neither of the examples I have described represents the self-help model for ending poverty that has been advocated by conservatives. Certainly, self-help through individual empowerment and collective initiative is a central element in both cases, but so too is strategic assistance. Neither Jamila nor the distressed Duddley neighborhood could have changed things without help. In both cases, allies with resources and a willingness to help were instrumental in making change possible. I believe a similar approach can be taken to transform urban public schools.

WHAT IS TO BE DONE?: EDUCATION, CIVIL RIGHTS, AND COMMUNITY EMPOWERMENT

In Chapter 1, I cited the example of my old friend, Amateka Morgan, the teacher at the Islamic school in Brooklyn who had left the public schools because he was tired of seeing educators accept the failure and loss of large numbers of students. His efforts to create a genuine educational alternative for students outside of public education is representative of an important trend in American education. Historically, efforts to provide poor children of color with access to quality education have been the preoccupation of activists and educators who connected their work in education to broader efforts to improve and uplift the condition of downtrodden and disadvantaged people. Recognizing the consistent failure of federal and state governments to ensure access to quality public schools, such individuals have played a crucial role in making educational opportunities available to the disenfranchised.

At the end of the Civil War many of the educators who traveled to the South to establish schools for the former slaves were driven by a missionary zeal to help those recently freed from bondage (Anderson, 1988). While their efforts led to some of the first schools and universities created for the purpose of educating African Americans, several critics now question the goals and intentions of these educators. Rather than conceiving of education as a means to empower those who had been enslaved, some of the early architects of African American education appear to have settled for an education designed to create a docile but useful servant caste (Watkins, 2001). Similar arguments have been made about the boarding schools that were set up for Native American children as part of the effort to "civilize" them and free them from their "savage cultures" (Prucha, 1973). As the German philosopher and playwright Berthold Brecht (1965) has written, "Education is a double-edged sword: it can be used to oppress or to liberate" (p. x). Similar arguments were made by Carter G. Woodson (1933), an African American historian and educator, who argued that the "mis-education" of Black people was instrumental in their oppression.

There is also a long legacy of educators who have dedicated themselves to serving subordinate populations in the United States and have envisioned their work as part of the effort to liberate and empower the oppressed. For some, this has taken on an overtly political dimension because they have attributed the cause of inadequate educational opportunities to an indifferent and unresponsive political system. Such a view has led many to take up the struggle for educational opportunity in the courts, an arena where, at certain times, overt forms of discrimination and institutional indifference have been challenged (Wolters, 1984). Others, like my friend Amateka, have focused their energies on establishing independent schools where they have sought to address the needs of children by providing them with the attention, love, and support they cry out for and deserve. Despite differences in approach, both strategies have conceptualized the educational dilemma in political terms, and both strategies have been linked to broader social movements aimed at improving the lives of the poor and disenfranchised in American society.

Since the U.S. Supreme Court's *Brown* decision in 1954, public education has been at the center of struggles for expanding and redefining civil rights in American society (Carnoy, 1994; Orfield & Eaton, 1996). The Court's landmark ruling to end apartheid in public education opened the door to protracted conflict and debate over the meaning of equality and equal opportunity in education and how these were to be achieved (Kirp, 1980). Although *Brown* failed to provide clarity to communities and school districts with regard to how the Court's mandate should be fulfilled, the Court's decision did bring about significant changes at the federal, state, and local level with respect to policies governing access to public education. With federal assistance and court enforcement, many public schools have been desegregated, and legally sanctioned racial segregation has been largely eliminated.[6]

Yet, despite this significant accomplishment, the limitations of *Brown* are glaring and obvious: Nearly 50 years after the Court's decree, large numbers of schools throughout the United States remain segregated, not only on the basis of race, but also on the basis of class (Orfield & Eaton, 1996). Segregation remains because in many parts of the United States *Brown* was never fully implemented. In cities like San Francisco, Berkeley, Richmond, and Oakland, the majority of White middle-class residents simply have opted out of the system altogether, even though they continue to reside in the city. Now, with the courts increasingly less willing to support desegregation plans that were adopted in the past, the limitations of *Brown* are even more obvious.

This is not to say that the changes brought about as a result of the *Brown* decision have not been significant. The precedent set by *Brown* and related court rulings has created a legal basis for promoting educational equity that extends well beyond racial justice. Since the *Brown* ruling, public education has become the most democratic and accessible institution in the United States. Gradually but steadily, groups and individuals that historically have been subject to discrimination and exclusion have been able to use the courts to press for the elimination of unjust barriers (Cuban & Tyack, 1995; Katznelson & Weir, 1985; Spring, 1994). Discrimination on the basis of language, disability, and gender has been eliminated, and even the rights of undocumented children have been upheld.[7] Genuine progress has been made in expanding the rights of children, and even those who decry the continued neglect and mistreatment of millions of children across the United States should acknowledge the gains.

Despite these advances, it would be a mistake to grow complacent, because conservative groups continue to challenge these victories through lawsuits and ballot initiatives.[8] Relying on justice from the courts clearly has its limitations. I was reminded of this by a recent conversation with the principal of Central High School in Kansas City, Missouri. In the 1980s and 1990s the district received nearly $500 million from that state as a result of a federal court order to upgrade facilities. In a novel approach to desegregation, Judge Clark ruled that in order to integrate the city's long-neglected schools, improvements would have to be made in facilities so that Whites would be attracted back into the system. The controversial court order resulted in significant physical improvements to the schools in the district, including Central High School, a place described by *60 Minutes* as the "Taj Majal" of schools. I visited the school in 1995 and was extremely impressed by its features: an Olympic-sized pool, a computerized robotics lab, and a fully equipped Greek-styled amphitheater. Yet, when I spoke recently with the new principal, I was shocked to learn that the robotics lab no longer existed because the equipment had been stolen (he believed by adults who worked at the school). He also informed me that school had no swim team or drama club to make use of the other facilities. "If I could have had some say in how to spend all that money back then I would have told them to invest in some competent teachers who knew how to teach our students. That's what we really need" (interview, July 30, 2002).

The limitations of legal remedies have become obvious elsewhere as well. For example, there are several cities, such as Boston, where schools continue to be segregated even after a bloody and protracted struggle to integrate them in the 1970s. This is why the approach epitomized by the work of my friend Amateka or the struggle for community-controlled schools in Brooklyn, New York, in 1968,[9] is appealing to so many people. For those frustrated by the slow pace of change in public schools or whose experience with these flawed institutions has led them to believe change is not possible, working outside of the system by creating independent alternatives has been attractive. While some pressed the courts to desegregate schools in the 1970s, other activists and educators formed the Council of Independent Black Institutions, representing a network of independent Black schools throughout the United States. The success of schools like Shelton's Primary in Oakland and Marcus Garvey in Los Angeles reminds us that providing quality education to poor children in the inner city is possible. The tireless efforts of the educators who keep these schools going also show that those who are unhappy about the state of urban schools can do more than wring their hands in despair as we wait for the courts or the government to do the right thing.

Yet, over 20 years later, many of these independent institutions no longer exist due to a lack of funds or because the activists who created them have burned out, passed away, or moved on. For this reason, even as we applaud their efforts, we must remember that the small number of successful independent schools do not constitute a genuine alternative to public schools. There simply aren't enough of them to address the needs of millions of poor children.

Moreover, as civil rights activists have understood for some time, it is a mistake to carry self-help initiatives too far. This is a point that I made to several close friends with regard to the Million Man March in 1995. While I was inspired by the sight of one million Black men marching in the name of personal responsibility, I couldn't help but note the irony that it occurred as the U.S. Congress, under the leadership of former Speaker Newt Gingrich, was preparing to enact the so-called Contract with America. By asserting that it was the responsibility of Black men to rebuild Black communities, the marchers inadvertently were letting the government shirk its responsibility to serve the needs of all its citizens. Black men and women do need to take initiative to help struggling communities, but personal responsibility alone cannot address the chronic problems plaguing the inner city, nor should it. American society as a whole has a responsibility to provide the resources and support needed to revitalize urban schools and communities. To accept anything short of this is shortsighted.

Those who seek to hold the government accountable for aiding urban schools, and those who direct their efforts toward grassroots community-building initiatives, share a common goal: to make quality education available to all poor children. Differences in outlook often have separated and divided these camps, but both strategies are important. While civil rights activists continue to pursue the goal of integration and access to all of the rights and privileges children deserve, independent educators and activists can continue to focus their efforts on community empowerment. Often, the differences between the two camps seem to mirror the divisions that separated W. E. B. Du Bois and Booker T. Washington as the two leaders debated the best way forward for African Americans after the end of Reconstruction (Twombly, 1971). Today, there is no need for the rivalry or acrimony that characterized the previous debate because there is simply too much to do.

Presently, some of the differences between the two camps have become manifest in conflicting stances toward the issue of vouchers and privatization. Whereas civil rights activists generally have opposed vouchers on the grounds that they would further undermine public support for education, independent school activists have been more likely to embrace vouchers as a means to provide educational alternatives to poor families. Vouchers also have been embraced by some as representing a means to obtain more stable support for financially strapped independent schools.

Although I am firmly opposed to vouchers, it is not because I oppose the idea of educating poor children in private schools. If vouchers would guarantee all children who need them access to high-quality schools of any kind, my conscience would require that I support the policy. However, this is far from the case. Rather than framing solutions to the educational problems facing poor children of color in dichotomous terms, I believe that concerned individuals should adopt a pragmatic approach as we consider various possibilities for change. Polarization on these issues often has had the effect of blurring the important commonalities shared by the two camps and undermining possibilities for concerted action.

As an educator and activist, I have worked without a sense of conflict, within both camps. My personal commitment has been to put the needs of children first, and I have worked in a variety of ways to provide quality education to poor children of color. For this reason I have experienced no sense of contradiction in supporting independent private and charter schools, even while working to support public schools. I am opposed to vouchers, not for ideological reasons but for practical ones: I know that few private schools have the space or the desire to serve poor children. When we put the needs of children first, defending an ideological position on how schooling should be provided becomes less important than doing whatever it takes to make quality education available to poor children.

Education is a political issue, and the question confronting all of those who are disturbed over the state of education for poor children in America is: "Which side are you on?" Education plays a special role in American society because it operates on more democratic principles than any other social institution (Carnoy & Levin, 1985). As the only public institution required to serve the needs of all children, it is all that remains of the social safety net for poor children in the United States. Without a doubt it would be a major blow to child welfare and civil rights generally if the flawed and feeble institution of public education were to be dismantled.

We can make significant improvements in the quality of public education available to poor children in urban areas. We have the resources, the know-how, and the models to do this. What is lacking is the will and conviction to make it happen. Those who understand the importance of education must work with creativity and a sense of urgency to find ways to generate the will, to make those who are presently indifferent or unconcerned understand what is at stake. What is at stake are children's lives and the kind of society we will become. For those who do not want to see entire cities written off as dangerous "no man's lands," who do not want to see incarceration rates continue to rise and executions of the most vulnerable continue to escalate, who are afraid of becoming a society that fears its own children, working to improve urban education is an imperative. The future of American society will be determined in large measure by the quality of its urban schools. We have the responsibility and the obligation to try to make that future far better than the present we now know.

Notes

CHAPTER 1

1. Several public opinion polls have shown that education is regarded as the number one domestic policy issue. Even after September 11, education follows closely behind concerns about security and terrorism. For an analysis of public opinion and the response of policy makers, see "The 29th Annual Phi Delta Kappa/Gallup Poll of the Public's Attitudes Toward Public Schools" in *Phi Delta Kappan*, September 1997, pp. 41–56.

2. Polls of parents reveal that while many are critical of public education in general, they tend to hold more positive views toward the particular schools their children attend. For a discussion of the polling data, see "31st Annual Phi Delta Kappa/Gallup Poll of the Public's Attitudes Toward the Public Schools" by L. C. Rose and A. M. Gallup in *Phi Delta Kappan*, September 1999, pp. 41–56.

3. In addition to education, a growing number of schools serving poor children frequently provide a variety of other services to children, including free lunch, health centers, immunizations, etc. See "Rising to the Challenge: Emerging Strategies for Educating Youth at Risk" by N. Legters and E. McGill in *Schools and Students at Risk* edited by R. Rossi (New York: Teachers College Press, 1994).

4. In a public lecture at a conference entitled Human Rights in the Americas (May 1993), the former Dean of Boalt Law School at UC Berkeley, Jesse Choper, used the terms *positive* and *negative rights* to distinguish between rights that constitute a social entitlement (e.g., housing, health care, etc.) and rights that are intended to prevent individuals from exercising certain "freedoms" (i.e., religious beliefs, gun ownership, speech, etc.).

5. Shelby Steele and John McWhorter are two of the better-known Black scholars who have argued that the failure of African Americans is explained largely by what McWhorter refers to as "self sabotage" and Steele describes as embracing "victim focused identity." See *Losing the Race* by J. McWhorter (New York: Free Press, 2000) and *The Content of Our Character* by S. Steele (New York: St. Martin's Press, 1990).

6. It is not uncommon for the best-paying jobs available in cities to be held by individuals who live outside of the city limits. For a discussion of the role cities play within regional economies, see "Cities and Uneven Economic Development" by M. Savage and A. Warde in *The City Reader* edited by R. Legates and F. Stout (New York: Routledge, 1996).

7. Part of the problem with most voucher and choice plans is that they fail to address the fact that most of the better suburban and private schools lack the

space to accommodate significant numbers of poor children from the inner city. For an analysis of choice plans and access to schools, see *Who Chooses? Who Loses?* by B. Fuller and R. Elmore (New York: Teachers College Press, 1996).

8. The Education Trust and the Heritage Foundation have identified a number of high-performing schools that serve minority children. Several of these are located in high-poverty, inner-city communities. However, these schools are relatively isolated, and their existence generally has been difficult to replicate. See *No Excuses, Lessons from 21 High Performing, High Poverty Schools* by S. C. Carter (Washington, DC: Heritage Foundation, 2000) and "New Frontiers for a New Century" in *Thinking K–12, 5*(2), Spring 2001.

9. For an analysis and discussion of academic programs that have proven effective in serving low-income minority students, see "Promising Programs for Elementary and Middle Schools: Evidence of Effectiveness and Replicability" by O. Fashola and R. Slavin in *Journal of Education for Students Placed at Risk, 2*(3), 1997, pp. 251–307.

CHAPTER 2

1. It is important to note that non-Whites constitute the majority in nine of the ten largest U.S. cities. See *The Atlas of American Society* by A. Andrews and J. Fonseca (New York: New York University Press, 1995).

2. The limitations faced by Black elected officials as they came to power in cities across the United States are analyzed by W. Tabb in *The Political Economy of the Black Ghetto* (New York: Norton, 1970).

3. The degree of racial imbalance in Berkeley public schools is particularly striking because of the historical commitment to integration in education and housing in the city. For a detailed discussion of Berkeley's efforts to promote integration in its public schools, see *Just Schools* by D. Kirp (Berkeley: University of California Press, 1980).

4. For an extensive analysis of widening disparities in wealth and living conditions throughout the United States, see *The Widening Gap* by J. Heyman (New York: Basic Books, 2000). For a similar discussion of the Bay Area, see *To Place Our Deeds: The African American Community in Richmond, California 1910–1963* by S. A. W. Moore (Berkeley: University of California Press, 2000).

5. For an explanation of how the academic performance index is calculated, see Education Data Partnership, 2001.

6. West Berkeley parents did get the funding to complete the construction of Columbus School, but not from the school district. They were compelled to raise $1 million over the original budget allocation with assistance from the Berkeley Public Education Foundation.

7. I have documented how the polarization of certain Berkeley neighborhoods contributed to difficulties in responding to drug trafficking in Berkeley in an article co-authored with Patricia Morgan entitled "Taking Chances, Taking Charge: A Report on a Drug Abuse Intervention Conceived, Created and Con-

trolled by a Community" in *International Quarterly of Community Health Education, 14*(4), 1993–94.

8. Although funding to support Healthy Start programs in schools has been limited, several schools throughout California were able to establish a number of school-based services for students and their families during the 1980s and 1990s. Many of these have been recognized as model programs. For a discussion of these efforts and the policies needed to support them, see *Community Schools: A Handbook for State Policy Leaders* (Washington, DC: Institute for Educational Leadership, 2002).

9. The decision to provide new shoes, which was made possible through donations from local businesses, came after teachers learned that a number of students did not want to come to school during the first week because they didn't have new clothing to wear.

10. Milbrey McLaughlin describes the role such schools play as "urban sanctuaries." In her book, *Community Counts: How Youth Organizations Matter for Youth Development* (Washington, DC: Public Education Network, 2000), McLaughlin explains how and why such schools should be expanded.

CHAPTER 3

1. It is important to note that the most prominent advocates of the idea that differences in academic performance can be explained by genetic differences, have not been geneticists. Charles Murray is a political scientist and his co-author Richard Hernstein was a psychologist. Similarly, Arthur Jensen is an educational psychologist.

2. The leading proponents of cultural explanations of Black crime and poverty have been Black social scientists. Starting with E. Franklin Frazier, one of the leading Black sociologists of the 1940s and 1950s, scholars such as Thomas Sowell and Elijah Anderson have emphasized the importance of culture in understanding the behavior of African Americans. See *Streetwise* by E. Anderson (Chicago: University of Chicago Press, 1990) and *Ethnic America: A History* by T. Sowell (New York: Basic Books, 1981).

3. Recent research by Marcello and Carolla Suarez-Orozco indicates that immigrant students are more likely to be overrepresented among both high achievers and low achievers. See *Children of Immigration* (Cambridge, MA: Harvard University Press, 2001).

4. For an analysis of the new percentage-based admissions policies and their impact on public universities in Texas, California, and Florida, see *Diversity Challenged* edited by G. Orfield (Cambridge, MA: Harvard Educational Review Press, 2001).

5. Several researchers have pointed out that there are significant differences between the Black middle class and the White middle class, especially in terms of wealth. White and Black families with similar incomes often have unequal wealth because Whites are more likely to benefit from inherited wealth. The Black middle

class is also more likely than the White middle class to have friends and relatives that are poor. For further discussion, see *Black Wealth, White Wealth* by M. Oliver and T. M. Shapiro (London: Routledge, 1997).

CHAPTER 4

1. Berkeley's busing plan was unique because it required that minority students from kindergarten through third grade (most of whom resided in the flatlands of Berkeley) be bused to schools in affluent neighborhoods in the hills. In grades 4–6, White students from the hills were to be bused to flatlands schools. For further discussion of the plan, see *Just Schools* by D. Kirp (Berkeley: University of California Press, 1982).

2. An indication of how many former private school students enter BHS is provided from the Diversity Project survey on the Class of 2000. Nearly 25% of ninth-grade students responding to the survey reported that they had attended private school prior to entering BHS. Also, whereas the percentage of White students in public elementary and middle schools in Berkeley is approximately 30%, the White student population at BHS is over 40%.

3. This sentiment has been expressed to me on numerous occasions by White parents in Berkeley. One Berkeley professor who was aggravated that her son entering kindergarten had not been assigned to the school she preferred, informed me, "I would think that the district should be happy to have White middle-class kids like my son. For heavens sake, I want to do all I can to support the public schools myself, but they've got to be more flexible in how they apply their rules" (interview, April 16, 1998).

4. I saw an example of this when I ran into a Berkeley professor one day at BHS who told me about problems that his son was having at the school. He informed me that his ninth-grade son had cut 36 classes in the spring semester and was in danger of flunking. He said that his son told him he had been reading poetry in the botanical gardens on the days he cut school, and he confidently asserted that he was on his way to a conference with his son's counselor and some of his teachers to determine what could be done to salvage the semester. A few days later the professor emailed me to let me know that his son's teachers were very understanding, and that they had assigned make-up work, which, if completed satisfactorily, would enable his son to still get "As" in most of his classes.

CHAPTER 5

1. 5 Cal. 3d 584 (1971).

2. The API is a rating system that assesses the performance of schools based on the average scores received by its students on the Stanford 9 achievement tests. For information on PSAA, see www.cde.ca.gov/iiusp/

3. In the past, the state of California has intervened in school districts only when they were fiscally insolvent. In 1995, the state took over management of Compton public schools and turned control back to the locally elected school board in 2001. However, there is little evidence that conditions in Compton's schools have improved. See "Accountability Won't Rescue Disadvantaged Students" in *California Educator, 5,* 2001.

CHAPTER 6

1. Homicide rates in the United States are about 10 times higher than in most European countries. In 1994 there were over 23,000 murders in the United States. A disproportionate number of these occurred in cities. For a detailed discussion of crime rates and international comparisons, see *The Real War on Crime* edited by S. Donziger (New York: Harper Perennial, 1996, pp. 10–12).

2. Following the murder of foreign tourists in Miami, car rental companies began distributing to their out-of-town customers maps that designated certain neighborhoods and exit ramps in red, an indication that these were unsafe areas. The practice of containing crime to certain neighborhoods rather than trying to eliminate crime is described by Katheryn Russell in *The Color of Crime* (New York: New York University Press, 1998).

3. A national report entitled *Indicators of School Crime and Safety,* published by the National Center for Education Statistics (Washington, DC) in 1998, indicates that fear of school-related violence has risen sharply among parents, teachers, and students since 1989. This has occurred even though incidents of violence in schools actually have declined.

4. See "For the Ultimate Safe Schools, Officials Turn Their Eyes Toward Dallas," by P. Applebome in the *New York Times,* September 20, 1995, p. A26.

5. In 1989, the Richmond Unified School District went bankrupt and was nearly forced to shut down its schools 6 weeks before the end of the school year. Two years later, the district installed metal detectors at each of its high schools at a cost of nearly one million dollars, even though the district budget was still in deficit. To change its image, the district changed its name to the West Contra Costa Unified School District. Many observers argued the name change was primarily intended to remove the strong connection to the impoverished city of Richmond, which constitutes most of the district. For a discussion of these issues, see "Violence on the Rise in Schools" by E. Shogren in *The San Francisco Chronicle,* January 6, 1996, p. 6.

6. Much of the violence that has occurred at Berkeley High School has been interracial. However, the district typically has downplayed its racial aspect, fearing the negative publicity that would be generated if news of racial violence was leaked to the public. For a description of violent incidents at BHS, see "Board Beefs up Safety at BHS" by J. Mar in *Berkeley Voice,* November 27, 1991.

7. The grounded theory approach to research has been especially useful for inductive inquiries. According to the premise of such an approach, theory is pro-

duced through empirical investigations, and can be tested through repeated observation or data collection.

8. Critics of this approach point to the rising number of complaints of police harrassment by citizens in New York City, and to more extreme examples of police shootings of unarmed individuals, as a drawback of aggressive policing strategies.

CHAPTER 7

1. In 1994 the school board reluctantly voted to eliminate music programs in the elementary schools as a cost-saving measure. The programs were saved and expanded by an initiative launched by members of the community to fund the program through private resources.

2. In 1986 the Berkeley City Council approved the creation of the Real Alternative Program as a strategy for addressing the large number of young people who had become involved in drug-related crime. Funded through revenue generated from parking tickets, RAP provided first-time offenders with tutorial and mentoring services, summer jobs and recreation opportunities, and a case worker who provided counseling. Although the program was very successful, the city was unable to expand it due to limited resources. For a description and analysis of the program, see "Taking Chances, Taking Charge" by P. Noguera and P. Morgan in *International Quarterly of Community Health Education, 14*(4), 1993–94.

3. Rod Paige was one of six superintendents of large urban school districts who drafted and signed a letter from the Council of Great City Schools (CGCS) calling on the person who would be named secretary of education to support a national urban policy that would address conditions in urban schools and social welfare issues facing young people in impoverished areas. Check the CGCS website for a copy of the statement: http://www.cgcs.org

4. I regard federal policies such as compensatory education and economic impact aid as palliative treatments because although they provide schools serving impoverished students with additional aid, the supplemental resources provided generally fail to truly mitigate the impact of poverty on schools and students. For a discussion of the limitations of these programs, see G. Orfield and E. H. DeBray (Eds.), *Hard Work for Good Schools: Facts Not Fads in Title I Reform* (Cambridge, MA: Harvard University, Civil Rights Project, May 1, 1999).

5. The name of the student has been changed.

6. It could be argued that certain federal policies, such as special ed and bilingual ed, actually allow for some degree of segregation.

7. Cuban and Tyack make this point very effectively in *Tinkering Toward Utopia* (1995). They point out that during the twentieth century there was a steady expansion in access to education at primary and secondary levels. With increased access, the rights of children also expanded, particularly after the *Brown* decision.

8. The English-only laws that have been adopted in several states as well as the ballot initiatives to ban affirmative action serve as a reminder that past gains in civil rights can be taken away.

9. The struggle for community control over schools in the Ocean Hill–Brownsville section of Brooklyn precipitated a city-wide strike by the United Federation of Teachers in 1968. Although the experiment was aborted as a result of the strike, initiatives to further decentralization and community controls of schools continued. See Fantini, Gittell, and Magat (1970) for an analysis of the movement for community control.

References

Accountability won't rescue disadvantaged students. (2001, June). *California Educator, 5.*

Anderson, E. (1990). *Street wise: Race, class and change in an urban Community*. Chicago: University of Chicago Press.

Anderson, J. (1988). *The education of blacks in the South, 1860–1935*. Chapel Hill: University of North Carolina Press.

Andrews, A., & Fonseca, J. (1995). *The atlas of American society*. New York: New York University Press.

Anyon, J. (1996). *Ghetto schooling: A political economy of urban educational reform*. New York: Teachers College Press.

Applebome, P. (1995, September 20). For the ultimate safe schools, officials turn their eyes toward Dallas. *The New York Times*, p. A26.

Asimov, N. (1994, January 6). Two students shot at Richmond high school. *San Francisco Chronicle.*

Ayers, W. (1997). *A kind and just parent*. New York: Beacon Press.

Ayers, W., Klonsky, M., & Lyon, G. H. (2000). *A simple justice: The challenge of small schools*. New York: Teachers College Press.

Banks, J. (1981). *Multi-ethnic education*. Needham Heights, MA: Allyn & Bacon.

Barry, D. (1993). Growing up violent. *Media and Values, 62*(2), 1–24.

Berkeley Alliance. (1999). *Report on student achievement in the Berkeley Unified School District*. Berkeley, CA: Author.

Berkeley Unified School District. (2001). *District profile*. Berkeley, CA: Author.

Blasi, G. (2001). *Reforming educational accountability*. Unpublished conference paper, Los Angeles.

Block, F., Cloward, R., Ehrenreich, B., & Piven, F. (1987). *The mean season: The attack on the welfare state*. New York: Pantheon Books.

Blumstein, A., & Wallman, J. (Eds.). (2000). *The crime drop in America*. Cambridge: Cambridge University Press.

Boykin, W. (1983). On the academic task performance and African American children. In J. Spence (Ed.), *Achievement and achievement motives*. Boston: Freeman.

Brecht, B. (1965). *The Messingkauf dialogues*. Berlin, Germany: Methuen.

Brookover, W., & Erickson, E. (1969). *Society, schools and learning*. East Lansing: Michigan State University Press.

Brown, P. (2001, August 24). Oakland's schools military bearing rankles some. *The New York Times*, p. A11.

Bush, R. (1984). *The new black vote*. San Francisco: Synthesis.
Carnegie Foundation. (1994/1995). *Quarterly report*. New York: Author.
Carnoy, M. (1994). *Faded dreams: The politics and economics of race in America*. New York: Cambridge University Press.
Carnoy, M., & Levin, H. (1985). *Schooling and work in the democratic state*. Stanford: Stanford University Press.
Carter, S. C. (2000). *No excuses: Lessons from 21 high performing, high poverty schools.* Washington, DC: Heritage Foundation.
Casella, R. (2001). *Being down*. New York: Teachers College Press.
Casey, D. (2002, July 8). Economic hard times hit Flint. *The New York Times.*
Castells, M. (1998). *Informational city*. Oxford: Blackwell.
Chubb, J., & Moe, T. (1990). *Politics, markets and America's schools*. Washington, DC: Brookings Institute.
Cibulka, J. (2001). Old wine, new bottles. *Education Next*. www.educationnext.org
City of Oakland. (1994). *West Oakland community—Existing conditions*. Office of Economic Development, Oakland, CA.
Clark, D. (1985). *Post-industrial America*. New York: Metheuen.
Clark, R. (1983). *Family life and school achievement: Why poor black children succeed or fail*. Chicago: University of Chicago Press.
Clark, W. (1998). *The California cauldron*. New York: Guilford Press.
Clinchy, E. (Ed.). (2000). *The new small schools*. New York: Teachers College Press.
Coleman, J. (1988). Social capital in the creation of human capital. *American Journal of Sociology, 94*(Suppl.), S95–120.
Coleman, J., Campbell, E., Hobson, C., McPartland, J., Mood, A., Weinfeld, F., & Yonk, R. (1966). *Equality of educational opportunity*. Washington, DC: U.S. Department of Health, Education and Welfare, Office of Education.
Comer, J. (1980). *School power*. New York: Free Press.
Commission for Positive Change. (1990). *Good education in Oakland*. Oakland, CA: Author.
Community schools: A handbook for state policy leaders. (2002). Washington, DC: Institute for Educational Leadership.
Conchas, G. (2001). Structuring success and failure: Understanding variability in Latino school engagement. *Harvard Educational Review, 70*(3), 475–504.
Council of the Great City Schools. (2001). *Foundations for success.* Prepared by the Manpower Research and Development Corporation, Washington, DC.
Cross, W., Parnham, T., & Helms, J. (1991). *Shades of black: Diversity in African American identity*. Philadelphia: Temple University Press.
Cuban, L., & Tyack, D. (1995). *Tinkering toward Utopia*. Cambridge, MA: Harvard University Press.
Currie, E. (1985). *Confronting crime*. New York: Pantheon Books.
Darling-Hammond, L. (1997). *The right to learn: A blueprint for creating schools that work*. San Francisco: Jossey-Bass.
Davidman, L., & Davidman, P. (1994). *Teaching with a multicultural perspective.* White Plains, NY: Longman.
Delpit, L. (1988). The silenced dialogue: Power and pedagogy in educating other people's children. *Harvard Educational Review, 58*(3), 280–298.

Devine, J. (1996). *Maximum security*. New York: New York University Press.
Diamond, M. (1999). *Magic trees of the mind: How to nurture your child's intelligence, creativity and healthy emotions from birth through adolescence*. New York: Penguin.
District profile. (2001). Unpublished report, Oakland, CA.
Diversity Project. (1999). *Project report*. Berkeley, CA: UC Berkeley.
Diversity Project. (2000). *Final report*. Berkeley, CA: UC Berkeley.
Donziger, S. (Ed.). (1996). *The real war on crime*. New York: Harper Perennial.
Donziger, S., Sandefur, G., & Weinberg, D. (1994). *Confronting poverty*. New York: Sage.
Dryfoos, J. (2001). Evaluation of community schools: An early look. www.communityschools.org/evaluation/evalbrieffinal.html
Durkheim, E. (1977). *Moral education*. New York: Free Press.
Earls, F. (1991). Not fear, nor quarantine, but science: Preparation for a decade of research to advance knowledge about causes and control of violence in youths. *Journal of Adolescent Health, 12*, 619–629.
Eccles, J., & Gootman, J. (Eds.). (2001). *Community programs to promote youth development*. Washington, DC: National Academy Press.
Ed Data. (2002). District financial statements. www.ed-data.k12.ca.us/fiscal/fundingsummary.asp
Edmonds, R. (1979). Effective schools for the urban poor. *Educational Leadership, 37*(1), 15–27.
Education Data Partnership. (2001). www.ed-data.k12.ca.us
Education Trust. (2002). *Dispelling the myth revisited: Preliminary findings from a nationwide analysis of high-flying schools*. Washington, DC: Author.
Elmore, R. (1996). The new accountability in state educational policy. In H. Ladd (Ed.), *Performance based strategies for improving schools*. Washington, DC: Brookings Institution.
Epstein, J. (1993). A response. *Teachers College Record, 94*(4), 710–717.
Fantini, M., Gittell, M., & Magat, R. (1970). *Community control and the urban school*. New York: Praeger.
Fashola, O., & Slavin, R. (1997). Promising programs for elementary and middle schools: Evidence of effectiveness and replicability. *Journal of Education for Students Placed at Risk, 2*(3), 251–307.
Fass, P. (1989). *Outside in*. New York: Oxford University Press.
Ferguson, R. (2000). *A diagnostic analysis of black–white GPA disparities in Shaker Heights, Ohio*. Washington, DC: Brookings Institute.
Fine, M. (1993). (Ap)parent involvement: Reflections on parents, power and urban schools. *Teachers College Record, 94*(4), 26–43.
Fordham, S. (1996). *Blacked out: Dilemmas of race, identity, and success at Capital High*. Chicago: University of Chicago Press.
Fordham, S., & Ogbu, J. (1986). Black students and school success: Coping with the burden of acting white. *Urban Review, 18*(3), 176–206.
Franklin, J., & Moss, A. (1988). *From slavery to freedom*. New York: Knopf.
Fredrickson, G. (1981). *White supremacy*. New York: Oxford University Press.
Freire, P. (1970). *Education for critical consciousness*. New York: Continuum.

Freire, P. (1972). *The pedagogy of the oppressed.* New York: Continuum.

Friedland, R. (1983). *Power and crisis in the city.* New York: Schocken Books.

Frost, B. (2003, March 29). A policy that depends on segregation. *The New York Times.*

Fuller, B., & Elmore, R. (1996). *Who chooses? Who loses?* New York: Teachers College Press.

Gans, H. (1967). *The Levittowners.* New York: Pantheon Books.

Garbarino, J. (1999). *Lost boys: Why our sons turn to violence and how to save them.* New York: Free Press.

Garcia, E. (2001). *Hispanic education in the United States.* Lanham, MD: Roman Littlefield.

Gibson, M. (1988). *Accommodation without assimilation: Sikh immigrants in an American high school.* Ithaca, NY: Cornell University Press.

Gilligan, J. (1996). *Violence: Our deadly epidemic and its causes.* New York: Gossett/Putnam.

Gittel, R., & Thompson, P. (2001). Making social capital work: Social capital and economic development. In S. Saegert, P. Thompson, & M. Warren (Eds.), *Social capital and poor communities.* New York: Russell Sage.

Glaser, B., & Strauss, A. (1967). *The discovery of grounded theory.* New York: Aldine.

Gold, E. (2001, August). Clients, consumers or collaborators? Parents and their roles in school reform. *Consortium for Policy Research in Education.*

Gormley, W. (Ed.). (1991). *Privatization and its alternatives.* Madison: University of Wisconsin Press.

Gottfredson, D. (2001). *Schools and delinquency.* Cambridge: Cambridge University Press.

Gratz, R., & Mintz, N. (1998). *Cities back from the edge.* New York: Wiley.

Greenberg, M., & Schneider, D. (1994). Young black males is the answer, but what was the question? *Social Science Medicine, 39*(2).

Harris, F., & Wicker, T. (1988). *The Kerner report: The 1968 report of the national advisory commission on civil disorders.* New York: Pantheon Books.

Haycock, K. (2002). Thinking K–16. In P. Barth (Ed.), *New frontiers for a new century: A national overview* (Vol. 5). Washington, DC: Education Trust.

Hebert, R. (2002, May 11). A rising tide of death. *The New York Times.*

Henig, J. R., et al. (1999). *The color of school reform: Race, politics, and the challenge of urban education.* Princeton, NJ: Princeton University Press.

Hernstein R., & Murray, C. (1994). *The bell curve: Intelligence and class structure in American life.* New York: Free Press.

Hess, F. (1999). *Spinning wheels: The unpolitics of urban school reform.* Washington, DC: Brookings Institute.

Hess, G. A. (1999). Community participation or control? From New York to Chicago. *Theory into Practice, 38*(4), 217–224.

Heyman, J. (2000). *The widening gap.* New York: Basic Books.

Horseman, R. (1981). *Race and manifest destiny.* Cambridge, MA: Harvard University Press.

Horton, M., & Freire, P. (1990). *We make the road by walking.* Philadelphia: Temple University Press.

Indicators of school crime and safety. (1989). Washington, DC: National Center of Education Statistics.
Jacobs, J. (1961). *The death and life of great American cities.* New York: Vintage Books.
Jencks, C. (1972). *Inequality.* New York: Harper Books.
Jencks, C., & Phillips, M. (1998). *The black–white test scores gap.* Washington, DC: Brookings Institute.
Jensen, A. (1969). How much can we boost IQ and scholastic achievement? *Harvard Educational Review, 39*(1), 1–123.
Johnson, T., Boyden, J., & Pitts, W. (2000). *Racial profiling and punishment in U.S. public schools.* Oakland, CA: Applied Research Center.
Kao, G., & Tienda, M. (1995). Optimism and achievement: The educational performance of immigrant youth. *Social Science Quarterly, 76*(1), 1–19.
Katz, M. (1989). *The undeserving poor.* New York: Pantheon Books.
Katznelson, I., & Weir, M. (1985). *Schooling for all.* Berkeley: University of California Press.
Kirp, D. (1982). *Just schools.* Berkeley: University of California Press.
Kozol, J. (1991). *Savage inequalities.* New York: Crown Books.
Ladson-Billings, G. (1994). *The dreamkeepers.* San Francisco: Jossey-Bass.
Lareau, A. (1989). *Home advantage: Social class and parental intervention in elementary education.* New York: Falmer Press.
League of Cities. (2002). *Municipal leadership in education.* Washington, DC: National League of Cities.
Ledesma, J. (1995). Another look at the model minority myth. Unpublished course paper, UC Berkeley.
Lee, S. (1996). *Unraveling the model minority stereotype.* New York: Teachers College Press.
Legters, N., & McGill, E. L. (1994). Rising to the challenge: Emerging strategies for educating youth at risk. In R. Rossi (Ed.), *Schools and students at risk* (pp. 23–47). New York: Teachers College Press.
Lehman, N. (1999). *The big test.* New York: Farrar, Strauss and Giroux.
Linn, R. (2000). Assessments and accountability. *Educational Researcher, 29*(2), 4–16.
Loury, G. (1995). *One by one from the inside out: Essays and reviews on race and responsibility in America.* New York: Free Press.
Luker, K. (1996). *Dubious conceptions: The politics of teenage pregnancy.* Cambridge, MA: Harvard University Press.
Maeroff, G. (1988). Whithered hopes and stillborn dreams: The dismal panorama of urban schools. *Phi Delta Kappan, 69*(9), 632–638.
Making the future different. (1990). Oakland: University of California Press.
Mar, J. (1991, November 27). Board beefs up safety at BHS. *Berkeley Voice.*
Maran, M. (2000). *Class dismissed.* New York: St. Martin's Press.
Maran, M. (2001, August). Damage control. *Teacher Magazine, 13*(1), 24–31.
Maslow, A. (1962). *Toward a psychology of being.* Princeton, NJ: VanNostrand.
Massey, D., & Denton, N. (1993). *American apartheid.* Cambridge, MA: Harvard University Press.

Matut-Bianchi, M. (1986). Ethnic identities and patterns of school success and failure among Mexican descent and Japanese American students in a California high school: An ethnographic analysis. *American Journal of Education, 95*(1), 233–255.

McGroarty, D. (1996). *Break these chains*. Rocklin, CA: Prima.

McLaughlin, M. (2000). *Community counts: How youth organizations matter for youth development*. Washington, DC: Public Education Network.

McWhorter, J. (2000). *Losing the race*. New York: Free Press.

Medoff, P., & Sklar, H. (1994). *Streets of hope*. Boston: South End Press.

Meier, D. (1995). *The power of their ideas*. Boston: Beacon Press.

Meier, K., Stewart, J., & England, R. (1989). *Race, class and education: The politics of second generation discrimination*. Madison: University of Wisconsin Press.

Miles, R. (1989). *Racism*. London: Routledge.

Miller, S. (1995). *An American imperative*. New Haven, CT: Yale University Press.

Moore, S. A. W. (2000). *To place our deeds: The African American community in Richmond, California, 1910–1963*. Berkeley, CA: University of California Press.

Murnane, R., & Levy, F. (1996). *Teaching the new basic skills*. New York: Free Press.

Murray, C. (1984). *Losing ground*. New York: Basic Books.

Nathan, H., & Scott, S. (1978). *Experiment and change in Berkeley*. Berkeley: Institute of Governmental Studies.

National Research Council. (2002). *Community programs to promote youth development*. Washington, DC: National Academy Press.

New frontiers for a new century. (2001, Spring). *Thinking K–12, 5*(2).

Newman, F. (1992). *Student engagement and achievement in American secondary schools*. New York: Teachers College Press.

Nieto, S. (1992). *Affirming diversity*. New York: Longman.

No Child Left Behind Act. (2002). hhtp://www.nclb.gov

Nocera, J. (1991). How the middle class helped ruin the public schools. *The Utne Reader*.

Noguera, P. (1993). Simple justice gets complicated. *Hastings Constitutional Law Quarterly, 20*(3).

Noguera, P. (1995a). Preventing and producing violence in schools: A critical analysis of responses to school violence. *Harvard Educational Review, 65*(2), 189–212.

Noguera, P. (1995b). Reducing and preventing youth violence: An analysis of causes and an assessment of successful programs. In *Wellness lectures*. Oakland: University of California, Office of the President.

Noguera, P. (1995c). A tale of two cities: School desegregation and racialized discourse in Berkeley and Kansas City. *International Journal of Comparative Race and Ethnic Studies, 2*(2).

Noguera, P. (1995d). Ties that bind, forces that divide: Berkeley High School and the challenge of integration. *University of San Francisco Law Review, 29*(3).

Noguera, P. (1996). Confronting the urban in urban school reform. *Urban Review, 28*(1), 1–19.

Noguera, P. (2001a). The role of social capital in the transformation of urban schools in low income communities. In S. Saegert, P. Thompson, & M. Warren (Eds.),

Social capital and poor communities. A volume in the Ford Foundation series on asset building. New York: Sage.

Noguera, P. (2001b, November). Racial politics and the elusive quest for equity and excellence in education. *Education and Urban Society, 34*(1).

Noguera, P., & Akom, A. (2000, June 5). Disparities demystified. *The Nation.*

Noguera, P., & Bliss, M. (2001). *A four year evaluation study of youth together*. Oakland, CA: Arts, Resources and Curriculum.

Noguera, P., & Morgan, P. (1993–94). Taking chances, taking charge: A report on a drug abuse intervention conceived, created, and controlled by a community. *International Quarterly of Community Health Education, 14*(4).

Oakes, J. (1985). *Keeping track*. New Haven, CT: Yale University Press.

Oakes, J. (2002). Adequate and equitable access to education's basic tools in a standards-based educational system. *Teachers College Record* [special issue].

Obiakor, F. (1992). Self-concept of African-American students: An operational model for special education. *Exceptional Children, 59*(2), 160–167.

Office of Economic Development. (1994). *Creating a community vision: Community goal statements and proposal implementation strategies.* Oakland, CA: Author.

Office of Economic Development. (2000). Unpublished report.

Ogbu, J. (1987a). Opportunity structure, cultural boundaries, and literacy. In J. Langer (Ed.), *Language, literacy and culture: Issues of society and schooling.* Norwood, NJ: Ablex Press.

Ogbu, J. (1987b). Variability in minority student performance: A problem in search of an explanation. *Anthropology and Education Quarterly, 18*(4), 312–334.

Ogbu, J. (1990). Literacy and schooling in subordinate cultures: The case of black Americans. In K. Lomotey (Ed.), *Going to school.* Albany: State University of New York Press.

Olsen, L. (1997). *Made in America: Immigrant students in our public schools.* New York: New Press.

Oliver, M., & Shapiro, T. M. (1997). *Black wealth, White wealth.* London: Routledge.

Olsen, L. (1997). *Made in America: Immigrant students in our public schools.* New York: The New Press.

Omi, M., & Winant, H. (1986). *Racial formation in the United States.* New York: Routledge.

Orfield, G. (Ed.). (2001). *Diversity challenged.* Cambridge, MA: Harvard Educational Review Press.

Orfield, G., & DeBray, E. H. (Eds.). (1999, May 1). *Hard work for good schools: Facts not fads in Title I reform.* Cambridge, MA: Harvard University, Civil Rights Project.

Orfield, G., & Eaton, S. (1996). *Dismantling desegregation.* New York: New Press.

Patterson, O. (1998, December 16). Boston's ten point program for reducing juvenile homicides. *The New York Times.*

Payne, C. M. (1984). *Getting what we ask for: The ambiguity of success and failure of urban education.* Westport, CT: Greenwood Press.

Payne, C. (2001). So much reform, so little change. Unpublished conference paper, Boston, MA.

Perkins, A., & Chen, A. (1988). *By the numbers: A public health dataview of Oakland.* Alameda, CA: City Health Profiles, Alameda County Health Department. www.co.alameda.ca.us/publichealth/information/info.htm

Perlstein, D. (1998). Saying the unsaid: Girl killing and the curriculum. *Journal of Curriculum and Supervision, 14*(1), 88–104.

Perry, T., & Delpit, L. (1997). The real ebonics debate. *Rethinking Schools, 12*(1).

Peshkin, A. (2000). The nature of interpretation in qualitative research. *Educational Researcher, 29*(9), 5–9.

Phelan, P., Davidson, A., & Yu, H. C. (1998). *Adolescents' worlds.* New York: Teachers College Press.

Phillips, K. (1983). *Post conservative America.* New York: Vintage Books.

Phillips, K. (2002). *Wealth and democracy.* New York: Broadway Books.

Phinney, J. (1990). Ethnic identity in adolescents and adults: Review of research. *Psychological Bulletin, 108*(3), 499–514.

Pinkney, A. (1984). *The myth of black progress.* Cambridge: Cambridge University Press.

Pollack, M. (1999, August 18). Changing student attitudes. *The New York Times,* p. A14.

Portes, A., Haller, W., & Guarnizo, L. E. (2002). Transnational entrepreneurs: An alternative form of immigrant economic adaptation. *American Sociological Review, 67,* 278–298.

Portilla, M. (1999). *Black picket fences.* Chicago: University of Chicago Press.

Prucha, F. P. (1973). *Americanizing the American Indians.* Cambridge, MA: Harvard University Press.

Putnam, R. (1995). Making democracy work: Bowling alone: America's declining social capital. *Journal of Democracy 6*(1), 65–78.

Report on College Admissions for the Class of 1996. (1996). *Berkeley High School College Advisor.*

Rose, L. C., & Gallup, A. M. (1999, September). 31st annual Phi Delta Kappa/Gallup poll of the public's attitudes toward public school. *Phi Delta Kappan,* pp. 41–56.

Rouce, C. (1999). *Rhetoric versus reality.* Washington, DC: Rand Corporation.

Russell, K. (1998). *The color of crime.* New York: New York University Press.

Sachs, J. (1989). *Developing country debt and the world economy.* Chicago: University of Chicago Press.

Saegert, S., Thompson, P., & Warren, M. (Eds.). (2001). *Social capital and poor communities.* New York: Russell Sage.

Sampson, R. (1998). What community supplies. In R. Ferguson & W. Dickens (Eds.), *Urban problems and community development.* Washington, DC: Brookings Institute.

Sandler, S. (2000). *Turning to each other, not on each other: How school communities prevent racial bias in school discipline.* San Francisco: Justice Matters.

Sarason, S. (1971). *The culture of the school and the problem of change.* Boston: Allyn & Bacon.

Savage, M., & Warde, A. (1996). Cities and uneven economic development. In R. Legates & F. Stout (Eds.), *The city reader.* New York: Routledge.

Schiraldi, V., & Ziedenberg, J. (2001). How distorted coverage of juvenile crime affects public policy. In W. Ayers, R. Ayers, & B. Dorhn (Eds.), *Zero tolerance*. New York: New Press.

Schorr, L. (1997). *Common purpose: Strengthening families and neighborhoods to rebuild America*. New York: Anchor Books.

Shogren, E. (1996, January 6). Violence on the rise in schools. *The San Francisco Chronicle*, p. 6.

Sizemore, B. (1988). The Madison Elementary School: A turnaround case. *Journal of Negro Education, 57*(3).

Skolnick, J., & Currie, E. (1994). *Crisis in American institutions*. New York: Harper Collins.

Smitherman, G. (1977). *Talkin' and testifyin': The language of black America*. Boston: Houghton Mifflin.

Solomon, P. (1992). *Black resistance in high school*. Albany: State University of New York Press.

Sowell, T. (1981). *Ethnic America: A history*. New York: Basic Books.

Spring, J. (1994). *American education*. New York: McGraw Hill.

Steele, C. (1997). A threat in the air: How stereotypes shape intellectual identity and performance. *American Psychologist, 52*(6), 613–629.

Steele, S. (1990). *The content of our character*. New York: St. Martin's Press.

Steinberg, L. (1996). *Beyond the classroom*. New York: Simon & Schuster.

Stone, C. (2001). *Building civic capacity*. Lawrence: University of Kansas Press.

Suarez-Orozco, C., & Suarez-Orozco, M. (2001). *Children of immigration*. Cambridge, MA: Harvard University Press.

Sue, S., & Okazaki, S. (1990). Asian American educational achievement: A phenomenon in search of an explanation. *American Psychologist, 45*(8), 913–920.

Suskind, R. (1999). *A hope in the unseen*. New York: Broadway Books.

Tabb, W. (1970). *The political economy of the black ghetto*. New York: Norton.

Takagi, D. (1992). *Retreat from race: Asian American admissions and racial politics*. New Brunswick, NJ: Rutgers University Press.

Takaki, R. (1989). *Strangers from a different shore*. New York: Penguin.

Tatum, B. (1997). *Why are all the black kids sitting together in the cafeteria?* New York: Basic Books.

Terry, W. (1995, August 14). US child poverty highest in Western world. *The New York Times*.

Thompson, C. (2001). Class struggle. *East Bay Express, 23*(27).

29th annual Phi Delta Kappa/Gallup poll of the public's attitudes toward public school. (1997, September). *Phi Delta Kappan*, pp. 41–56.

Twombly, R. (1971). *Blacks in white America*. New York: David McKay.

Tyack, D. (1980). *The one best system*. Cambridge, MA: Harvard University Press.

U.S. Census Bureau. (2000). Available at www.census.gov

Valencia, R. (1991). *Chicano school failure and success*. New York: Falmer Press.

Valle, V., & Torres, R. (2000). *Latino metropolis*. Minneapolis: University of Minnesota Press.

Vigil, J. (2002). *A rainbow of gangs*. Austin: University of Texas Press.

Wacquant, L. (1998). Negative social capital: State breakdown and social destitution in America's urban core. *Netherlands Journal of Housing and the Built Environment, 13*(1).

Wade, R. (1995). The enduring ghetto: Urbanization and the color line in American history. In R. Caves (Ed.), *Exploring Urban America.* London: Sage.

Wagner, T. (1994). *How schools change*. Boston: Beacon Press.

Waters, M. (1990). *Ethnic options*. Berkeley: University of California Press.

Watkins, W. (2001). *The white architects of black education: Ideology and power in America, 1865–1954*. New York: Teachers College Press.

Weinstein, R., Madison, S., & Kuklinski, M. (1995). Raising expectations in schooling: Obstacles and opportunities for change. *American Educational Research Journal, 32*(1), 121–159.

Wilgoren, J. (1997, April 27). Young blacks turn to school vouchers as civil rights issue. *The New York Times.*

Wilson, W. (1978). *The declining significance of race*. Chicago: University of Chicago Press.

Wilson, W. (1987). *The truly disadvantaged*. Chicago: University of Chicago Press.

Wolters, R. (1984). *The burden of Brown: Thirty years of school desegregation*. Knoxville: University of Tennessee Press.

Woodson, C. G. (1933). *The mis-education of the Negro*. Washington, DC: Associated Publishers.

Woolcock, M. (1998). Social capital and economic development: Toward a theoretical synthesis and policy framework. *Theory and Society, 27,* 151–208.

Index

About the Author

Pedro A. Noguera is the Judith K. Dimon Professor of Communities and Schools at the Harvard Graduate School of Education. Previously he was a professor in Social and Cultural Studies at the Graduate School of Education and Director of the Institute for the Study of Social Change at the University of California, Berkeley. For 19 years, Dr. Noguera lived in the Bay Area where he engaged in collaborative research with several large urban school districts, and served as an elected member of the Berkeley School Board from 1990 to 1994. He has been an activist on issues related to social justice in the United States and internationally for many years. He is married (Patricia Vattuone) and the father of four children (Joaquin, Amaya, Antonio, and Naima).

Dr. Noguera has done extensive field research and published several articles on the role of education in political and social change in the Caribbean. He is also the author of *The Imperatives of Power: Political Change and the Social Basis of Regime Support in Grenada* (Peter Lang, 1997).

Dr. Noguera has served as a member of the U.S. Public Health Service Centers for Disease Control Taskforce on Youth Violence, and as Chair of the Committee on Ethics in Research and Human Rights for the American Educational Research Association. Dr. Noguera was a K–12 classroom teacher for several years and continues to teach part-time in high schools. In 1995 he received an award from the Wellness Foundation for his research on youth violence, in 1997 he was the recipient of the University of California's Distinguished Teaching Award, and in 2001 he received an honorary doctorate from the University of San Francisco for his work in the field of education.